LAST MAN STANDING

LAST MAN STANDING

THE 1ST MARINE REGIMENT ON PELELIU

SEPTEMBER 15–21, 1944

DICK CAMP

ZENITH PRESS

First published in 2009 by Zenith Press, an imprint of MBI Publishing Company, 400 First Avenue North, Suite 300, Minneapolis, MN 55401 USA

Hardcover edition published 2009.
Softcover edition 2011.

Zenith Press titles are also available at discounts in bulk quantity for industrial or sales-promotional use. For details write to Special Sales Manager at MBI Publishing Company, 400 First Avenue North, Suite 300, Minneapolis, MN 55401 USA.

To find out more about our books, visit us online at www.zenithpress.com.

ISBN-13: 978-0-7603-4127-8

The Library of Congress has cataloged the hardcover edition as follows:

Camp, Richard D.
 Last man standing : the 1st Marine Regiment on Peleliu, September 15-21, 1944 / Dick Camp.
 p. cm.
 Includes bibliographical references and index.
 ISBN-13: 978-0-7603-3493-5 (hbk.)
 1. Peleliu, Battle of, Palau, 1944. 2. United States. Marine Corps. Marines, 1st. 3. World War, 1939-1945--Regimental histories--United States. I. Title. II. Title: 1st Marine Regiment on Peleliu, September 15-21, 1944. III. Title: First Marine Regiment on Peleliu, September 15-21, 1944.
 D767.99.P4C36 2008
 940.54'2666--dc22
 2008024341

Editor: Scott Pearson
Design Manager: Brenda C. Canales

About the Author:
Dick Camp is a retired Marine Corps colonel and the author of *Lima-6*, his memoir as a Marine infantry company commander at Khe Sanh. He has written several combat histories focusing on the U.S. Marines, including *The Devil Dogs at Belleau Wood, Battleship Arizona's Marines at War, Iwo Jima Recon, Operation Phantom Fury*, and *Battle for the City of the Dead*. He is also the author of *Leatherneck Legends: Conversations with the Marine Corps' Old Breed* and *Boots on the Ground: The Fight to Liberate Afghanistan from Al-Qaeda and the Taliban, 2001–2002*. His writing has appeared in various military-oriented magazines, including *Vietnam, World War II, Marine Corps Gazette*, and *Leatherneck*. Camp is currently the vice president for museum operations at the Marine Corps Heritage Foundation, overseeing the National Museum of the Marine Corps in Triangle, Virginia.

On the cover: U.S. Marines in the blasted landscape of Peleliu. USMC Photo

Printed in the United States of America
10 9 8 7 6 5 4 3

Richard David "Chip" Camp III
Beloved Son
1970–2007

CONTENTS

INTRODUCTION

In 1969, I accompanied Maj. Gen. Ray Davis to Albany, Georgia, where he addressed a luncheon of senior officers. Afterward we returned to the VIP quarters to relax. Nothing further was on his schedule and I was desperately searching for something to occupy the time—an aide de camp abhors a vacant schedule. I noticed a *Leatherneck* magazine lying on the coffee table, its masthead trumpeting "25th Anniversary of Peleliu." I handed it to Davis, saying, "General, it's your anniversary." I knew the "Old Man" had been a battalion commander in the 1st Marine Regiment, under the famous Lewis B. "Chesty" Puller. He got a pensive look on his face as he leafed through the article, scrutinizing closely the half-dozen photographs. After several moments, he sat back and said, "Dick, it was a terrible battle—casualties were just unbelievable."

Peleliu was a battle that should not have happened. Initially planned to support MacArthur's return to the Philippines, the bloody assault on this small seven-square-mile coral island was declared to be unnecessary by Adm. William F. "Bull" Halsey, Jr., after his fast carrier strike force found the Philippines ripe for the picking. He recommended canceling the operation but was overruled by Fleet Adm. Chester Nimitz—a controversial decision that signed the death warrant for thousands of Americans and Japanese.

On September 15, 1944, twenty-five thousand men of the famed 1st Marine Division stormed ashore. Six days later, after suffering more than 50 percent casualties, one of its regiments was taken off the line over the strenuous objections of the division commander, Maj. Gen. William H. Rupertus, and replaced by soldiers of the 81st "Wildcat" Division. Rupertus, an acerbic, contentious officer, was vehemently opposed to using soldiers and had to be ordered to use them by his superior, Maj. Gen. Roy S. Geiger.

Even before the operation, Rupertus did not enjoy the confidence of his officers. One of his battalion commanders called him "Rupe the Dupe" and another thought he was "a jackass." His boast that Peleliu would be captured within "two days, three at the most," was wildly optimistic.

When the attack stalled, he ordered his commanders to make fruitless assaults against impregnable defenses. Ten thousand battle-hardened Japanese soldiers of Col. Kunio Nakagawa's 2nd Infantry Regiment waited in the nearly impregnable caves and bunkers of the Umurbrogol Mountain, promising to "bleed the Americans white." The 1st Marines, led by the legendary Chesty Puller, were ordered to attack head on into the teeth of Nakagawa's defenses. Puller launched his infantry in attack after bloody attack, fulfilling Nakagawa's wishful objective. Two of Puller's battalions lost 50 percent of their men, while Davis' 1st Battalion lost seven out of ten men—70 percent—the greatest number of casualties for a single unit in Marine Corps history.

Puller's famed reputation was severely tarnished. One survivor complained bitterly that "the only scheme of maneuver he knows is 'fix bayonets and charge!'" Many thought Puller was simply out of touch with the actual conditions on the ground. His daily "continue the attack!" orders flew in the face of reality. His rifle companies were being savaged. C Company, 1st Battalion, reported fourteen men present for duty after one fruitless attack. Its company commander stated angrily, "Why Puller wanted us dead on that hill has never been clear to me." Other detractors thought the loss of his brother on Guam colored his fanatical obsession with coming to grips with the Japanese. On Pavuvu, Puller erected a sign in the mess hall reading "Kill Japs, Kill Japs, Kill Japs." He reminded his men to "destroy the bandy-legged little bastards." Ray Davis said he was "terribly bitter, because of the loss of his brother."

For the men of the 1st Marine Regiment on that September morning, Peleliu was nothing more than another storm landing. The division commander told them, "We're going to have some casualties but let me assure you this is going to be a fast one, rough but fast." Their regimental commander was a certified hero with years of combat experience—an officer they could trust. Yet as the assault waves neared the beach, plumes of water rose in the air as Japanese gunners found the range. By the end of the first day, even the most optimistic Marine could sense this landing was going to be hell—five hundred of the regiment's Marines were casualties. Bull Halsey had made an ominous—and accurate—prophesy: "I felt [Peleliu] would have to be bought at a prohibitive price . . . and I was right."

CHAPTER 1

BREAKWATER OF THE PACIFIC

Hundreds of half-naked soldiers toiled in the broiling sun, sweat pouring off their torsos as temperatures soared into triple digits. One slumped to the ground, overcome with heat exhaustion. A comrade hurried to assist him but was brought up short by the angry bark of a non-commissioned officer, "Shigoto ni kaere *(Back to work)!" Medical personnel quickly gathered up the unconscious soldier and bundled him off to one of the many camouflaged emplacements, out of the sun. The relentless digging continued at a frenzied pace; it was a matter of life and death—the Americans were coming. One Peleliu defender said, "The enemy has planned to land. Let them come if they're coming. Who is afraid of the Americans? We will defend Peleliu to the death!"*

"On this small island, we must fortify until it is like a big warship," one officer emphasized, "a large, unsink-able warship." So-cho (Sergeant Major) Masao Kurihara,

1

Imperial Japanese Army, remembered, "At various battalion meetings I overheard the officers stress the importance of constructing fortifications. They said that Peleliu Island is the most important island in the Pacific for Japan." The Japanese pledged to break the Americans on their defenses—"Make the American Marines come to you, and when they do, kill them!"

Peleliu (known as Periryu by the Japanese) is one of six large islands and numerous islets in the Palaus group, the westernmost extremity of the vast Caroline Islands chain spanning thirty-three degrees of longitude just north of the Equator. Palaus group's one hundred to two hundred separate islands lie along a generally northeast–southwest axis roughly 500 miles east of the Philippines and an equal distance from New Guinea. Covering some 175 square miles of ocean, they vary from flat atolls in

■ Artist Tom Lea: "Last evening he came down out of the hills. Told to get some sleep, he found a shell crater and slumped into it. He's awake now. First light has given his gray face eerie color. He left the States thirty-one months ago. He was wounded in his first campaign. He has had tropical disease. There is no food or water in the hills, except what you carry. He half-sleeps at night and gouges Japs out of holes all day. Two-thirds of his company has been killed or wounded, but he is still standing. So he will return to attack this morning. How much can a human being endure?" *U.S. Army Center for Military History, Washington, D.C.*

■ Japanese soldier bending to with a will—the Americans are coming! *Marine Corps History Division*

the north, to volcanic central islands, to coral-limestone composition at the southern end. A great coral reef encircles them, forming a barrier reef on the west coast and a fringing reef on the east coast.

A navy intelligence report noted that the Palaus were hot and humid, "seldom less than eighty or more than eighty-two degrees Fahrenheit . . . [R]elative humidity (eighty-two percent) remains high at all times and is most discomforting and debilitating. As is typical of equatorial climates, dengue fever and dysentery are quite prevalent. Surprisingly, malaria is not present. Sand flies and red mites are widespread, particularly on Peleliu. Red, brown, and green snakes are also common on the trees and ground. The two former may be poisonous and are feared by the natives. Crocodiles are common in the waters around Babelthuap and Koror Islands; cases of attack on man are known."

First discovered by the Spanish in the mid-1500s, the Palaus' remoteness kept them from being developed well into the eighteenth century, until they were sold to Germany in 1899 for four million dollars. The Germans promptly exploited the islands' resources, mining phosphates and producing coconut oil. However, with its defeat in World War I, Germany surrendered them to Japan, a member of the victorious Allies.

■ Earl H. Ellis was considered to be a brilliant but flawed strategist. He predicted how the Pacific war would be fought and what role the Marine Corps would play. However, his abuse of alcohol may have led him to an early grave on a remote island in the Palaus. *Marine Corps History Division*

■ **LT. COL. EARL ELLIS** The mystery surrounding Lt. Col. Earl H. "Pete" Ellis' travel to and subsequent death on Peleliu has never been satisfactorily explained, although there have been a number of investigations and a detailed account of his last days in *Pete Ellis: An Amphibious Warfare Prophet 1890–1923*. The most commonly accepted explanation is that he was on a secret intelligence-gathering mission and was poisoned by the Japanese secret police to keep him from reporting on his observations. One New York paper's front page carried a photo of Ellis in his dress uniform. The caption read, "Was Marine Murdered by Japs While on U.S. Spy Mission?" A Washington D.C. paper headlined, "Marine Hero Dies Mysteriously on Japanese Island."

Another less known version has Ellis drinking himself to death. Whatever account is true, he was considered to be a brilliant staff officer who, according to historian Col. Robert Debs Heinl, USMC, "outlined much of the Pacific war to come and forecast with remarkable prevision the role the Marine Corps would play." Ellis' 1921 "Advanced Base Operations in Micronesia" predicted that Japan would attack first. "Considering our consistent policy of nonaggression, [Japan] will probably initiate the war," he wrote, [and] "it will be necessary for us to project our fleet and landing forces across the Pacific and wage war in Japanese waters." Ellis went on to say that "To effect [an amphibious landing] in the face of enemy resistance requires careful training and preparation to say the least; and this along Marine lines. It is not enough that the troops be skilled infantrymen or artillerymen of high morale; they must be skilled watermen and jungle-men who know it can be done—Marines with Marine training."

Japan quickly consolidated control by encouraging twenty thousand mainland Japanese—three times the number of local Palauans—to emigrate. Émigré men were encouraged to marry the daughters of prominent Palau families to further cement ties to the homeland.

Xenophobic Japan kept its activities in the islands secret and attempted to exclude all foreigners. In 1923, Marine Lt. Col. Earl H. Ellis attempted to penetrate this veil of secrecy and paid for it with his life.

The principal islands of pre-war interest to the American military were Babelthuap, the largest and most heavily defended; Koror, the administrative, commercial and communication hub of the islands with

■ A close-up view of the scrub growth covering the ridge. Even though heavily shelled and bombed, vegetation still shrouds the high ground—and the Japanese defenses. Days and days of continued shelling would finally denude the area, exposing the incredibly difficult topography. *Marine Corps History Division*

a deep-water lagoon, anchorage and sea plane facilities; Angaur, suitable for the development of air facilities; and Peleliu, with its two-strip, hard-packed coral surface airfield, complete with taxiways, dispersal areas and turning circles. A second airfield was under construction on Ngesebus (Ngedebus) Island off the northern tip of Peleliu.

It was the airfield development that attracted the attention of American planners and intelligence experts in early 1944. Aircraft launched from Peleliu posed a threat to MacArthur's imminent return to the Philippines. The airfield, located on the only flat ground in the southern sector of the island, was a branch air arsenal and the home of Japan's 26th Air Flotilla. It was well developed, complete with barracks, hangars, large water cisterns, machine shops, a power plant, a radio station and a large two-story administrative building. The main runway was over 1,675 meters long, with a shorter fighter strip of 1,220 meters intersecting it at a ninety-degree angle. Revetments and trenches lined the runways, with concrete reinforced air-raid shelters positioned near the administrative area.

Photo interpreters identified more than twenty dual-purpose (air and ground) anti-aircraft guns in and around the airfield complex. Their tell-tale circular and semi-circular revetments arranged in a triangular pattern made them readily identifiable from the air. The aerial photographs also showed numerous machine-gun positions interspersed among the heavy guns to provide defense against both high-and low-level attack.

Barely six miles long from northeast to southwest, with a maximum width of slightly more than two miles, Peleliu is essentially a coralline-limestone formation, shaped roughly like a lobster claw. The island is heavily wooded with a thick scrub jungle growth, except on the thin top-soil of the ridges, which only supports sparse, scraggly vegetation. Water is a problem. It has no rivers or lakes, and except for a few swamps, its soils drain within a few hours after a heavy rainfall. The inhabitants depend on rain water stored in cisterns.

The Joint Army-Navy Intelligence Service (JANIS) erroneously described Peleliu's terrain as "low and flat," except for the high ground along the upper half of its western pincer. This ridge system took its name from the almost unpronounceable Umurbrogol Mountain, a 550-foot irregular series of broken coral ridges, narrow valleys and rugged peaks. Erosion wore away the rock formations, leaving a razor edge to its jagged crags.

It was this nightmare of crags, pinnacles and coral rubble, honeycombed with natural caves, that the Japanese used to bolster their defense. A Leatherneck wounded in the fighting described the

7

■ Japanese bunkers were extremely difficult to see until the vegetation was burned or blasted away. Even then, debris often concealed the emplacement until the advancing Marines were right on top of them. Often the first notice was a burst of fire that killed or wounded the lead men. *Marine Corps History Division*

Umurbrogol, nicknamed "Bloody Nose Ridge," as "a place that might have been designed by a maniacal artist given to painting mathematical abstractions—all slants, jaggeds, straights, steeps, and sheers with no curve to soften or relieve. The Umurbrogol was a monster Swiss cheese of hard coral limestone pocked beyond imagining with caves and crevices. They were to be found at every level, in every size—crevices small enough for a lonely sniper, eerie caverns big enough to station a battalion among its stalactites and stalagmites."

Thick jungle scrub cloaked the slopes, masking the Umurbrogol's rugged contours from aerial observation. Colonel Merwin Silverthorn thought

"They looked like a normal ridge. But when we denuded it through gunfire and aerial bombardment, we found that there were these funny shaped ridges that were as steep as the roof of a house. And instead of one ridge as it appeared under the foliage, there might be three or four parallel ridges with deep ravines in between." Brigadier General Oliver P. Smith, assistant division commander, declared that, "There was never any question in the minds of the 1st Division planners but that the high ground was the key terrain feature of the island."

During July and August 1944, dozens of photo reconnaissance missions were flown over the island by both navy carrier aircraft and New Guinea–based planes of the Fifth Air Force. Photo interpreters analyzed hundreds of these photographs but did not spot a single Japanese position in the Umurbrogol, although the defenders had created a nightmare of mutually supporting concrete blockhouses, machine gun emplacements, entrenchments and individual riflemen's positions. Captain W. J. "Jasper" Holmes of the Joint Intelligence Center Pacific Ocean Area (JICPOA) expressed regret that "Information concerning the beaches was fairly good, but dense tropical foliage that aerial photography was unable to penetrate concealed jagged limestone ridges, honeycombed with caves, behind the beaches." "Inadequate knowledge of the terrain," he bluntly asserted, "was partly responsible for the heavy casualties." One after-action report indicated that "in the 20% of the area the 1st Marines captured, there were 144 prepared caves which had not been identified." What little the interpreters did discover elsewhere on the island showed that the Japanese were rapidly digging in. In a one-month period, they identified twenty-one new artillery positions, seventeen pillboxes, seven anti-boat guns and five blockhouses.

Intelligence experts attempted to piece together a comprehensive map of the island using pre–World War I German reports, Office of Naval Intelligence (ONI) studies, sketchy information from Japanese POWs and photographs from reconnaissance aircraft. "The navy produced those photographs," Silverthorn recalled, "all sorts of angles and different areas that weren't simple to obtain." But there was still a lack of planning information. To help fill this intelligence gap, the U.S. submarine *Seawolf* lay off the island and photographed its profile and landing beaches.

The final map produced by the 64th Engineer Topographical Battalion showed the high ground to be a single more or less continuous ridge system running about two-thirds of the way up the peninsula, flanked by a good road on either side. Hundreds of the maps were printed in special moisture-resistant paper and distributed to the division, mostly in 1:10,000 and 1:20,000 scale (1 inch = approx. 1/8 and 1/4 nautical mile). In addition, each assault battalion was issued a composite mosaic of terrain and identified enemy installations. The map and intelligence gained from submarine and aerial reconnaissance was also incorporated into the Palau Information Bulletin, which was disseminated to all the major units just prior to the operation. Jasper Holmes lamented that despite their best efforts it was incomplete—"no one could be found who had ever visited the Palaus, and nothing much had been written about them for a century or more."

In one incredible stroke of luck, a captured Japanese officer on Saipan led a patrol to a cave that contained the records of Japan's 31st Army, which had overall responsibility for the defense of the Palaus. The treasure trove included muster rolls and ration reports for the units stationed on Peleliu. The reports listed the approximate enemy strength but not, unfortunately, their location. They turned out to be remarkably accurate. The only discrepancy was three small units—a mortar company, a machine cannon company and a heavy rocket unit— that had little bearing on the outcome of the battle.

Eventually, over fifty tons of documents were recovered, showing that the Japanese had a well-developed predilection for record-keeping but little concern for security. The Saipan bonanza was verified when a message from the Palau garrison was intercepted and decoded. Titled "Disposition of Forces," the message listed the strength of every unit in the Palaus.

The "low and flat" eastern claw tapered off into a series of islets, separated from each other and the western peninsula by a complex of swamps and shoal coral. The area adjacent to the airfield was flat ground choked with mangroves and scattered coconut groves in a tidal coral flat. The southernmost part of the island terminated in two promontories with a cove between. The southwestern promontory, sometimes called Ngarmoked Island, was larger and more rugged than the southeastern one, which was connected to the mainland by a spit of land. At the northern tip of the western peninsula, a wooden causeway connected the small islands of Ngesebus and Kongaruru, where a small airstrip was being constructed. It was known that Peleliu was surrounded by a fringing reef up to one thousand yards wide; however, there was a scarcity of hydrographic information—depth of water over the reef, obstacles, both natural and man-made, surf conditions, soil composition of the beach and trafficability. The amphibious planners were desperate to have this information because the 1st Marine Division had never conducted an opposed landing, and the Tarawa debacle was foremost in the planner's minds.

Assistant Division Commander Brig. Gen. O. P. Smith commented that "Photographs furnished considerable information but they could not tell us the depth of the water over the reef, nor could they disclose the coral heads hidden under the surface of the water." It was decided to perform a physical reconnaissance using an underwater demolition team, "one of the most remarkable developments of the Pacific War," according to Smith.

On the night of 11 August, the USS *Burrfish* surfaced off Peleliu's southeastern shore. Minutes later, a rubber boat was launched with a five-man team led by Lt. (junior grade) M. R. Massey and Chief Gunner's Mate Howard L. Roeder. The team paddled the boat to within a few hundred yards of shore. Four swimmers entered the water and swam in to the beach, under the very noses of the island's defenders. After completing the mission, the team returned and reported. "The beach was found to be satisfactory for LVTs [landing vehicles, tracked], DUKWs [amphibious trucks (manufacturer's designation)] and possibly LCTs [landing craft, tanks]. Any smaller landing craft would have

■ **TARAWA** In August 1943, the 2nd Marine Division assaulted the tiny island of Betio in the Tarawa atoll. It was the Corps' first test of its amphibious doctrine, and it proved to be a costly affair. In seventy-six hours, the Marine Corps and Navy lost 3,407 men, including over 1,100 dead and missing (1,085 Marines and 30 navy corpsmen). The December 3, 1943, *Time* magazine reported, "Last week some 2,000 to 3,000 United States Marines, most of them now dead or wounded, gave the nation a name to stand beside those of Concord Bridge, the Bon Homme Richard, the Alamo, Little Big Horn, and Belleau Wood. The name was Tarawa." The graphic description of the assault waves wading ashore through murderous machine gun fire sent the nation into shock.

The operation's planners thought there would be enough water (five feet) for landing craft to float over the reef fronting the landing beaches. Unfortunately, a "dodging tide" occurred that limited the depth of the water to three feet, grounding all the landing craft, except for the amphibian tractors. There were only enough tractors for the first three waves. The following waves had to wade ashore through chest-deep water. Author Robert Sherrod was among the waders: "No sooner had we hit the water than the Japanese machine guns really opened up. There must have been five or six of these machine guns concentrating their fire on us . . . It was painfully slow, wading in such deep water. And we had seven hundred yards to walk slowly into this machine-gun fire, looming into larger targets as we rose onto higher ground. I was scared, as I have never been scared before."

difficulty in the surf." This was the last physical reconnaissance of the island because, according to the Joint Expeditionary Force intelligence report, "The other beaches were not checked, as heavy Japanese plane activity and many radars in the vicinity made submarine operation extremely hazardous."

In 1935, there were only an estimated 650 natives on Peleliu. They were described as Micronesians, a blend of Polynesian and Melanesian, with some Malay blood mixed in due to the proximity of the Netherland Indies to the west. Their dialect had a characteristic Malay digraph—a pair of letters that represents a single speech sound, such as "ng" in "ring"—in many of their place names, like Ngesebus or Ngarmoked. Most Americans simply ignored these unfamiliar pronunciations and hung their own moniker on the terrain, such as "Bloody Nose Ridge," "Hill 200," "Five Sisters," "The Horseshoe," or "Walt Ridge." The Japanese did the same, naming the topography after the Kanto planes, their home prefecture. The islanders were described in an intelligence report as having "a gentle disposition and good physique. They are large, move quickly, and are especially skillful in various underwater operations. They speak a Malay dialect which is difficult to understand. It is said that the natives are inclined to steal."

With the build-up of the island's defenses in the spring of 1944, the Japanese forced all able-bodied natives, whom they called "Kanakas," to work as laborers. They wore Japanese uniforms and were given armbands that proclaimed, "Training for Victory." One laborer, Kebekal Ngirchobong, was unhappy with being conscripted to unload supplies. "The Japanese often treated us like slaves," he said. Another complained that "the Japanese had run out of food and there were constant fights between soldiers looking for something to eat. If a Palauan fisherman went out in the morning to catch fish, he stood a good chance of having his catch taken by hungry soldiers when he returned."

As the war came closer to the islands, the natives became more skeptical. Ito Ngirabekuu-Iechad initially thought the Japanese would win; however, in July 1944, he visited his brother on Peleliu and was surprised to find the island under daily air attack. He was shocked to see the damage to the airfield and all the destroyed aircraft. Several stranded Japanese pilots were there, and he asked them, "I thought you told me that you would win easily when the Americans arrived?" They answered rather disconcertedly, "They're a hell of a lot stronger than we had thought."

By late summer, carrier-based aircraft had virtually eliminated Japanese air power. Ngiruous Rull, a conscripted native, remembered that "The newly arrived Japanese soldiers were very cocky until the bombing started . . . Their attitude changed somewhat, but they remained confident in their unit." One soldier wrote home, "I cannot help feeling that fate is closing in on us who are in the Palau Sector. We are imbued

■ ROEDER'S LAST MISSION Shortly after the Peleliu reconnaissance, Chief Gunner's Mate Howard L. Roeder volunteered to lead a five-man team on a beach reconnaissance of Gagil Tomil, an island in the Yap Group. They arrived on the night of 18 August 1944 aboard the USS *Burrfish*, a Balao-class submarine. At 2006 on the night of 18 August 1944, the team and two boat handlers passed through the gun access hatch onto the deck, where they retrieved the rubber boat from its storage cylinder. After inflating it, they launched the small rubber craft and paddled through heavy surf until they reached a point approximately five hundred yards from shore. After anchoring the boat, Roeder and three others entered the water and swam toward the beach. One exhausted swimmer returned to the boat twenty minutes later, but the others failed to show up for the rendezvous.

Four days after the men vanished, a Japanese message was intercepted, which explained their disappearance:

> Annansaki 22 August 1944
> Special Unit Gotto Unit
> Intelligence Office (Jokoshitsu)
>
> On the 20th we seized 3 American prisoners at the TOBARU Battery on Yap. They belong to the FIFTH Demolition Unit. The men were transported by submarine. They jumped into the sea at points several miles distant from shore and by swimming reached the reefs off Tobaru Island, Leng and Lebinau. When they tried to return they lost sight of their submarine and swam back to the sea coast. They were captured while hiding. In view of this situation we must keep a strict watch especially in regard to infiltration of these various patrols and spies from submarines.
>
> In view of the case, every lookout, whether it be night or day, shall carefully watch the nearby coast line, and if he observes any examples of the above, shall report it immediately without fail. He should with-out hesitation emulate the above captures. We are confident there is safety in this manner.

On September 2, Roeder, MacMahon, and Black were placed aboard a Japanese sub-chaser for transfer to Davao and Manila in the Philippines. Nothing more was ever heard of them. They were posthumously awarded the Silver Star. After the war it was learned that they were tortured and executed.

with the firm convictions that even though we may die, we will never let the island fall into enemy hands. Our morale is sky high."

One officer bragged that "being a picked Manchukuoan (Manchurian) regiment that does not expect to return alive [we] will follow to the death an imperial order . . . [W]e vow with our unbreakable solidarity to establish the 'Breakwater of the Pacific.' "

CHAPTER 2

THE EMPEROR'S COMMANDERS

Chujo (Lieutenant General) Sadae Inoue, the fifty-five-year-old commanding general of the 14th Division (*Hohei Ju-yon*), was a product of the Imperial Japanese Army's pre-war training system. According to the 1944 Handbook on Japanese Military Forces, the training was "somewhat narrow, arbitrary, and inflexible in its system of indoctrination. Its rigidity often has inhibited originality of thought and action." Inoue graduated from the Military Academy (*Rikugun Shikan Gakko*) and attended the General Staff College (*Rikugun Daigakko*). Author Bill Ross described Inoue as "Hollywood's vision of a Japanese general officer . . . a strict disciplinarian in his mid-fifties, medium-tall, husky, balding, myopic, stern-voiced, and fiercely dedicated to the heritage of five generations of [his] ancestors who had been military officers."

Inoue was the handpicked choice of Gen. Hideki Tojo, the Japanese War Minister, to command the defense of the Palaus: "The Palau Sector Group Commander will secure the islands, which must be held to the

17

very last as the final position barring the enemy from penetrating into the Pacific." This operational strategy recognized that the United States was advancing rapidly across the central Pacific. In September 1943, the Caroline Group, including Peleliu, was included within the Zone of Absolute Defense, Japan's attempt to constrict her strategic perimeter to counter the American threat.

Tojo defined Inoue's orders. "Your objective is to hold the island as long as possible to deny its use by the enemy to support their future plans, and kill as many Americans as you can before the last Japanese soldier dies at his post." Colonel Tokuchi Tada, chief of staff of the 14th

■ Japanese army officers were instilled with the spirit of bushido, the way of the warrior. It was a set of military virtues that stressed absolute loyalty to the Emperor, bravery in battle and a willingness to die rather than surrender. *Marine Corps History Division*

■ **WAY OF THE WARRIOR** The Japanese military prided itself on *bushido*, the "way of the warrior," which traced its origin to the late twelfth and thirteenth centuries when the Chinese brought their chivalrous ideals to Japan. The philosophy was codified into a set of military virtues by the Samurai in the seventeenth century. The code valued compassion for the weak, consideration for wounded enemies and even allowed for honorable surrender. During the Russo-Japanese War of 1904–1905, the Japanese earned high marks for their treatment of the Russians. One British observer wrote, "The chivalry displayed by the Japanese soldier to a fallen foe has been demonstrated on innumerable occasions . . . I have witnessed the considerate treatment accorded to Russian prisoners."

In the 1930s, the Japanese military changed. It stressed brutal discipline and hatred of the enemy, while extolling the offensive and a lust for battle. Surrender was considered to be disgraceful not only to the soldier, but to his entire family. It was believed death in combat was honorable. In combat, this code was used to rally troops into suicidal *banzai* charges, or to encourage encircled troops to take their own lives before capture.

According to Robert B. Edgerton in *Warriors of the Rising Sun*, "Bravery was thought essential, and an honorable death became idealized as a means by which a man's spirit could become a god, eternally to protect his family or clan. Suicide emerged as an honorable way to die, but the Japanese insisted that suicide—by disembowelment—be painful." *Seppuku*, or *hari-kari*, was highly ritualistic. A very sharp disemboweling knife was thrust deep into the left side of the belly, draw across to the right, with a sharp upward cut at the end. A trusted assistant often delivered a killing blow with a sword as the cut was made.

On Peleliu, General Inoue said, "There were no orders to fight until death. However, in the Japanese army, it has been a practice of long standing to indoctrinate all troops so that they do fight until death."

Division, was more succinct about the guidance. "Stated simply, it was planned to defend Palau to the death."

One officer who knew the hard-nosed Inoue said that "He was the type of senior officer who would carry out his tasks without flair, but with tenacity. He wouldn't crumble under the most adverse circumstances." In a sense Inoue typified the senior Japanese officer. They were

■ SUBMARINE INTERDICTION In early August 1944, the USS *Batfish* (SS 310) began its fourth war patrol in the Palau Island group. After an eleven-day transit, she arrived off Peleliu on 20 August. Just after surfacing, "a Japanese 'Betty' popped out of the clouds about three miles astern crossing our track from starboard to port." Describing their emergency crash-dive, the skipper quipped, "[We] dove with our fingers in our ears."

The next day the *Batfish* spotted a Japanese *Minekaze* (Summit Wind) class destroyer and fired a three-torpedo spread—bow, middle and stern. All three hit, leaving the ship sinking rapidly. *Batfish* went deep and rigged for silent running as vengeful patrol craft (PC) headed her way. Fortunately, reef noises were so loud that the Japanese PC couldn't hear the American submarine. Four days later *Batfish* put two torpedoes into another destroyer and "broke her in half." The force of the explosions threw debris two hundred feet in the air and practically sheared the stern off.

The *Batfish* stayed in the area until September 5, watching the bombing of the island while acting as a plane guard for ditched pilots. The skipper stated in his patrol report, "The impression I took away with me from this once very active area is that the enemy never recovered from the carrier raid of last spring. The absence of [ship] patrols and fighter opposition is significant . . . and if an attempt is made to take these islands the opposition will be surprisingly light." He wasn't the only one fooled.

inspired by emotion and impulse, often displaying a disastrous rigidity, rather than cool calculation. British General William Slim wrote that "the Japanese were ruthless and bold as ants when their designs went well but if those plans were disturbed or thrown out, they fell into confusion, were slow to adjust themselves, and invariably clung to their original schemes."

Inoue sat quietly on Babelthuap, while forty miles south the 2nd Infantry Regiment fought to the death because he was convinced Peleliu was a diversion—despite evidence to the contrary. His belief in the Japanese military code of *bushido* did not allow him to consider the cost his decision would have on the lives of his men.

The backbone of Inoue's command, crack troops of the 14th Division, was one of the oldest and best military units in the Japanese Army.

■ The average Japanese soldier stood 5 feet 3 inches tall and weighed between 116 to 120 pounds. His army training inured him to hard work and privation. Seen here, he is wearing a winter uniform with field gear, including magazine pouches, bayonet, gas mask and 7.7mm Arisaka Type 99 rifle. *National Archives*

Nicknamed the Shining Division (*Sho Heidan*), it traced its battle lineage from the Sino-Japanese War (1894–1895), the siege and capture of Port Arthur during the Russo-Japanese War (1904–1905) and the Siberian Intervention (1919–1922), where several hundred of its men were massacred by Bolshevik irregulars at Nikolayevsk. In 1932, during the "1st Shanghai Incident," its soldiers came in contact with members of the 4th Marine Regiment, then guarding the International Settlement.

The division was originally part of the Eastern District Army, one of four army geographical districts in Japan proper. Its headquarters in Tokyo gave the division a more prestigious reputation. Colonel Tada bragged that "Our division was famous for its strength and loyalty to the Emperor." In the Japanese military system, units were recruited from a specific area. The 14th Division was enlisted from the Utsunomiya Division (*Shikan*) District, where its twenty-thousand–plus men were conscripted for an initial period of two years; with the onset of war the term of service was extended indefinitely.

The division was initially mobilized for service in China but ended up in Tsitsihar, Manchuria. According to Tada, "it was engaged in training for its defense in case of Russian attack." After a series of military reversals in the Pacific, the Japanese high command shifted some of its elite forces to counter the American onslaught. In February 1944, the 14th Division was ordered to Biak to counter MacArthur's advance northwestward from New Guinea. The orders were changed to Saipan prior to deployment, but while en route the convoy was further rerouted to the Palaus. American intercept stations picked up this coded message and passed it to the U.S. Army Signal Security Agency for decryption, translation and analysis. The actual message read, "The 14th Division is deleted from the Third Area Army Order of Battle and enrolled in the Second Area Army Order of Battle." American Order of Battle specialists determined the division's final destination by comparing this message snippet with other intelligence sources at the Joint Intelligence Center Pacific Ocean Area (JICPOA).

The division's sixteen transports and cargo ships reached their destination on 24 April, after a long circuitous voyage to avoid prowling U.S. submarines. By this time in the war, the movement of Japanese reinforcements was extremely hazardous. Unbeknownst to the enemy, the U.S. Navy had broken the four-digit *Maru* "S" code, encrypted merchant ship routing messages that gave the route, schedule and destination of each convoy. Ships radioed positions where they estimated they would be as of noon on the next few days. This priceless intelligence achievement enabled American submarines to locate them anywhere in the vast Pacific.

Convoys were routinely intercepted and torpedoed with the loss of thousands of Japanese soldiers and tons of badly needed equipment. Lt. Gen. Holland M. "Howlin' Mad" Smith related that "A few days before the invasion of Saipan, a wolf pack nearly annihilated a convoy of the Japanese 13th Infantry Division. Five out of seven transports were sunk by our submarines." The same fate befell the 28th Individual Garrison Infantry Battalion off Guam and the 118th Infantry Regiment two weeks later. One frightened Japanese survivor said there was a feeling among his shipmates that "You could walk from port to port on American periscopes." By the end of the war, Japan had lost some 2,500 transports, sixty-two thousand crewmen and eight million tons of shipping.

Inoue made his headquarters on Koror, the traditional capital of the island chain, but deployed the bulk of his men on Babelthuap, the largest island, where he intended to make his final stand. He firmly believed that Babelthuap and Koror, the South Seas Administrative Authority headquarters, would be the primary objective of the American landing; however, to protect his southern flank, he ordered the elite 2d Infantry Regiment to defend Peleliu and its valuable airfield. The 6,500 soldiers of this "A" type reinforced regiment were made of strong stuff; in an interview after the war, Inoue recalled, "All the officers and men carried in mind the meaning of our sacred war, and the leaders, burning with the will to be 'Breakwater of the Pacific.' [They] do not expect to return alive [and] will follow to the death an imperial order and devote themselves to the endeavor of being the type of soldier who can fight hundreds of men."

Forty-four-year-old Col. Kunio Nakagawa, the aggressive commander of the 2d Infantry Regiment, was noted for his courage in action. He received nine medals for bravery and leadership as a commander in China and was considered to be one of the best in the Japanese Army, slated for higher rank. He was also an authority on the employment of armor. Peleliu islander, Ngiruous Rull, met Nakagawa after being conscripted by the Japanese and put in charge of the native contingent. He described him as a "stocky—5-foot 6-inch—serious man," who never seemed to smile. "Although there were army photographers around, he would permit no pictures of himself. He lacked any humor [but] I don't

■ Colonel Kunio Nakagawa, the aggressive commander of the 2nd Infantry Regiment. His stubborn defense of Peleliu ranks with that of Iwo Jima as being the most enduring resistance of the Pacific war. *Marine Corps History Division*

think this was a result of knowing that he was about to lay down his life and the lives of his fine regiment but simply a result of his military training and his own personality."

Rull attended two briefings by Nakagawa:

> We stood quietly in ranks . . . and although it was hot and humid, he always dressed in full uniform with all his ribbons. He spoke with much emotion about the coming battle. He reminded us that we were Japanese, that success depended on each of us doing our part,

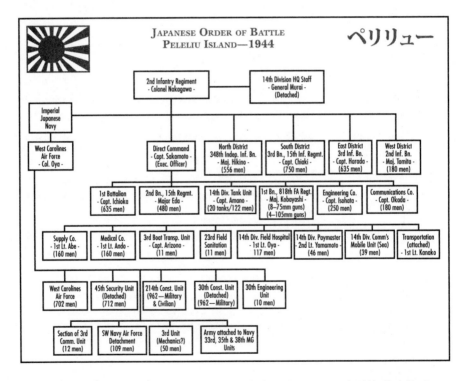

Table of organization of the 2nd Infantry Regiment commanded by Col. Kunio Nakagawa. The regiment had a long and distinguished history and was made up of combat-hardened troops of the Manchuria Army. Its 6,500 men were willing to die to keep the Americans from taking the island. *History of War.org*

and that we needed to look out for the welfare of one another. He always reminded us that we had a fine unit. His talks were designed to exhort the troops before battle. No questions were allowed of the colonel, and as

```
  HEADQUARTERS, EXPEDITIONARY TROOPS, THIRD FLEET
                  IN THE FIELD.


                                    28 August, 1944

    SECRET

                PELELIU and NGESEBUS

            CG is Maj Gen MURAI, Kenjiro.

        Army
14th Div
        2d Inf Regt including 1 Arty Bn          3,283        (a)
        One Bn 15th Inf Regt including
          one Arty Bty (4 x 75mm) and one
          Mortar Co (10 x 81mm)                  1,030        (b)
        Tank Unit, less 1 Pl (12 Tanks)            100        (c)
        Sig Unit, 1 Radio Squad                     10        (d)
        Intendance Duty Unit                        30        (e)
        Fd Hosp                                    250        (f)
53d Ind Mixed Brig
        One Ind Inf Bn                             685        (g)
                                                 5,388

        Navy, Combatant
45th Guard Force Det                        200 -   400       (h)
114th and 126th AA Units                    600              (i)
                                            800 - 1,000

        Navy, Labor
204th and 214th Const Bns        )
Elements of 43d and 235th Const Bns)       2,000 - 2,200     (j)
        Navy, Airbase Personnel
PELELIU                                          1,270        (k)
NGESEBUS                                           950        (k)
                                                 2,220

                Recapitulation

    Army, Combatant               5,300
    Navy, Combatant                 800 - 1,000
    Total, Combatant              6,100 - 6,300   6,100 - 6,300

    Navy, Labor                                   2,000 - 2,200
    Navy, Airbase Personnel                       2,200
                                                 10,300 -10,700
```

■ Third Fleet classified Japanese troop list for Peleliu and Ngesebus.
Expeditionary Troops Third Fleet, Intelligence Report dated 30 September 1944

■ Marine engineer defusing anti-boat mines scattered among the dozens of steel stakes the Japanese emplaced to disrupt the landing. Fortunately for the assault troops, the sixteen-ton amphibious tractor easily plowed over the obstacles. *Marine Corps History Division*

soon as he was through talking, we would leave and go back to our jobs. I was a little perturbed that not once did Colonel Nakagawa or any Japanese officer ever thank the Peleliu labor force for the work they had done.

Upon reaching the island, an additional 5,300 navy combatants, labor and airbase personnel swelled the defenders' ranks to between 10,300 and 10,700 men.

■ Barbed wire entanglements, designed to slow down the assaulting troops or channelize them into prepared fire lanes. Heavily laden troops would be hard pressed to move quickly through this tangle of barbed wire—some of which was shoulder high. At times, the wire would be booby-trapped to add an extra dimension of devilry. *Marine Corps History Division*

Shortly after arriving in the Palaus, Inoue took the two-hour boat trip from Koror to Peleliu. He closely studied the island's shoreline through his high-powered binoculars. "[As] I circled the island in a large barge," Inoue recalled, "I could see nothing wrong with the defensive positions." As his barge approached the southwestern shore, he paid close attention to the working parties erecting anti-landing obstacles. He determined this area was the only feasible landing site on the island and had ordered his men to prepare a special welcome for the invading

Americans. Steel poles and tetrahedrons were positioned to pierce the bottom of landing craft, wide belts of barbed wire were strung on the beach and in the water to slow and channelize the attackers into prepared fire lanes. Hundreds of land mines and improvised booby traps (artillery and huge aerial bombs rigged as mines) were scattered below the water between the reef and the shoreline. Long anti-tank ditches

■ Heavily camouflaged coral bunker containing either a machine gun or riflemen. The vegetation in front of this emplacement has been torn away, exposing the firing ports. They were positioned to take advantage of the terrain and were mutually supported by other similar positions. They were almost impossible to spot and difficult to knock out except by infantry assault. *Marine Corps History Division*

■ Japanese land mine—designed to destroy a tank or armored vehicle. Fortunately on Peleliu, most of the mines on the beach had not been armed. *Marine Corps History Division*

paralleled the beaches to prevent tanks from moving inland. The beaches themselves were covered by fields of fire from dozens of casemates, pillboxes and bunkers. The casemates mounted 37mm or 47mm anti-boat and anti-tank guns and were made of reinforced concrete with coral packed against the sides and over the top. Not only were they difficult to spot, but they were almost impervious to anything but a direct hit with a large-caliber gun.

Peleliu's defenses were prepared in accordance with Inoue's "Palau Sector Group Training for Victory" order. Issued on 11 July 1944, the document incorporated a new defensive strategy designed to "bleed the Americans white." In a break with traditional Japanese tactics of uselessly expending lives in a suicidal *banzai* attack, Inoue tried to indoctrinate his officers against the use of these tactics. "After the Americans had landed, I issued strict orders the banzai attack was not to be employed," he said. His guidance was put to the test during the battle when one of his subordinates proposed an all-out attack on the airfield. Inoue responded with a mild rebuke. "It is easy to die, but difficult to live on. We must select the difficult course, and continue the fight because of the influence on the morale of the Japanese people." He went on to explain his rationale. "Saipan was lost in a very short time because of vain *banzai* attacks, with the result that the people at home suffered a drop in morale." He ordered the subordinate to "fight a delaying action from prepared positions, causing as many enemy casualties as possible."

CHAPTER 3

MANIACAL RAMPARTS

"The Japs were in deep caves, which had small holes for
fixed machine gun fire. We were being hit from all sides
with no way to get at them."
—Maj. Raymond G. Davis
Commanding officer, 1st Battalion, 1st Marines

Inoue expected that "at least three American divisions would land
on either the southern or the eastern beaches because they were
unguarded by reefs." When the 2d Infantry Regiment landed on Peleliu,
they were "astonished at the weakness of this island." Colonel Tada
explained in a matter-of-fact manner that "we had no airpower to
oppose the American air force; we had no tanks capable of defeating
American tanks; we had no hopes of receiving any supplies whereas
the Americans had anything they desired." In typical Japanese fashion,
he used an analogy to describe the situation. "[It] closely resembled a
contest between a large man armed with a long spear and a small man
armed with a sword. The man armed with the short sword must crowd
in close to the large man so that his spear is useless . . . We had to attempt
to infiltrate into the American lines to render American air attacks,
naval bombardments, and tank attacks ineffective." Tada was under no
illusions. "We did not believe that this method of attack would succeed, but
we believed that the great number of American losses would cause them

31

to think the price was not commensurate with the value of Peleliu and therefore withdraw."

With this strategy in mind, Colonel Nakagawa divided the island into four independent defensive sectors. The northern sector was defended by eight hundred soldiers of the 346th Independent Infantry Battalion, 53rd Independent Mixed Brigade, under the command of Major Hikino. His battalion was responsible for half of the western claw, including Ngesebus Island. Captain Harada's 3rd Battalion, 2nd Regiment, held the eastern claw, while the southern end of the island belonged to the 3rd Battalion, 15th Infantry Regiment, commanded by Captain Chiaki. Chiaki's one-thousand-man battalion was reinforced with four 75mm guns and a mortar company of ten 81mm mortars. The vital western sector was defended by a thousand men of the 2nd Battalion, 2nd Infantry Regiment. Captain Ichioka's 1st Battalion, 2nd Infantry Regiment, the 14th Division tank unit (minus one platoon), and the Engineer Company were held in reserve. The regimental second in command, Captain Sakamoto, was in direct control of this force.

Colonel Nakagawa's command post was "placed on the southern end of the ridge [Umurbrogol Mountain] along the western side of the island." His pioneer (labor) unit carved out an elaborate cave, complete with electricity, ventilation and wooden stairways for easy access to the various levels of the complex. His immediate staff—fifty-five officers and enlisted men, consisting of administration, code and intelligence, ordnance and the headquarters guard—worked in complete safety beneath the impenetrable coral surface. The entranceway was heavily camouflaged and almost unnoticeable in the dense vegetation and broken terrain. Several machine guns and snipers were positioned to provide security. Food and ammunition were stored in every nook and cranny, and troughs were constructed to collect water.

A secondary headquarters was prepared on Oyama, the northern end of the same ridge. It was the highest hill on the island, at ninety-eight meters above sea level. From here Colonel Nakagawa "held meetings

and issued normal battle orders from this position until at least D + 15,"
according to prisoner of war reports.

Nakagawa quickly devised an initial defense plan, which he reviewed
with General Inoue. "On my first trip to Peleliu, about July, I examined the
defense plan with Colonel Nakagawa," Inoue recalled. "In order to effectively repel an invasion, infantry troops were to be deployed in strongly
prepared positions along the beaches, the artillery battalion was to be
emplaced along the slopes of the ridge on the western side of the island,
and the tank company was to remain in a central position, so it could be
deployed in any spot in danger of being captured."

Colonel Nakagawa issued the Peleliu District Unit Defense Plan on
May 27. In it, he outlined his overall philosophy. "Defensive positions
should be completed—key strong points and at the water's edge within
one month. Positions should be prepared in an interlocking fashion and
defended with fierce fire and counterattack to destroy enemy at water's
edge." He spelled out in detail how his men were to fight an invasion:

> If the enemy secures a foothold on the beach, we
> will attack with the reserve units and troops diverted
> from other sectors. We will direct firepower [small arms
> and indirect weapons, artillery and mortars] from other
> areas and annihilate them. Each area will reinforce the
> others with fire, while each section will annihilate the
> enemy facing it. Taking advantage of the enemy's insecure
> bridgehead, we will attack and destroy him that night at
> the latest . . . If the situation becomes bad, we will contrive
> to hold out. We will maintain a firm hold on the high
> ground and prevent the enemy from establishing or using
> an airbase. We will commence a daring guerrilla warfare
> and, in cooperation with the Naval Landing Force, we will
> wipe out the enemy troops at all times, and will carefully
> guard the breaks in the high ground.

■ ■ ■

Nakagawa's plan articulated the new Japanese defensive doctrine learned from the fighting on Saipan and Guam. "Although there is a need for beach positions to disrupt the enemy landing," a staff officer reported, "it is dangerous to depend on them too much. There is need for preparation of strongpoints from which to launch counterattacks, and for deep resistance zones adjacent to waterfront positions." Nakagawa would not willingly give the Americans a pass on gaining a toehold on the island. His troops would still try to annihilate the invading force, but they would also organize a defense in depth, including prepared positions to fall back to if the counterattack was not successful. From these positions, they would wage a war of attrition. Every foxhole and cave position would be defended to the death. Futile "suicide charges" would not be allowed, although coordinated counterattacks would be employed if tactically advantageous. The strategy was designed to inflict maximum casualties. The Japanese believed this high cost would strain the enemy's will to fight, while at the same time boost sagging morale at home.

Construction started immediately. Nakagawa established an aggressive schedule. "The area should prepare as rapidly as possible for an enemy attack in close conjunction with the Naval Unit. Rapidly complete temporary positions within one month [and] within two months, fire positions and firm field positions to be completed. These fortifications should be continually strengthened." Sergeant Major Kurihara lamented, "From the moment we landed on the island, we worked night and day building fortifications. Day in and day out, all we did was dig!" However, trouble soon developed between Colonel Nakagawa and Vice Adm. Seiichi Itou, the naval commander, who was senior. The admiral refused to cooperate. He would not allow the army to use any of his equipment, construction material, nor existing caves and installations. Army 2nd Lt. Ei Yamaguchi related sarcastically that "the building materials were rich in the navy area; the army units [had] to bow three times and then nine [more] times [before] receiving it."

The rift was symptomatic of a long-standing inter-service rivalry, which plagued the Japanese war effort. The army and navy were at loggerheads. They did not agree on strategy. The navy formulated its plans on confronting the U.S. Navy, while the army looked upon Russia as the principal enemy. In addition, the two services maintained secrecy so tight that it was impossible to determine what was happening in the other's domain. For example, Admiral Nobutake Kondo related that the Battle of Midway was "a defeat so decisive and so grave that the

■ Japanese emplacement hewed out of coral rock. It is lined with logs to further strengthen it against bombardment. This photo shows the effects of fire on its interior, probably the result of a flamethrower . . . a weapon that absolutely terrified the Japanese defenders. *Marine Corps History Division*

details were kept the guarded secret of a limited circle, even within the Japanese Navy. The army did not find out about the debacle for months." Another naval officer bitterly criticized both services. "Instead of cooperation, the army had studied how to protect its position against the navy, and vice versa. The spirit of rivalry just got the better of both of them. This attitude is among the most important causes that led to our swift defeat." (At Midway the IJN lost four aircraft carriers, a heavy cruiser and over three hundred of its best pilots—a defeat so stunning that many historians consider it the turning point of the war.)

In order to resolve the impasse, Inoue sent fifty-three-year-old Maj. Gen. Conjiro Murai, the youngest general officer in the Japanese Army, to Peleliu in mid-July. "He was charged with directing the operations on the island," according to Colonel Tada, "and acting as liaison between Colonel Nakagawa and General Inoue." However, records indicate that Colonel Nakagawa retained command of the garrison and the two acted in concert for the island's defense. Sergeant Major Kurihara, assigned to the 2nd Regiment headquarters, said that "General Murai, an authority on fortifications, had been sent to the Palaus to supervise the construction of the defenses of the area. Because his return to the north was cut off, he attached himself to Colonel Nakagawa as an adviser." Despite the conflicting testimony on Murai's role, American intelligence agree that the two army officers conducted a brilliant defense. Both men committed suicide on the same day in the same location and were posthumously promoted to the grade of lieutenant general by special promotion. After the battle, a captured Japanese orderly identified Murai's remains to a patrol from the 81st Division. The body was found in the headquarters cave "in a very decomposed state" and could only be identified from personal items.

With Murai's assignment the navy acquiesced and construction proceeded at a faster pace. As Sergeant Major Kurihara lamented, however, there were still problems. "[Although we] undertook the responsibility of transportation and construction without a murmur, machine power

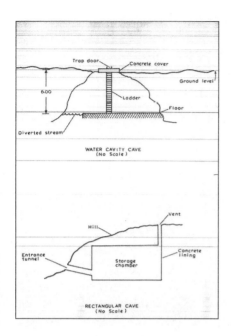

WATER CAVITY CAVE
(No Scale)

RECTANGULAR CAVE
(No Scale)

■ Sketches of various types of Japanese caves. The resourceful defenders took advantage of the island's natural erosion to construct hundreds of gun positions, shelters and bombproofs. The fighting positions were mutually supporting and located to take advantage of the terrain. *Expeditionary Troops Third Fleet, Intelligence Report dated 30 September 1944*

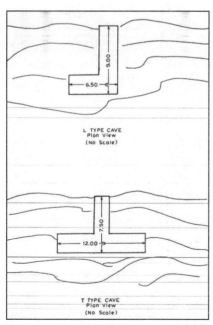

L TYPE CAVE
Plan View
(No Scale)

T TYPE CAVE
Plan View
(No Scale)

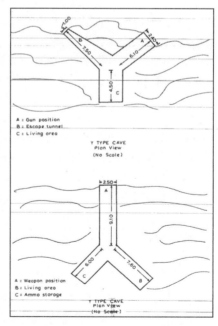

A : Gun position
B : Escape tunnel
C : Living area

Y TYPE CAVE
Plan View
(No Scale)

A : Weapon position
B : Living area
C : Ammo storage

Y TYPE CAVE
Plan View
(No Scale)

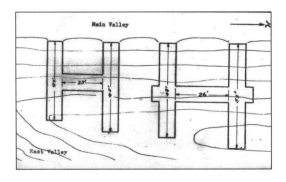

■ Japanese naval shelter. One such position sheltered over a thousand men and was impervious to bombardment. It had to be taken by direct infantry assault—with the resultant casualties from the Japanese defenders. *Expeditionary Troops Third Fleet, Intelligence Report dated 30 September 1940*

and materials were scarce. At the time we were very worried about the shortage of manpower; many soldiers died due to the lack of medical supplies and illness and exhaustion." Another soldier complained that "construction material was unsuitable and difficult to use. Therefore only important fortifications were built. We spent many days and nights in constructing pillboxes, although the thickness of the cement was not up to expectations due to the lack of manpower and machinery." Despite the soldiers' bellyaching, Umurbrogol's coral subsurface was soon honeycombed with over two hundred interconnected artificial caves and hardened weapons positions. In addition, the Japanese made use of over three hundred naturally formed caves and caverns to augment their system of concrete pillboxes, entrenchments and gun emplacements. The elite 214th Naval Construction Battalion (*Setsueitai*) was sent to help blast out many of the caves. This special all-Japanese naval unit (*Suidotai*) was made up of former civilian miners and tunnel workers. The BABA Unit (a labor unit that worked on caves and tunnels) of the Kobayashi Labor Force (*Setsubutai*) was also used for construction. An intelligence report stated that "this unit was considered inferior because more than half its force was Koreans."

■ Flamethrower operator sends a stream of jellied gasoline into an emplacement while wary riflemen keep watch. This cagy veteran has "camouflaged" the tell-tale tanks by pulling canvas over them to keep the Japanese from specifically targeting him. *Marine Corps History Division*

The Japanese were masters at hewing the coral ridge into a near impenetrable stronghold. They constructed myriad positions, from one-man spider holes to enormous four- or five-story caves capable of housing hundreds of men. Many of the caves had secondary entrances and escape routes. Narrow entrances were lined with blast walls of coral and barrels filled with stone or concrete. All caves were either naturally

39

twisting or were so constructed to provide protection from bomb and artillery blast and direct fire. Several large caves were constructed with staggered levels; one of them had nine separate galleries. Firing ports were carved into the walls, and those on the lower slopes often housed a field piece. Rooms for ammunition and sleeping quarters were prepared. Some natural caves on the peaks were used as observation posts and provided with telephone communications. A number of the caves had sliding steel doors and blast shutters.

One "H" style navy cave was constructed in the side of a hill. A POW reported that "On 3 September when [he] first entered the cave there were over a thousand men in it. The cave was built in such a way that it could not be bombed nor destroyed by naval gunfire. It had to be taken by direct infantry assault, primarily with demolitions and flame throwers." Eugene B. "Sledgehammer" Sledge, in *With the Old Breed at Peleliu and Okinawa,* described a typical flamethrower attack: "The assistant reached up and turned a valve on the flamethrower. Womack then aimed the nozzle at the opening . . . He pressed the trigger. With a *whooooooosh,* the flame leaped at the opening. Some muffled screams, then all quiet." One Japanese soldier, seeing a Marine point his flame-thrower, killed himself with a hand grenade. Toward the end of the battle, gasoline was poured into the cave and set afire; however, even that failed. The last hold-out of the caves did not surrender until 1 February 1945, almost five months after the initial landing.

Colonel Nakagawa prepared the caves for a last-ditch stand by stock-piling them with ammunition, food and clothing. The Division after-action report noted that "Scattered clothing dumps were found in the southern and extreme northern portions of the island. Food, particularly canned fish, canned meat and rice was abundant. Ammunition was plentiful for all weapons . . . [S]upply dumps were small and well-dispersed." The Japanese did suffer from a shortage of water when they were cut off from their wells and storage tanks.

The cleverly camouflaged positions took maximum advantage of terrain features and were located to provide mutual support

and overlapping fields of fire. A III Amphibious Corps Operations
Report stated:

> The outstanding feature of the Palaus Operation was
> the difficulty of reducing the cave defenses. A fanatical
> enemy had retired to a coralline hill mass comprised of
> many pinnacles, sharp ridges, sheer cliffs, and narrow
> ravines, honeycombed with caves. Many of these caves
> were high on the sides of the cliffs or precipitous slopes.
> They faced in all directions, were on different levels, and
> were frequently reinforced with concrete and with steel
> doors covering entrances which were practically invis-
> ible. Often they were provided with many chambers and
> multiple entrances. They were stocked and located as to
> be self-supporting as well as mutually supporting and
> were almost inaccessible to an attacking force.

Major Nikolai Stevenson witnessed their deadly effect. "Our objective was a group of spiny intertwining coral and limestone ridges, heavily
fortified by pillboxes and caves designed to permit murderous interlocking
machinegun fire. The men struggled forward, yard by yard, always with a
cry, 'Corpsman, Corpsman!' and always the stretchers came back full." The
positions were constructed with openings that sloped downward or with
sharp turns to protect the defenders from direct-fire weapons. Entrances
and firing slits were small and expertly camouflaged, which made them
almost impossible to see from a distance. The highly disciplined Japanese
held their fire until they could not miss and then opened up from several
directions at once. An exasperated Lt. Col. Jeff Fields related, "The Japanese
had developed this cave system with various levels and openings. You just
couldn't get to them. They could kill guys before you could get to them."

On September 3, Lieutenant General Inoue was notified of the
American assault. Japanese intelligence officers estimated that it would
be a division-size unit and gave the time and place of the landing. He

immediately issued an eloquent call to arms. "This battle may have a part in the decisive turn of tide in breaking the deadlock of the 'Great Asiatic War.' The entire Army and the people of Japan are expecting us to win this battle. There will never be another chance as these few existing days for the people living in the empire to repay the Emperor's benevolence again. Rouse yourself for the sake of your country! Officers

■ Unbelievably precipitous terrain stymied normal tactical formations. Men had to climb up the jagged slopes any way they could, under the unrelenting fire of the defenders. Often the men fought their way up a difficult slope only to find it ended in an impossibly steep cliff. *Marine Corps History Division*

and men, you will devote your life to the winning of this battle, and attaining your long cherished desire of annihilating the enemy."

Colonel Nakagawa ordered his troops to take up defense positions. Morale was high. One soldier wrote in his diary, "At last the enemy has come to make a landing! I realize that I will die . . . and in a way, it's too bad, but it is a glorious thing to do!" Another wrote, "I cannot help feeling that fate is closing in on us . . . but we will defend Peleliu. We are imbued with the firm conviction that even though we may die, we will never let the airfield fall into enemy hands. Our morale is sky high!"

■ Even with the camouflage stripped away by the bombardment, the Japanese emplacements were almost impossible to spot until they opened fire—and even then, they might remain concealed by debris. This photo shows several potential positions in the face of this bluff. At lower left of the photo, several Marines cautiously examine an enemy position. *Marine Corps History Division*

■ MARINE WRITER TELLS OF CAVE FIGHTING ON PELELIU

BY STAFF SGT. WARD WALKER

Peleliu, Palau Islands, September 19—(Delayed)—As they did at Guam and Saipan, the Japs are fighting the Marines here from the bottoms of their caves—the last desperate stratagem of a beaten soldier.

Caves big enough to hold 250 or more men, caves running for more than one hundred yards inside a ridge, caves with many entrances and shelves, caves reinforced with concrete, little caves cleverly camouflaged—they've used them all with the same result: death.

Most of their caves are proof against Naval gunfire and bombing, although a direct hit may knock out one entrance. But Marines with blocks of TNT, a flame thrower, or a tank, can—and have—solved the best of them.

The caves on Peleliu are fashioned in the limestone ridges. These are for the most part merely improvements on interior faults of the coral ridges—deep black holes where the Japs huddle. They snipe at the Marines until they're discovered. They refuse to surrender, chatter in their native tongue, scream foul words in English. And then they die.

One Marine tank rolled up to the mouth of a cave. The snout of its artillery piece swung into the hole. Jap bullets bounced like hail off its thick sides. The piece fired shot after shot. From a camouflaged hole more than one hundred yards away, smoke rose. Marine engineers with TNT blew all the openings shut, sealing the Japs inside.

At the edge of the airport during the first day's fighting, two Marines were killed by Jap snipers in a cave. Leathernecks tossed in grenades. Still the Japs fired. Heavy charges of explosives were thrown in. Still the Japs fired. A flame thrower was summoned. Its scorching blast was squirted in. Two Japs broke, screaming, from another entrance to be met with rifle fire. But it took another blast from the flame thrower to kill the two who remained in the cave, which ran for fifty feet inside a low coral ridge. [U.S. Marine Corps news release]

CHAPTER 4

OPERATION

STALEMATE

"Everything about Stalemate left a bad taste in my mouth."

—Brig. Gen. Merwin Silverthorn

By the summer of 1944, the United States was advancing on Japan's home islands in a two-prong attack through the Central and Southwest Pacific Theaters. Japan's first line of defense in the Marshall and Mariana Islands had been shattered. The country was now desperately pouring men, weapons and equipment into a second line, the Zone of Absolute Defense, extending west of the Marianas–Carolines–Western New Guinea line, where each Japanese soldier was expected to fight to the death. General MacArthur's southwestern forces had reached the western extremity of New Guinea and were preparing for a move into the Philippine island of Mindanao, to honor his "I shall return" promise. In the Central Pacific, Admiral Chester W. Nimitz's amphibious forces had seized Saipan in the Marianas and were planning to move toward Iwo Jima in the Volcano Island Group—only 800 miles from Tokyo. First, however, MacArthur's advance had to be secured.

Admiral Nimitz directed the seizure of the southern Palaus in the western Carolines to "remove a definite threat from MacArthur's right

■ Admiral William F. "Bull" Halsey, the aggressive commander of the U.S. Navy's Third Fleet, recommended cancellation of the Peleliu operation because of the weakness of the Japanese air strength in the Philippines. His recommendation was not accepted, and the landing went on as scheduled. *Marine Corps History Division*

flank, and to secure a base to support his operation into the southern Philippines." On 7 July he designated it Operation Stalemate II and assigned Phase I (Peleliu) a target date of 15 September 1944.

Admiral William F. "Bull" Halsey was charged with the conduct of the Palau operation under the title of Commander Western Pacific Task Force. His immensely powerful Third Fleet consisted of 800 ships, 1,600 aircraft and an estimated 250,000 soldiers, sailors and Marines. His attack force alone included 14 battleships, 16 fleet carriers, 20 escort carriers, 22 cruisers, 136 destroyers and 31 destroyer escorts.

Halsey, the consummate warrior, launched his fast carrier task force to "seek out and destroy hostile air and naval forces that threaten Stalemate II." His far-flung sweeps ranged from the Bonins south to the Philippines—Iwo Jima 31 August–2 September; Palaus, 6–8 September; and Mindanao on 9–10 September. Halsey was surprised at the extent of his success and the weakness of the Japanese. "Enemy's non-aggressive attitude unbelievable and fantastic, we had found the central Philippines a hollow shell."

After carefully considering the situation, Halsey composed a message to Nimitz recommending the cancellation of the Peleliu operation because there was no serious threat to MacArthur's flank. "I'm going to stick my neck out," he remarked, adding later that, "Such a recommendation would upset many apple carts, possibly all the way to Mr. Roosevelt and Mr. Churchill." However, Nimitz did not concur and ordered the operation to go as planned.

Task Force 58 launched a seventy-two plane fighter sweep that hit the airfields at dawn, catching the Japanese with their Zeros down. Following close on their heels were three squadrons armed with magnetic mines which they planted in the main exits of Palau's anchorages, trapping thirty-two ships inside the lagoon. A third strike hit the oil storage tanks, docks, radio stations, runways and warehouses. Large fires were burning as the American aircraft exited the target area.

General Inoue was caught in the raid on Peleliu:

> Just as I completed my tour, the American air force made its first raid. From the northern end of the island I saw smoke rising from the air field sector. The naval headquarters had suffered a direct hit and all of the Navy staff officers had been wounded; the fuel depot had been hit and was burning fiercely, blackening the sky with smoke.

Halsey's scope of responsibility was so large that he delegated the amphibious phase of the operation to Vice Adm. Theodore S. Wilkinson, while tactical control of the Peleliu Attack Group was given to Rear Adm. George H. Fort. Major General Julian C. Smith, USMC, deputy of Fleet Marine Force Pacific (FMFPAC), was designated as commander of the expeditionary troops. Under him, Maj. Gen. Roy Geiger's III Amphibious Corps (IIIAC) was designated the Western Attack Force. It fell to Geiger's command to attack and seize Peleliu and Angaur, a small island seven miles south. His ground forces consisted of the 1st Marine Division and the Army's 81st Division.

Geiger's IIIAC was formed in the spring of 1944. Brigadier General Merwin Silverthorn, his chief of staff, said it was "a field organization and never did have a roof over its head, until it established a headquarters near Naha, Okinawa, in May 1945." At the time it was formed, its headquarters was located on Guadalcanal, which Silverthorn described as, "rather primitive, under canvas, in a jungle grove of miscellaneous trees—very

■ MAJ. GEN. ROY S. GEIGER

Roy Geiger enlisted in the Marine Corps in 1907 and attained the rank of corporal before being selected to attend the Marine Officer School of Application. After receiving a commission as a second lieutenant in 1909, he served for seven years in a variety of posts and stations before applying for flight training. He received his wings in 1917 and was designated the fifth Marine Corps aviator and only the forty-ninth naval aviator. Captain Geiger cut a dashing figure, wearing highly polished knee-high boots, leather flying jacket and riding breeches—a true knight of the air.

A year later he took his squadron to France as a part of the 1st Marine Aviation Force. For distinguished service, he was awarded the Navy Cross, the first of many decorations for bravery and leadership. The period between World War I and II found him serving in various aviation commands in Haiti, Nicaragua and the United States.

When World War II broke out, Geiger commanded the 1st Marine Air Wing on Guadalcanal. In 1943, he was selected to command I Amphibious Corps, which was later redesigned III Amphibious Corps. He led it during the campaign for Guam, Peleliu and Okinawa. During the last operation, he assumed command of an entire United States Field Army, the first and only Marine to achieve the distinction. After the campaign, he commanded the Fleet Marine Force Pacific until his untimely death in 1947, a week before retirement. He was posthumously promoted to the rank of four-star general.

thick, not near any town of any kind. General Geiger lived in a tent. I guess you would call it a storage tent—maybe twenty feet by twenty feet."

Geiger invited Silverthorn to move in with him, which greatly benefited their association. Silverthorn recalled that his "office tent was of the same size and about fifty feet from his [Geiger's], and the other staff officers were in similar tents with a bunk in their tent that they slept in. So their working quarters and their living quarter[s] were synonymous." Geiger and his staff were immediately immersed in planning Operation Stevedore, the assault of Guam, scheduled for June 14, 1944, just as the warning order for Peleliu made its way down the chain of command.

Brigadier General O. P. Smith, assistant commander, 1st Marine Division, said that, "IIIAC had very little time to think about the Palau operation before embarking for the Guam operation. It was difficult to

■ Lieutenant General Roy S. Geiger was one of the Corps' outstanding wartime leaders. An aviator, he pioneered the introduction of close air support of the infantry, commanded the "Cactus Air Force" on Guadalcanal and then went on to serve as the amphibious force commander for the capture of Guam, Peleliu and Okinawa. In this last assignment, he commanded a United States Field Army, the first and only Marine to do so. *Marine Corps History Division*

coordinate planning at the higher echelons." Admiral Halsey, Vice Adm. Wilkinson and Maj. Gen. Julian Smith were thousands of miles away at Pearl Harbor, where they had established temporary headquarters. One of O. P. Smith's aides reported flippantly, "It was almost like jungle tribes talking to each other with tom-toms." To help solve this problem, "The IIIAC chief of the planning section, Col. Dudley Brown, was sent to Pearl Harbor," O. P. Smith recalled, "where he would be more closely associated with the Third Amphibious Force and the other various

■ Insignia of the III Amphibious Corps. During the war, the Marine Corps authorized the wearing of patches on the left shoulder of the service uniform, denoting the Marines' service in a major unit—Corps, Division, Wing and certain support units. *Author collection*

staffs." However, "Dudley just wasn't able to get it done by himself," Julian Smith recounted. "He had to have more help. I worked half a day on Peleliu and my other job half a day, which didn't leave much time for sleeping. We got the thing going, and then Geiger finished up on Guam and took over planning for the operation."

OPERATIONAL PLANNING

O. P. Smith was assigned to the 1st Marine Division by the Commandant of the Marine Corps. In a personal letter to the division commander, the Commandant wrote, "I am sending out to you O. P. Smith. He is a very senior colonel, and I wanted him to have some experience with a division prior to his becoming a brigadier general." Smith joined the division on May 8 and was surprised to find that "General Rupertus [division commander] and Selden [chief of staff] were leaving for Washington the following day, partly for the purpose of taking leave and partly on business . . . and I was left temporarily in command of the division."

Smith was also left with the job of planning Operation Stalemate II. "On June 2nd, while General Rupertus was still absent, we received the Joint Chiefs of Staff concept for the Palau Operation," Smith wrote. He continued:

> There were many changes to the plan. At first it was quite an operation that included not only Peleliu, Angaur, Babelthuap; but at one time Yap was in it. There was a complete Army corps taking part, plus the 1st Marine Division. It was then that the aviators from Admiral Halsey's fleet found that Leyte was not too strongly held, and they made a quick decision to cancel everything except Peleliu and Angaur. That meant we could go ahead and plan without reference to directives from higher headquarters, because our mission never

51

changed—capture Peleliu. The real work on planning
was started by the lowest echelon [1st Marine Division]
before it was started at the top. By the time higher
commands were able to organize staffs or return from
intervening operations, the Division had a concrete plan
to offer.

Smith immediately started the staff working on an operation
plan that was quite different from any the division had previously
developed. "In its two previous operations, Guadalcanal and New
Britain, the beaches were not surrounded by a 600–700 yard reef and,
while the terrain was difficult, Peleliu had some of the most rugged and
easily defended ground yet encountered by American forces. After much
discussion between Col. Harold D. 'Bucky' Harris (G-2), Lt. Col. Lewis J.
'Jeff' Fields (G-3) and myself [Smith], we drew up a brief analysis of the
different courses of action."

Fields thought there wasn't much choice:

> The width of the island was such that the only thing
> we could do was go in and then go north or south. We had
> quite a discussion as to how we would take the island.
> There was a swamp on the east side, with only a narrow
> strip of land, so we couldn't go in from that side. The
> southern promontories were heavily mined and blocked
> by concrete tetrahedrons. It was doubtful if boats or
> amphibian tractors could discharge troops because of the
> surf and sharp ledges. The western beaches promised
> to be the best, with a broad front to quickly maneuver
> forces and it was only a few hundred yards to the other
> side of the island, which would split it in two.

Fields spent a great deal of time studying the western beaches. "The
protection of the flanks of the division was given considerable study and

■ A wide fringing reef, framed by the white water in the photo, fronted the southwestern landing beaches. The development of the amphibious tractor, with its cleated treads, enabled the machines to climb over the reef. The White beaches are located in the top right, directly across from the runway. The small tip of land on either end contained anti-boat guns that caused heavy damage during the landing. *Marine Corps History Division*

attention. The high ground to the north of the airfield, dominating the landing beaches . . . presented a most difficult problem. There was no question as to the necessity of knocking out enemy positions in these areas." Fields emphasized the importance of concentrated fire support on this flank during the initial planning. "This fact was impressed upon the staff of [Rear Adm. George H.] Fort on many occasions. Numerous conferences were conducted between the naval gunfire, air support,

■ Overhead view of the Umurbrogol ridge, which contained the bulk of Colonel Nakagawa's 2nd Infantry Regiment. Their cleverly camouflaged positions were invisible in the pre-landing aerial reconnaissance photographs. The location of this hill mass on the flank of the landing beaches gave the Marine planners fits. The smoke in this photograph is from bombing. *Marine Corps History Division*

amphib officers and the respective regimental commanders and their staffs. The flank regiment [1st Marines] was allocated additional fire support forces, including ships and LVT(A)s [LVTs, armored]. Liaison officers from these units were assigned to the ships working close in."

Rupertus returned to Pavuvu on June 21 and was presented with the Peleliu concept of operations. "We gave Rupertus a briefing on the plan and he approved it," Smith related. What Smith did not know was that before Rupertus approved the division plan, he exchanged correspondence with Julian Smith, the Expeditionary Force Commander. In a five-page, Top Secret letter, Rupertus continually stressed that "the seizure and occupation of island 'P' [code letter the two correspondents used for Peleliu] can be done by this division alone . . . [W]ith any luck, I think this can be done by about D plus 3 or at the most D plus 4." He continued to express confidence when he wrote, "This division is a Marine amphibious unit and we sincerely hope that we will . . . quickly seize, occupy, and turn over to the Army the objective . . . and be withdrawn immediately, reorganized, and made ready for another striking operation."

Julian Smith acknowledged the point and responded that "one RCT [regimental combat team] of the 81st [Division] would be attached to the division as a reserve." Rupertus expressed his dismay, replying, "I do not consider this attachment to be necessary. I assure you that there is little chance of the division needing it." He did not believe that he would even need the division reserve. "I do not think that it will be necessary for me to commit this battalion . . . in the action on island 'P.' " This time Julian Smith replied, "I concur in your opinion that the First Division can do this job alone." Both men were very, very wrong.

In his letter Rupertus also addressed serious concerns about the main enemy force on Babelthuap:

> Now as you know, while we are doing this job on Island "P," there exists to the north on Island "B" approx- imately 35,000 enemy who will have small boats that can

be used in quickly coming to the south to reinforce the enemy on "P." Until I can get my ground forces set in position to combat this attack . . . I consider it definitely the job of the Navy . . . to prevent [this] from taking place. The greatest danger, of course, will be at night, and it would be necessary . . . to use star shells . . . to keep the north-south boat passageway under observation.

In fact, General Inoue thought the landing on Peleliu was a precursor to the main landing on Babelthuap, which kept him from sending large-scale reinforcements to Nakagawa.

General Rupertus approved the Division Operation Plan No.1-44 on August 15 and distributed it to its subordinate commands. It called for "a landing of three regiments abreast (five battalion landing teams) on a 2,200 yard beach on the southwest coast of Peleliu on D-day at H-hour." (In an amphibious operation, H-hour is the planned time for the first wave to land on the designated beach.)

In accordance with standard amphibious doctrine, the landing beaches were color coded and numbered. The landing plan called for the 1st Marines (code named "Spitfire") to land two battalions abreast on White Beach 1 (3/1) and White Beach 2 (2/1) with one battalion in reserve (1/1); the 5th Marines ("Lonewolf") on Orange Beach 1 (1/5) and Orange Beach 2 (3/5) with one battalion in reserve (2/5); and the 7th Marines ("Mustang") to land in column (3/7 followed by 1/7, with 2/7 in division reserve) over Orange Beach 3. The division's goal was to land 4,500 men in the first nineteen minutes. The initial eight waves were to be landed in amphibious tractors (LVTs), designed to carry twenty troops, preceded by a wave of amphibian tanks (LVT)(A) mounting 75mm howitzers or 37mm anti-tank guns.

The division scheme of maneuver gave the 1st Marines the toughest nut to crack. It was to drive inland, pivot left, and attack northeast, straight at the Umurbrogol massif and into the teeth of the Japanese defense. In the center, the 5th Marines was to attack straight across the island, secure the airfield, and continue the attack north to seize the northeastern peninsula and the outlying islands. The 7th Marines on the right would drive across the island and wheel right to seize the southern tip of the island.

The landing was to be proceeded by three days of pre-assault bombardment and air strikes. Rear Admiral Jesse B. Oldendorf's Fire Support Group, consisting of five old battleships, four heavy cruisers, four light cruisers, and fourteen destroyers, blasted away at all known targets. In three days the ships expended 519 rounds of 16-inch shells, 1,845 rounds of 14-inch, 1,427 rounds of 8-inch, 1,020 rounds of 6-inch, and 12,037 rounds of 5-inch, for a total of 2,255 tons of ammunition. In addition, carrier planes dropped many tons of bombs on the Japanese defenses. Despite this impressive expenditure, O. P. Smith complained that Oldendorf "hit all the visible targets, but the cut-up, jungle-covered terrain concealed many targets that the infantry had to overrun at heavy cost." In effect, the three-day bombardment accomplished little more than to rearrange dirt and strip foliage.

The unexpected Japanese resistance on Guam delayed Geiger's departure until the morning of August 12, when he, Silverthorn and key members of his staff flew to Guadalcanal to meet with Julian Smith and go over the plan that he and Brown had worked out. "There were very cordial relations between Geiger and Smith," according to Silverthorn. "They were close personal friends." The meeting started well when Smith announced, "I'm just here as a spectator. It's true I am in overall command, but I don't intend to inject myself and my headquarters into this Peleliu operation. You just go ahead and fight this battle the way you want to." Geiger was presented the plan, which he readily accepted. "So we sort of inherited the plan for the Palau operation," Silverthorn remarked matter-of-factly. "We were relieved of all the preliminary planning and all we had to do was put the Corps plan on top of the division's concept."

Unfortunately the spirit of cooperation among the top Marine commanders did not extend to the Navy's Attack Force Commander.

■ Maj. Gen. William H. Rupertus

■ UNEXPLAINED ABSENCE

In *Peleliu: Tragic Triumph*, Bill D. Ross declares that "there is no known case to match that of Rupertus," a division commander who was absent just before an operation. The official Marine Corps monograph simply noted that "Major General William H. Rupertus, and Colonel John T. Selden, his chief of staff, obtained orders to proceed Stateside to place their needs [for replacements] before Headquarters Marine Corps, and hence were absent during the planning process." Ross wrote that some senior officers suspected that the Commandant showed compassion for his old friend and brought him back to spend time with an infant son he had never seen. Rupertus' first wife and child died in 1929 of scarlet fever while he was stationed in China. Many who knew Rupertus said that the tragic incident changed him from a hale fellow well met to a demanding introvert.

"We flew to the Russell Islands to confer with Admiral Fort," Silverthorn remembered. "The meeting did not go well. The very first thing that Admiral Fort told us was that 'you're not going to get all the gunfire support here [on Peleliu] that you got on Guam. I don't have the ships, and we don't have the ammunition.' " He announced that there would be two days of preliminary bombardment. Geiger found this unacceptable and argued forcefully for at least one more day, which was grudgingly accepted. Fort remarked sarcastically, "The idea which some people seem to have of just firing at an island is an inexcusable waste of ammunition." Silverthorn responded that "it was the same old navy story."

The Marines accused the Navy of giving them short shrift by providing inadequate naval gunfire support. In one famous exchange, two naval officers described in great boring detail how their heavily armored fire support ships would close to within one thousand yards of the beach. Julian Smith had heard enough, rose from his chair, stared around the room filled with navy officers, and said softly, "Gentlemen, when the Marines meet the enemy at bayonet point, the only armor a Marine will have is his khaki shirt."

CHAPTER 5

MARINE
COMMANDERS

MAJ. GEN. WILLIAM H. "BILL" RUPERTUS

At the time of the Peleliu Operation, fifty-five-year-old William H. "Bill" Rupertus had been a Marine officer for thirty-one years. During that time he served at sea and expeditionary duty in Haiti and China, where he was commended for his "display of excellent tact, judgment and leadership" during the 1937 Sino-Japanese hostilities. A crack rifle shot, he was a distinguished marksman, member of the prestigious Marine Corps Rifle Team and author of "My Rifle: The Creed of a U.S. Marine." In 1942, he was assigned to the 1st Marine Division under his old friend and mentor Maj. Gen. Alexander A. Vandegrift.

During the Guadalcanal campaign, Rupertus commanded the force that captured Tulagi, Gavutu and Tanambogo in the Solomon Islands, for which he was awarded the Navy Cross. There were some who felt that he did not rate it. Clifton La Bree in *The Gentle Warrior* wrote, "It was common knowledge that many of the men in the division had a very low opinion of Rupertus, especially for his poor performance on

Guadalcanal." La Bree cited a battalion commander who claimed that Rupertus "just sat on his duff in a bunker and let others do the dirty work."

When Vandegrift was detached in July 1943, Rupertus assumed command of the division and led it in the Cape Gloucester campaign. Afterwards, Halsey had sent Rupertus a congratulatory message: "The entire Third Fleet extends its sincere admiration for the cave smashing, hill blasting extermination of eleven thousand slant eyes. It has been a tough task extremely well done." General Vandegrift wrote to Rupertus, saying, "You will be pleased to know that Admiral Bill Halsey very much wanted to have you."

Major Gordon D. Gayle, however, was surprised by the

■ Major General William H. Rupertus, controversial commander of the 1st Marine Division. A protégé of Marine Corps Commandant Gen. Alexander A. Vandegrift, many thought that he received the command because of their close association. Rupertus injured his ankle just prior to the operation and had his superior Maj. Gen. Roy Geiger known about it, he might have relieved him. Rupertus was unable to visit the frontline units to see firsthand what they were experiencing and was convinced that the operation would be quick—two or three days—and pushed his commanders to attack, despite fearsome casualties. Rupertus died of a heart attack shortly after the war and did not achieve the high rank he thought he deserved. *Marine Corps History Division*

promotion. "I had it in mind that someone other than General Rupertus would take command. For one thing, he was only a brigadier general, who they made a major general the day he took command. His interest and everything we had from him by way of communications seemed to be in writing . . . an awful lot of training directives . . . but except to see and read those directives we got not much other feel from him. He didn't make a strong impact on us." It didn't help that Rupertus took over from the very active, well respected Brig. Gen. Lemuel C. Shepherd. Gayle recalled that Shepherd's "impact was more immediate and more personal and much stronger. He seemed to have boundless energy in the vigor and activity with which he attacked the assistant division commander's training job."

Bill Rupertus was a controversial leader who did little to inspire confidence in his abilities as a commander. Lieutenant Colonel Harold O. Deakin, who served on his staff said, "Rupertus was a very opinionated, difficult man to serve with and for . . . [H]e ran the gamut from extreme coldness to warm friendship . . . [H]e was a strange one, very self-centered." Colonel Russell Honsowetz was more outspoken, calling Rupertus "Rupe the dupe." He described the last officers' conference on Guadalcanal before embarking for Peleliu: "[Rupertus said,] 'Now, I'm sending General Smith ashore early, but I don't want anyone to go to him for advice or commands, because I'm just sending him there to set up my CP [command post], and then I'll be ashore. But while he's doing that, you call back to the ship. He's not to enter this thing at all.' Smith got pretty well whipped. For some reason, 'Rupe' just landed on him." In an interview years later with Fox News, Ray Davis was asked about the division commander. "Rupertus," he replied, "what a jackass."

A circumspect O. P. Smith elaborated:

> General Rupertus had a fixation about the assistant
> division commanders; he didn't want them underfoot.
> I was never consulted about anything tactical or

anything like that. I went around, inspected training and periodically I'd come in and tell the general about what I saw. Our relations weren't exactly buddy-buddy, but there was no bitterness or anything like that. I had to argue quite strenuously with the General to get a minimum staff to land with me . . . I told the General frankly that to send me ashore in advance of himself with no authority to control the situation put me in a very anomalous situation; that in spite of such orders, as senior officer ashore, I could not escape responsibility for what transpired.

Rupertus finally backed down and allowed Smith to form his own small command group, with representatives from the various staff sections, a communications officer, and one half of the division signal company. Smith was to go ashore at "H plus three hours, following the reserve battalion of the 5th Marines, and set up an advance CP, a short distance inland from Orange 2, behind a small hill. General Rupertus expected to land about H plus four hours, by which time the advance CP would be in operation." Smith recalled that "events were to prove this estimate to be more than twenty-four hours out of line," which was not the only element of the operation about which Rupertus would be wrong.

Rupertus confidently told his staff that he believed the operation would only last three days. "We're going to have some casualties but let me assure you that this is going to be a short one, a quickie. Rough but fast. We'll be through in three days. It might take only two." Gordon Gayle was at the meeting. "I never understood why he said such a thing like that because it was pretty obvious from the terrain information that we had that while we might make the assault in seventy-two hours and might establish ourselves in a position so that there was no question about the outcome . . . the terrain was such that inevitably there would be an awful lot of Japanese to dig out of that place." Honsowetz "didn't have much confidence in the briefing where he said it was going to be over in seventy-two hours. I was worried about [Rupertus]. I wondered what was making him tick at that stage of the game. None of us, among the people I talked to, were inspired one damn bit. In fact, we were all a little bit worried about the operation after listening to that speech." Ray Davis was left with the impression that "we were expecting to go ashore, secure the airfield, upgrade it, get some exercise, and get back on the ship."

O. P. Smith thought Rupertus was "very, very optimistic" about the length of the operation:

> Apparently he wrote letters to the regimental commanders—they were pep talks—and to newspaper correspondents, in which he pointed out that this was going to be a quickie, probably faster than Tarawa [which took ninety-six hours]. I didn't go along with that kind of optimism. I'll admit that it never occurred to me that one month after the landing we'd still be fighting within sight of the airfield, but I didn't figure any two-day job. But that's what he felt, and that's what he told the newspaper correspondents, and it didn't go over very big because then some of them shoved off. They said, "What's the use of sticking around?" He got some bad press out of that.

The fact that Rupertus commanded the division at Peleliu was controversial. He broke his ankle just prior to the operation. O. P. Smith said that "[Rupertus] started to climb up into one of the amphibian tractors and the handhold gave way and he fell backward onto the rough coral rocks, and he badly fractured his ankle." Rupertus' official medical report indicated that "an x-ray showed no bone or ankle broken, but the ligaments had been severely torn." Regardless, the injury incapacitated him at a critical time; the division was conducting its final pre-deployment training and did not have the division commander's attention. Rupertus was confined to a bed, even during a visit by the commandant, Lt. Gen. Alexander A. Vandegrift, in mid-August. Smith said, "General Rupertus was still unable to leave his quarters, so I took the general around." The historian Harry A. Gailey said that Rupertus "ought to have been relieved from command before going to Peleliu." Others thought the same. Julian Smith was questioned about what he would have done, had he known about the injury. "Well," he said, "I'm going to tell you the truth—I don't know. But what should have been done was that Rupertus ought to have been relieved."

The most controversial issue involved Rupertus' delay in bringing in the U.S. Army. He simply did not want them on Peleliu and finally had to be ordered by his superior to use a regiment of the 81st Division to replace the decimated 1st Marine Regiment.

BRIG. GEN. OLIVER PRINCE "O. P." SMITH

Fifty-one-year-old Oliver Prince Smith, nicknamed the "professor" by contemporaries, was considered by his friends to be an intellectual because of his serious, studied approach to problem solving. Calm and deliberate, Smith was soft-spoken and unfailingly courteous. He was known as a man who would not speak unkindly of another—a man who kept his own counsel. His biographer Clifton La Bree wrote, "General Oliver P. Smith was an intellectual with common sense. He never forgot that his most important weapon was the individual rifleman, and he had the knack of obtaining the best his troops had to give by setting an example of confidence and faith in their ability to succeed." In a letter to Rupertus, Vandegrift wrote, "I know [Smith has] done good work and I believe him to be one of our ablest officers."

At the time of the Peleliu operation, Smith had served in a number of important staff and command assignments. After being commissioned in 1917, Smith was assigned to the Marine Barracks, Guam, while many of his contemporaries went to the battlefields of France. He always felt "left out" from the officers who fought "in the big one." However, it did not preclude him from being promoted or picked for choice assignments. In 1921, he was hand-selected for sea duty aboard the battleship *Texas*, followed by a tour at Marine headquarters, where he had "an awful time making ends meet." Washington was and still is a financial millstone around the necks of those assigned to the "head shed."

■ Brigadier General Oliver P. "O. P." Smith, assistant division commander of the 1st Marine Division. A scholarly officer and gentleman, he did not complain about the shoddy treatment he received at the hands of the division commander, Maj. Gen. William H. Rupertus. Smith went on to command the same division in the frozen mountains of North Korea in the winter of 1950. *Marine Corps History Division*

His next assignment took him to the Caribbean for detached duty with the Gendarmerie d'Haiti. "The Gendarmerie provided law and order," Smith recalled. "We had roads all over the place; we had an excellent hospital and medical service; we had an operating telephone network . . . [T]he Occupation down there did a tremendous amount of good."

Following his return from Haiti in 1931, Major Smith was assigned to attend his first professional military school, the army's ten-month Field Officer's Course. The school counted many of the military's bright lights. Lieutenant Colonel George C. Marshall was the assistant commandant. Major Omar Bradley and Lt. Col. Joseph W. Stilwell served as instructors. His classmates included Capt. Bedell Smith, who became Eisenhower's chief of staff, and the eminently quotable Capt. Lewis B. "Chesty" Puller. "You just simply cannot learn warfare in a schoolroom, or anywhere else except in combat," Chesty maintained.

Upon graduation, Smith was assigned as an instructor at the Marine company officer's school at Quantico, Virginia, and a year later as assistant operations officer, 7th Marine Regiment. In recognition of his intellectual ability, Smith was picked to go to the prestigious French military school, *École de Guerre*, a two-year military course of study conducted entirely in French. With only high school French as a base, Smith "hit the books." "I went to every lecture that I could find just to get my ear trained . . . and finally got to where I could understand the speaker." In 1939 he was assigned as the operations officer of the Fleet Marine Force, an embryonic organization dedicated to the development of amphibious warfare.

With war clouds looming, Smith longed to command troops. He approached his friend Lt. Col. Bill Ashurst, commander of the 1st Battalion, 6th Marines, and asked if he would like to trade jobs. "I talked him into it. We went to General Vogel who commanded the Brigade and he approved, and Bill came up and took over my job. Shortly after that he was ordered to Peking and was locked up as a prisoner of war in 1941 . . . my conscience hurt a little bit on that."

In May 1941, Great Britain asked for American troops to protect Iceland so its troops could be used in active combat. President Roosevelt agreed, and the mission was given to the 6th Marine Regiment. Smith commanded the 1st Battalion for the nine months of the deployment. When war broke out against the United States, he briefed his officers on the situation as he saw it—correctly predicting the strategic implications of the Japanese attack. "I told them that Pearl Harbor could not be a main effort but was a raid; also the Japanese main effort in the Far East was probably the Malaya Peninsula rather than the Philippines. I pointed out to them that we could not hold Guam, and in the pre-war planning no one considered that Corregidor could hold out more than six months." He also predicted that offensive war in the Pacific would probably require two years. He said, "the information I gave them was considerably different than they heard over the radio."

Smith returned, not to the battlefield, but to another assignment at Headquarters until January 1944, when he was tentatively assigned as the 1st Marine Division's chief of staff under General Rupertus. Smith recalled that after his transfer from Washington the commandant told him that "all Marine colonels wanted to command regiments . . . but that I was getting along in years and that duty as the chief of staff was a more suitable assignment." Rupertus had other ideas, however, and promptly gave him command of the 5th Marine Regiment then in combat on Cape Gloucester. Smith led it during the Talasea phase of the operation, which he summed up as, "a small affair, but it was not simple. It was the longest small boat shore-to-shore operation conducted by Marines in World War II. [It] was conducted against opposition without the benefit of air or naval gunfire support . . . and [with] a tenuous supply line." At the conclusion of the operation, Smith was promoted to brigadier general and assigned as the assistant division commander.

COL. LEWIS B. "CHESTY" PULLER

The feisty warrior Col. Lewis B. "Chesty" Puller commanded the 1st Marine Regiment, aptly codenamed "Spitfire." Only 5 feet 6 inches tall, he had a barrel chest that earned him his nickname. However, his friends called him Lewis or Lewie. A loving husband and father, he was

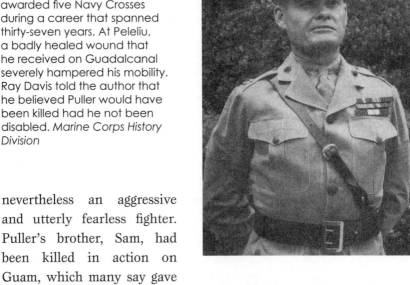

■ Lewis B. "Chesty" Puller, legendary Marine and combat leader. One of its most highly decorated officers, he was awarded five Navy Crosses during a career that spanned thirty-seven years. At Peleliu, a badly healed wound that he received on Guadalcanal severely hampered his mobility. Ray Davis told the author that he believed Puller would have been killed had he not been disabled. *Marine Corps History Division*

nevertheless an aggressive and utterly fearless fighter. Puller's brother, Sam, had been killed in action on Guam, which many say gave him such a burning hatred of the Japanese. Sergeant James Merrifield vividly remembered the signs that Puller placed in the mess halls on Pavuvu, "Kill Japs, Kill Japs, Kill Japs," and that he constantly reminded them to destroy "the bandy-legged little bastards."

Newsweek correspondent Bill Hipple had a special relationship with Puller because his brother fell dead in the newsman's arms. Hipple recalled telling Puller about his brother's painless death. "This seemed to comfort Chesty, who then, with a trace of tears, removed a corncob pipe from his clenched lips and began a half-smiling reminiscence of their happy boyhood in the faraway days and hills of Virginia, and their boisterous times together as young enlisted Marines in the 1920s."

Puller had a reputation that transcended almost any other Marine colonel of his day.

He was known for his "Pullerisms," catchy one-liners that endeared him to his men. On one memorable occasion he was given a demonstration of a flamethrower. After watching the jellied gasoline roast the target, Puller shrugged and nonchalantly remarked, "Where's the bayonet fit?" In China before the war, Puller faced down a large party of Japanese with just his .45 pistol. Afterward he said of the Japanese officer, "I wish now I had killed him. It would have started the war, perhaps, but we'd have lost only one regiment, instead of all those men and ships at Pearl Harbor."

He was a darling of the enlisted men and the bane of junior officers. One day he noted that a young lieutenant used most of the water that several enlisted men had sweated hard to put in a makeshift shower. Puller intercepted the officer and made him personally replace the water, much to the delight of the working party. On Guadalcanal, Puller found a young private lying in the grass, not shooting. The miscreant boasted proudly that Puller "gave me a good one right in the cheeks" and snarled, "Get the hell up theah, an' doan lemme se youah shirttail touch youah ass until you do!" Puller was wounded on Guadalcanal when an enemy shell landed in a group of wiremen that he was helping. A Corpsman patched him up and started writing out an evacuation tag. Puller tore it up. "Go label a bottle with that goddam tag," he roared.

Russ Honsowetz first met Puller as

> a brand new second lieutenant in 1936 at the Philadelphia Navy Yard . . . Captain Puller was the drill instructor there and also a tactics instructor and taught a "Small Wars" course which was very interesting. But the first day, they fell us in on the parade ground and the first sergeant turned us over to Captain Puller. All he said was, "I am Captain Puller, Squads Right." He drilled the hell out of us for about a half hour or so. But then he took us in and gave us an introductory talk about the Marine Corps, told us a little about what to expect and talked to us more like a father. All throughout the year that we were there in the Basic School, he was the

one person—from the colonel on down—who was the most impressive.

Puller was 2nd Lt. Ray Davis' company commander at the Basic School. "Sartorially, you had to pass the Puller inspection of your uniforms," Davis recalled, "and if there was room to breathe, it was too loose! When one of the lieutenants said his uniform was made by an exclusive men's shop, Puller told him, 'You go down there and tell old man Jacob or old man Reed or whoever the hell is in charge that I said that uniform is not going to pass.' Puller was perfectionist in all things, and especially in his way!"

Brigadier General Edwin H. Simmons, Director Emeritus, Marine Corps History Division, described seeing Puller for the first time when he came to address the officer candidates at Quantico. "This was the man we were going to hear speak . . . not very tall, he stood with a kind of stiffness with his chest thrown out, hence his nickname 'Chesty.' His face was yellow-brown from the sun and Atabrine, the anti-malaria drug that we used then. His face looked, as someone has said, as though it were carved out of teakwood. There was a lantern jaw, a mouth like the proverbial steel trap, and small, piercing eyes that drilled right through you and never seemed to blink."

Puller was no stranger to combat, having seen action during the banana wars in the 1920s and 1930s where he received two Navy Crosses, the nation's second highest award for bravery in action. "Puller was known as a fearless patrol leader in Nicaragua, [he was nicknamed] *El Tigre*," according to Marine Brig. Gen. Gordon Gayle. Puller joined a generation of Marines who learned their trade-craft pursuing bandits in the jungles of the Caribbean. They became the backbone of the 1st Marine Division in the early days of World War II. Their experience was particularly valuable on Guadalcanal in America's first offensive action of the war.

At the head of a battalion on the "Canal," Puller proved his worth on the night of October 24–25, 1942, in a desperate three-hour fight to protect the critical airfield. He repeatedly exposed himself to direct the defense and encourage his outnumbered men. After reinforcements arrived, he commanded the augmented force until the next afternoon. Over a thousand Japanese were killed, while Puller's Marines suffered only seventy casualties. He was awarded a third Navy Cross for the action, justifiably building on his reputation as the consummate small unit leader.

On Cape Gloucester in January 1944, Puller was awarded a fourth Navy Cross for taking over a second battalion after its commander had been wounded, and leading them in taking a heavily fortified enemy position. He was known for leading from the front and believed that his officers should also: "There will be platoon commanders in front of platoons, company commanders in front of companies . . . and the battalion commanders will be in front of their battalion."

As a small unit leader—company and battalion—Puller was second to none; however, his detractors thought he might not have been suited for higher command. Lieutenant Colonel Deakin thought that Puller "did not have a total grasp of the use of naval gunfire, artillery and supporting arms in general. That's as charitable as I can put it." A man who served with him on Peleliu said, "I believe that his only scheme of maneuver was 'Fix bayonets and charge.' " O. P. Smith was of a similar opinion. "Lewie Puller's strong point was fighting," and Smith had to "convince him that in a unit the size of a regiment, a staff was essential and should be used." Smith felt better when Lt. Col. R. P. "Buddy" Ross, Jr., became the executive officer of the 1st Marines. "I had had Ross in the 1st Battalion, Sixth Marines," Smith said. "For a short period he had been my executive officer and he was an exceptional one. He was exactly what Puller needed."

On Peleliu, Puller the fighter was in his element, a straight-ahead assault—"high diddle, diddle, right up the middle"—no finesse, no grand strategy. It was infantry work, pitting his crack 1st Marine Regiment against the elite Japanese 2nd Infantry Regiment. It was a slug fest, a meat grinder that savaged his regiment, leaving it shattered on the slopes of "Bloody Nose Ridge," the entryway to the Umurbrogol.

■ ■ ■

MAJ. RAYMOND G. DAVIS

Ray Davis, gunnery expert turned infantryman, earned his spurs on Peleliu. He entered the Marine Corps at the end of the Depression because of "near-starvation wages" after attending Georgia Tech. "My job had fallen apart just before graduation . . . and I had gone to the army ROTC instructor, to see if I could get active duty. He said the Marine Corps is offering a regular commission. I went down and took the test. I wasn't even sure of what I was getting into, except that the Marines had a great reputation." He reported to the Basic School in June 1938, along with "Pappy Boyington," legendary Marine fighter pilot and Medal of Honor recipient. Chesty Puller was on the staff—"a great inspiration," according to Davis. "He had a course of instruction in which the students would ask him to continue through the lunch hour! He would walk in with his lesson plan—I guess a lesson plan was required—put it aside and pick up a cue stick which he used as a pointer and proceed to talk about the things that make or break men in combat."

Upon graduation Davis reported aboard the heavy cruiser USS *Portland,* where he served as the fire control director for a battery of 5-inch, 25-caliber, anti-aircraft, dual-purpose guns. After fifteen months, he was transferred to the 1st Antiaircraft Machine Gun Battery, 1st Marine Division, and later to 1st Special Weapons Battalion, Camp Lejeune, North Carolina. Immediately after Pearl Harbor, Davis received his first war mission. "Reports of a hostile German airship over the Atlantic led me to organize anti-aircraft defense over the camp. We deployed our guns and dug them in," but the Germans failed to materialize. In June 1942, his unit received secret orders to deploy, objective unknown. Davis later remembered, "We had no idea that our destination was Guadalcanal."

Davis boarded the SS *Erickson,* a converted passenger liner, at San Francisco for the month-long voyage to Wellington, New Zealand. "This ship was not prepared for the load of troops and supplies . . . We had trouble with the food; some of it was bad. People vomiting all over the ship, and there were inadequate head [toilet] facilities." The ship's civilian crew gouged the embarked troops and "there were threats against

■ Major Raymond G. Davis' 1st Battalion was assigned as the regimental reserve but still had to fight its way ashore. Wounded within the first few minutes of landing, Davis refused evacuation and continued to lead his men until the remnant of his battalion was evacuated from the island. First Battalion suffered 70 percent casualties in less than a week, the highest ratio of any unit in the Marine Corps. *Marine Corps History Division*

the crew and even rumors that Marines were ready to throw them overboard," Davis reported. Upon reaching Wellington, he was designated the transport quartermaster and had to remain aboard the "Good Ship Vomit" for an extra six days. *Erickson* had been commercially loaded and all the cargo had to be offloaded before it could be reloaded aboard other ships in a combat configuration. "It rained constantly," Davis remembered, "and all the cardboard packing boxes and all the paper items on the dock got wet, melted down, and trampled over." The dock was soon covered with drifts of mushy cornflakes, thousands of rolling "C" ration cans, and cases of water-logged cigarettes and pogey bait (candy). Within days he was heading for combat.

At eight minutes past nine on August 7, 1942, the 1st Marine Division stormed ashore on Guadalcanal. Much to their relief, the beaches were undefended and they landed "standing up." Ray Davis went ashore an hour and a half later. "As we loaded into boats and were heading for shore, a formation of Japanese torpedo bombers attacked us. This was our first engagement for these American ships, and shot and shell were flying . . . it seemed like everybody was shooting . . . the sky was full, just full of bullets. I felt very uneasy out there with the Japanese aircraft strafing and bombing, and our own ships firing machine guns and AA guns. Indeed, I was happy to get ashore." Davis' battery deployed around the half-completed Japanese airfield, soon to be named Henderson Field for Maj. Lofton R. Henderson, who had been shot down leading Marine dive-bombers at Midway.

For the next six months, Davis was caught in the "V" ring, the bull's-eye of the Japanese attacks. "Enemy troops were trying to capture that airstrip by attacking overland . . . [T]hey also sent airplanes over every day, and sailed warships down to shell us. During the month of October, there were thirty-one consecutive days during which we were bombed . . . and shelled every night from battleships, cruisers. It was a very busy time." Davis learned quickly. "We could see the enemy bomb bays open and hear the clicks of the bomb release before we jumped into our holes. At night, we absorbed fire from ships . . . [that] were out of range of my guns, but we watched carefully to see the ships' gun flashes because they would signal the time to go for the holes." One very dark night Davis found himself on the horns of a dilemma. "I dived into my hole to come face-to-face with a large screaming bat. I told him, as I recovered from the terror and shock: 'Buddy—yell all you want—I'm staying!'"

Davis thought October was the toughest month. Vice Admiral Robert L. Ghormley had withdrawn the fleet and said the division had permission to surrender. The Marine commander, Maj. Gen. Alexander A. Vandegrift, vehemently refused. Davis remembered that "At that point there was no food, and we had to eat captured rice. The cook said that the black spots in the rice were weevils, but some of us ate them anyways, as a source of protein. The cook put a few raisins to camouflage them. We were sick with dengue fever, dysentery and malaria." The 1st Marine Division was pulled off the island in January 1943 and shipped to Australia. It was out of action for eight to nine months—about 5,000 to 6,000 Marines were down with malaria, including Davis. He had both types, plus hepatitis. Fortunately he had a friendly surgeon who kept him out of the hospital and on his feet.

In early 1944, the division was put on alert for another operation and started loading the assault shipping. One morning Davis ran into Puller and complained that

> all my units had been doled out and I was being left behind. Puller replied in his characteristic fashion: "It's a hell of a note when a man wants to go to war and no one will let him. Get in that ship over there!" Puller hired me to be his 1st Battalion commander. Thus on 24 April 1944 I took off with the 1st Marine Regiment for Pavuvu where I would re-equip and train my infantry battalion, 1/1, for one of the bloodiest battles in Marine Corps history: Peleliu!

MAJ. RUSSELL E. HONSOWETZ

Major Russell E. Honsowetz, while he had not been in combat, had seen more Japanese than any of the other battalion commanders. Honsowetz had been a "China Marine" and former member of the 4th Marine Regiment, which had been stationed in Shanghai, China, from the late 1920s until November 1941. His first assignment came during the Sino-Japanese War of 1937–1938, when he observed firsthand the Japanese proclivity toward brutality. They were known to use live Chinese prisoners for bayonet practice and routinely raped and terrorized the local population. In their most celebrated violation of international law, Japanese aircraft attacked and sank the USS *Panay*, causing several American casualties, including three dead, almost starting a war. Honsowetz and his platoon manned defensive works around the international settlement during this tense period. Soon the Japanese apologized, paid a large indemnity compensation and backed off.

■ Lieutenant Colonel Russell E. Honsowetz's 2nd Battalion landed on the right flank of White Beach 1 and fought its way toward the airfield. Together with a battalion of the 5th Marines, they stopped the Japanese tank-led counterattack late in the afternoon of D-day. Honsowetz led his men throughout the operation and received a Navy Cross for heroic actions. *Marine Corps History Division*

Honsowetz came home, but after a brief stay, returned to China, where he served another three years as a company commander. In late fall, early winter of 1940–1941, Japanese pressure on the Marines escalated, and Honsowetz knew that war could break out at any moment. He became actively involved in planning for the regiment to fight its way through the large Japanese garrison that surrounded them. Three weeks before Pearl Harbor, the regiment was withdrawn and sent to the Philippine island of Corregidor, in the middle of Manila Bay. On May 6, 1942, the Philippines surrendered and the men of the 4th Marines went into captivity. Honsowetz fortunately was spared their fate. In late summer 1941, the USS *Henderson* delivered replacements and picked up men who had completed their tour. Honsowetz was one of those lucky men.

Honsowetz returned home and was assigned as an instructor at the Basic School, Philadelphia, and then at the Marine Corps Schools, Quantico, Virginia. "I thought I was going to spend the whole war teaching

■ Lieutenant Colonel Stephen V. Sabol's 3rd Battalion landed on the left flank of White Beach 1 and immediately ran into heavy resistance from several strongly fortified Japanese bunkers. One of his companies launched an immediate assault against the high ground and succeeded in capturing it but suffered heavy casualties in the process. *Marine Corps History Division*

there, but finally in the spring of '44, I went to the Pacific and got to the 1st Marine Division. Colonel Puller had the 1st Marines, and since I'd served with him several times before, he gave me a battalion." Honsowetz remembered that "After Peleliu, Chesty called me and said, 'Well, Honsowetz, you did a pretty good job. I'm going to give you a Navy Cross for the job that you did.' But then he said, 'I have to admit I was worried about you. You've been around them goddamn schools so long.' "

LT. COL. STEPHEN V. SABOL

Thirty-year-old Lt. Col. Stephen V. Sabol led Puller's third battalion. Sabol, a Marine officer since 1936, had only commanded the battalion for four months at the time of the landing but was "well respected by Puller," according to Russ Honsowetz. A teacher by trade, Sabol joined the Corps one month after graduating from North Carolina State College, with a degree in education. Upon completion of Marine Officers Basic School at Philadelphia in July 1937, he was assigned as an infantry officer with the 10th and 6th Marines at the Marine Corps Base San Diego. Reassigned in November 1939, he served at Marine Barracks, Bremerton, Washington, for a short time before being transferred to the Naval Air Station, Kodiak, Alaska. A recruiting tour, instructor duty and attendance at the Marine Corps Command and Staff School followed. In May 1944, he assumed command of the 3rd Battalion, 1st Marines. Peleliu would be his first combat action.

CHAPTER 6

THE OLD BREED

On 1 February 1941, the 1st Marine Division was born at sea, which seemed entirely appropriate because Marines are commonly referred to as sea soldiers. The date of its designation made it the first division in Marine Corps history and earned it bragging rights among those divisions that followed, no small matter among proud Leathernecks. The 1st Marine Brigade, consisting of the 5th Marine Regiment, was headed for Culebra in the West Indies for Fleet Landing Exercise 7, under the command of Brig. Gen. H. M. "Howling Mad" Smith, when the message arrived designating it the 1st Marine Division. Three other regiments, the 1st and 7th Marines (infantry regiments), the 11th Marines (artillery regiment) and support units were quickly added, completing its complement.

Marine historian Col. Robert Debs Heinl, Jr., wrote that "the birth of the division required the blessing of the Judge Advocate General of the Navy—someone demanded that he search the statutes to be sure it was legal for the Marines to have an outfit as big as a division; he did;

■ 1st Marine Division shoulder patch designed by Col. Merrill B. Twining, division operations officer, upon returning to Australia after the Guadalcanal operation. Superimposed on a blue background are five stars representing the Southern Cross, a red figure one (1st Marine Division) in the center of the patch with the word Guadalcanal in its center. *Author collection*

it was." After completing maneuvers, the division hoisted its flag at the newly created East Coast base at New River, North Carolina, "111,710 acres of water, coastal swamp and plain, theretofore inhabited largely by sand flies, ticks, chiggers and snakes."

New River was an isolated, remote coastal lowland that lacked even the basic amenities—no bus service, no civilian entertainment, and no liberty. The men lived under canvas in a place aptly named Tent City. George McMillan described the living conditions:

> The winter, there on the edge of the coastal swamp, was bitterly and inescapably cold. Against the cold each tent was furnished with a kerosene stove—a smelly, ornery, and often dangerous contraption. If the stoves did not set tents afire—and they often did—they would at some time or other cover everything, including the sleeping men, with sooty smoke. There were wooden decks for the tents, but cracks were wide and unsealed. Many men stuffed newspapers, magazines and comic books into these chilly vents, for it were not until late in

the winter, that the division quartermaster issued tar
paper for flooring.

The foul weather, lack of facilities and remote location brought out
the usual gum-beating. One exasperated rear-rank private lamented,
"This is the way they want things. You don't make good fightin' men if
you're in love with everybody. You gotta be mad, so sore at everything
you'd slug your best buddy at the drop of a hat." However, the men soon
got used to the primitive conditions. A lieutenant observed that "The
men grew proud of being able to take it. To tell the truth, I think morale
went up during the New River days, bad and lonely as they were." The
division hardened, mentally and physically, into a team, with a strong
unit *esprit*. "They were second to none," Russ Honsowetz declared. "It
was a great outfit . . . all in good shape. We all felt confident, just like a
good football team feels confident. We were going to kick the hell out
of the Japs. There was not a doubt in our minds." As the winter chill
receded, rumors of impending orders swept the ranks. The aggressive
division intelligence officer, Lt. Col. Frank B. Goettge, groused, "We're
the first team, and we should be the first sent in."

Goettge got his wish. In mid-April 1942, the division received orders
to Wellington, New Zealand, "at the earliest possible moment." The
word spread like wildfire among the keyed up men. "They are full of
patriotism and have the 'up and at 'em spirit,'" one officer wrote. "When
a person is young and filled with the spirit of adventure, it is fairly easy
to pick up and shove off to war." He went on to say that "It is an entirely
different matter when you are older and have the responsibility of a
family." Within thirty days the last of the division pulled away from
the docks and sailed to war. Ninety days later, August 7, 1942, the first
waves of the division stormed ashore on Guadalcanal and Tulagi in the
Solomon Islands.

After four months of bitter jungle fighting, the Japanese abandoned the island, leaving behind 30,000 of its best soldiers moldering
in unmarked graves. The division's casualties amounted to 2,138, with

more than 5,000 cases of malaria and hundreds more sick with various other tropical diseases. George McMillan wrote that "many [Guadalcanal veterans were] so weak they could not climb the cargo nets to get back aboard ship." The division had certainly earned its Presidential Unit Citation.

The division sailed away to the "land down under" to refit. "We arrived in Australia to retrain and re-equip before getting back into the war," according to Ray Davis, "but we were there for eight months. No one was prepared for the long, long, long stay that we had." The division was in bad shape and needed the recovery time in Australia. From the onset, Australia welcomed "its Yanks," particularly the citizens of

■ The division struck tents, packed equipment and prepared to embark for "destination unknown." Hundreds of men, by squad, platoon and company, marched to the railhead and boarded troop trains bound for Norfolk, Virginia, the port of embarkation. Troop ships stood alongside the pier, ready to take them aboard. *The Old Breed: A History of the 1st Marine Division in World War II*

Melbourne where the division was billeted. On the day of their arrival, the city's newspapers trumpeted the Marines as "The Saviors of Australia."

The people opened their homes, extending invitations to the lonely men. "My hosts were so solicitous," a sergeant given the run of a large country house reported, "that at noon they would rap on my bedroom door to ask if I wanted lunch in bed." The arrival of the battle-hardened Australian 9th Infantry Division from the Middle East had the potential to strain relationships because the two groups competed for the same

■ When the Australian 9th Infantry Division returned, tensions between them and the "Yanks" threatened to spill over into bloodshed. Both groups were competing for the same girls and watering holes. The Marines threw a beer party attended by more than nine thousand men, half of whom were Australians. The party was a huge success and Allied solidarity was restored. *The Old Breed: A History of the 1st Marine Division in World War II*

Cited in the Name of
The President of the United States
The First Marine Division, Reinforced
Under command of
Major General Alexander A. Vandegrift, U.S.M.C.
Citation:

The officers and enlisted men of the First Marine Division, Reinforced, on August 7 to 9, 1942, demonstrated outstanding gallantry and determination in successfully executing forced landing assaults against a number of strongly defended Japanese positions on Tulagi, Gavutu, Tanambogo, Florida and Guadalcanal, British Solomon Islands, completely routing all the enemy forces and seizing a most valuable base and airfield within the enemy zone of operations in the South Pacific Ocean. From the above period until 9 December 1942, this Reinforced Division not only held their important strategic positions despite determined and repeated Japanese naval, air and land attacks, but by a series of offensive operations against strong enemy resistance drove the Japanese from the proximity of the airfield and inflicted great losses on them by land and air attacks. The courage and determination displayed in these operations were of an inspiring order.

girls and watering holes. To restore unity, the division threw a huge beer party—Allied solidarity was restored!

In July 1943, Gen. Douglas MacArthur's staff issued a warning order for the 1st Marine Division to prepare for another operation, naming the little known island of Cape Gloucester as the target. Code-named Dexterity, the operation proved to be another debilitating jungle campaign. "In the memory of the men who fought there, American, Australian, Japanese, it will remain one of the evil spots of this world," Lt. Col. Frank O. Hough wrote in *The Campaign on New Britain*. The division after-action report noted, "Water backed up in the swamps in rear of the shore line, making them impassible for wheeled and tracked vehicles. The many streams which emptied into the sea in the beachhead area became raging torrents. Some even changed course. Troops were soaked to the skin and their clothes never dried out during the entire operation." At the end of the campaign, it was a worn down, disease-ridden outfit that sailed away from Cape Gloucester. Scuttlebutt had it that the division was returning to Australia. "Now hear this," the ship's loudspeakers suddenly blared. "All hands, listen up! We will anchor tomorrow at the island of Pavuvu, where the Marines will disembark! That is all!" Stunned silence—no Australia!

CHAPTER 7

REST AND

RECUPERATION

"I think God has forgotten where Pavuvu is."
"God couldn't forget, because He made everything."
"Then I bet He wishes He could forget He made Pavuvu."
—Anonymous Marine

Pavuvu, a steamy pest-hole located approximately sixty miles north of Guadalcanal, was picked by General Geiger as a training and rest area. Larry J. Woodward wrote that "with its romantic sounding name, it conjures up an image of beautiful coral beaches, hula-skirted young women, good food, cold beer, and warm nights." Unfortunately Pavuvu had none of them. It was a "rain-soaked, rat-infested hunk of real estate," a terrible location to recover from a debilitating jungle campaign. Lieutenant Colonel Lewis Fields thought that Pavuvu "was one of the great mistakes as far as I am concerned in the whole war, stationing a division in such a place."

Rupertus complained to his old friend "Archer" Vandegrift, who responded, "Had I known prior to the arrival of the First [Division] that it was a virgin area, I certainly would have used every effort I could to have the rehabilitation area changed. Knowing the Russells, or part of them at least, to be a very pleasant place to be located, I assumed that the camp area was all laid out, which just shows that you can't go on assumptions." One disillusioned Marine groused, "If you were gonna give the world an enema, that's where you would put it." The men faced deplorable conditions but there was little they could do about it. James W. Johnston said that "At some point in his tour of duty, a Marine learns to think like a Marine [by] developing a fatalistic resignation . . . [and] applies himself primarily to the immediate and elemental pursuits of survival: Where is the water and food? How do we get it? What's the best way to stay warm and dry? Who's shooting at us, and from where?"

■ Pavuvu looked like a tropical paradise from the air, but on the ground it was a nightmare. Roads turned into axle-deep quagmires, and the island was infested with rats, land crabs, and other associated creepy crawlies. The worn-out veterans found there were no lights, no streets, no tents—nothing but acres and acres of coconut trees, whose rotting nuts gave off a sickening smell. *The Old Breed: A History of the 1st Marine Division in World War II*

Colonel John T. Selden recalled that "it was General Geiger's idea to base the division in the Russells in order to avoid having to furnish large working details, as was the rule on Guadalcanal [average of 1,000 men a day], which would interfere seriously with the training program. Unfortunately, [Geiger's] reconnaissance was made by air and failed to disclose the more serious terrain difficulties."

Soon after the division arrived on the island, Lieutenant Colonel Fields was invited to the general's mess, which was located on

■ To make the island habitable, hundreds of men were shanghaied to form working parties. They hauled ton after ton of coral from the beaches to make roads, streets and tent platforms. The work continued for weeks, to the detriment of training. *The Old Breed: A History of the 1st Marine Division in World War II*

Guadalcanal. Geiger asked him how things were going. Fields blurted out how amazed and disgusted he was with the training on Pavuvu and couldn't understand how the division ever got there. General Geiger turned to his chief of staff, Colonel Silverthorn, and asked pointedly, "But you told me that was a good place." Silverthorn responded rather penitently, "Well, that's what it was, I flew over the place and it looked all right." There was a long pregnant pause. Silverthorn sternly eyed Fields, who wanted to slip under the table. After what seemed like hours, the subject was dropped and the innocent junior officer escaped.

The debilitating Cape Gloucester campaign left the men of the 1st Division in poor physical condition. Hundreds of men were sick with

tropical diseases, dysentery and fungus infections because of poor food and the constant wet weather. E. B. Sledge "was appalled at their condition: most were thin, some emaciated, with jungle rot in their armpits and on their ankles and wrists. So many of them needed attention that they had to treat each other under a doctor's supervision." Malaria was rampant among the weakened veterans. Captain Richard B. Watkins remembered that

■ Cape Gloucester, like Guadalcanal, was a debilitating jungle campaign that took its toll on men and equipment. Hundreds were felled by tropical disease and jungle rot, equaling the number that fell from Japanese fire. The stress and strain of the campaign showed in the faces of the men coming off the line. *The Old Breed: A History of the 1st Marine Division in World War II*

MALARIA

After the Guadalcanal operation, the disease-riddled 1st Marine Division had been able to withdraw to Brisbane, Australia, to recover and prepare for the next campaign. One officer described the veterans as they debarked from the transports. "The men were ragged, still dirty, thin, anemic, sallow, listless. Just about one out of every ten of them fell down, tumbling limply down the steep ladder on their backs, landing pitifully on the dock." They were rife with malaria. "Everyone had it," according to Maj. Ray Davis, "The malaria reoccurrence was such that the troops would be in the hospital for two to three weeks to recover from the initial attack; get out of the hospital, spend all their time in the pubs and on the town in Melbourne and in two weeks' time be back in the hospital. The 'rotation' was about five thousand troops, that is, five thousand in the hospital and another five thousand out. In two weeks time another five thousand would go back in and replace the original five thousand. The result was that the division took eight months to recover instead of eight weeks." General Vandegrift ordered the troops to be "force-fed with Atabrine, a preventive pill that tinged the skin yellow, nauseated the stomach, and caused the ears to ring."

Brigadier General O. P. Smith's routine was "one tablet at breakfast for six days. Many of the men, myself included, acquired an Atabrine tan—a sickly yellowish-brown color." A rumor swept the division that Atabrine caused sterility and many of the men stopped taking it. Soon, NCOs were required to pop a tablet into each man's mouth and watch him swallow it. Although Pavuvu was supposed to be free of malaria, there was no relaxation of the Atabrine discipline—one tablet per day for six days.

"many Guadalcanal veterans contracted malaria and would often break out with sweat and start to shake violently. Not to be outdone, I had my turn at it and was pretty well out of it for five days." Major Gordon Gayle knew of an officer who, he thought, committed suicide because of the disease. "He lay in his bunk and took a .45 and blew his brains out. Those of us who'd had malaria, and most of us had, felt that it was caused by malaria-induced depression. It could drive a man to the point where he wasn't really himself."

Instead of rest and relaxation, the men had to build a camp from scratch. There were no streets, no mess halls, no lights, no decks for tents—nothing but acres and acres of coconut palms. O. P. Smith complained that "decayed coral rock underlay the coconut groves and the abundant rainfall did not readily drain through it . . . [F]oot and vehicle traffic churned the turf into mud . . . and the roads soon became impassible. There was no surface water until we eventually dug seven wells, with a daily output of 200,000 gallons, which did not provide much water for bathing." Abandoned coconut plantations covered the island, littering the ground with tons of rotting nuts. The stench was overpowering. One unfortunate moaned, "We could even taste it in the drinking water, and you had to scrub like hell to get the awful smell from our clothes and body. I'm still repulsed by the sight of coconuts in the supermarket, and I get sick to my stomach when I think about the smell of their damned milk!"

■ Row upon row of closely packed coconut trees covered the island. Billeting and training areas had to be squeezed into the available space. Large-scale exercises could not be conducted, and even squad- and platoon-sized units had to jury-rig their tactical training. Everyone was involved in working parties to make the island habitable—not the sort of location to rehabilitate sickened veterans. *The Old Breed: A History of the 1st Marine Division in World War II*

Unenthusiastic Marines were dragooned into working parties to gather the rotted husks, which usually cracked when handled, drenching the unfortunates with rancid milk. Richard Watkins remembered, "Ten thousand men formed into a line and the coconuts were passed hand to hand out to sea. Soon the bay was awash with them and I pictured the whole mass making a surprise arrival at, say, Hawaii!"

Several varieties of loathsome creatures inhabited the island. E. B. Sledge described the land crabs:

> Their blue-black bodies were about the size of the palm of a man's hand, and bristles and spines covered their legs. These ugly creatures hid by day and roamed at night. Before putting on his boondockers each morning, every man in the 1st Marine Division shook his shoes to roust the land crabs. Many mornings I had one in each shoe and sometimes two. Periodically we reached the point of rage over these filthy things and chased them out from under boxes, seabags, and cots. We killed them with sticks, bayonets, and entrenching tools. After the action was over, we had to shovel them up and bury them, or a nauseating stench developed rapidly in the hot humid air.

Hundreds of thousands of repulsive looking rats also populated the island. Their numbers simply overwhelmed every effort to eradicate the filthy beasts—poison, explosives, even flamethrowers. "We killed upward of 400," a disheartened officer reported, "but the next night I saw we hadn't even dented Pavuvu's rat population. I got discouraged and forgot about the scheme." One Marine wag wrote about the island's ecology. "Land crabs ate rotted coconuts—rats ate the land crabs—Marines killed the rats. Everyone thrived in harmony!"

The island was so small that it was impossible to hold large-scale field maneuvers. Even company-size units were forced to skirmish through the streets of the tent camps and "found themselves dodging among heads and mess halls and tripping over the guy ropes of their own tents." Eugene B. Sledge thought "it was funny to see a company move forward in combat formation through the groves and become intermingled with the rigid ranks of another company standing weapons inspection, the officers shouting orders to straighten things out." One frustrated battalion commander groused, "This would have been fine if we were getting ready to fight the Nips hiding in tents, but it was useless as hell as a training exercise if you were expected to blast the little bastards from caves and fortified bunkers." Russ Honsowetz remembered that Puller "would march us around and around [Pavuvu], up and down the few hills that were on it. The head of the column and the tail weren't very far apart when you get a 5,000-man regiment going."

In June, about a third of the veterans were picked by lot to go home. Many had been overseas for twenty-four months or longer and had been through two debilitating jungle campaigns. Colonel John T. Selden, division chief of staff, was instrumental in making it happen. "I moved right in on the personnel section in Washington and made a nuisance of myself. I told them our twenty-four-months men simply had to be sent home." As a result, 260 officers and 4,600 enlisted men were marked for rotation. However, as George McMillan noted, "264 officers and 5,750 enlisted men would have to go into the division's third campaign." For those men lucky enough to go home, it was an unbelievable reprieve from the horrors of combat. But as McMillan reported, "there was a lack of jubilation among the men who were to go home. It was simply not fitting nor in good taste to gloat in front of the men who had to stay on. The men going home went around to ask their buddies if there was any favor they could do; they filled notebooks with addresses of sweethearts, wives and families and promised to call them."

Replacements by the thousands poured into the division. Most were youngsters just out of boot camp without combat experience, but the cadre of seasoned campaigners—veterans of Guadalcanal and Cape Gloucester—quickly took them in tow. McMillan wrote that "The NCOs went to work on the new men who would have to be tested even more harshly, to prove themselves worthy of the Corps' first and finest fighting unit." One officer noted that "They were a strange breed, this bunch that came busting in after Pearl Harbor. Many of them, we discovered, were officer caliber, and could have easily gained that rank it they hadn't volunteered. There's no doubt about it but they wanted to fight."

Private Eugene B. "Sledgehammer" Sledge was one of the new breed. He dropped out of college to join the Corps because of "a deep feeling of uneasiness that the war might end before I could get overseas into combat." After boot camp and infantry training, he joined the 1st

■ With new replacements filling up the division, training started in earnest. After long days spent on troop ships, the new men needed toughening up—and early morning calisthenics was just the thing to get the blood flowing. Under hawk-eyed NCOs, the men performed the Marine Corps way of exercising—or else! *The Old Breed: A History of the 1st Marine Division in World War II*

97

A MARINE SHORT COURSE ON PERSONAL MANNERS

Many of the rotating Marines read an anonymously written and sur-reptitiously distributed spoof on how to act at home. It began with "You can still be a gentleman even if you were in the South Seas":

FOOD ETIQUETTE: "Your first meal in the morning will be breakfast. You will find a strange assortment of foods—such as cantaloupe, fresh eggs and milk—are likely to grace the table. DO NOT be afraid of them; they are highly palatable. If you wish some butter, turn to the nearest person and say, 'Please pass the butter.' DO NOT say, 'Throw down the grease!'

"If, while dining at a friend's home you wish more dessert, merely stare at your empty plate until some-one catches on. If this doesn't work, try rattling your spoon against the side of the dish. DO NOT say, 'How about seconds on the slop?'

PARTY BEHAVIOR: "It is not considered good taste to wink at an escorted lady and motion with your hand toward the door, even if she nods her approval. Her escort will immediately develop a strong dislike for you which might lead to bloodshed.

"It is exceedingly bad form to open a beer bottle with your belt buckle, regardless of how anxious you are to get at the contents.

"DO NOT serve your friends grain alcohol mixed with grapefruit juice or Aqua Velva strained through a loaf of bread, they may not survive the experience.

GENTLEMANLY CONDUCT: "DO NOT go about hit-ting everyone of draft age in civilian clothes—he might have been released on a medical discharge. First ask for his credentials, and if he has none, then go ahead and slug him!

"DO NOT whistle at every female over eight or under eighty.

"DO NOT sprinkle sand between the sheets (cov-ers for beds) to make them more comfortable, civilians like smooth surfaces."

Feeling at odds with the civilian world was an inescapable effect for those who fought in the war. Another story describes a group of returning veterans. One turned to his buddy and said, "By God, I'm a little afraid of what it's gonna be like at home. I'm afraid of what I'm gonna be like. Maybe it'd just be best for a fella to stay over here . . ."

Marine Division on Pavuvu. "The fact that I was assigned to the very regiment and division I would have chosen was a matter of pure chance. I felt as though I had rolled the dice and won."

Gordon Gayle marveled at the difference between the replacements and the veterans. "The troops that were arriving by and large were bigger. They had white skin, whereas those that were leaving were thin, gaunt and yellow with Atabrine. Their whole posture and attitude was entirely different than the new men. [The departing troops] seemed to be about three times as alert . . . they walked on their toes, as alert as cats . . . [T]hese were the survivors that had lasted through two campaigns. The new men were not nearly so alert . . . [T]hey walked on their heels . . . and were heavier. The picture of the contrast between the two groups made a terrific impression on me. One hoped that they could get to be as capable as the veterans in a short period of time."

With the arrival of the new men, training started in earnest. Ray Davis "found an area where we could assault four or five positions with total freedom of action. We employed mortars overhead with live ammo, plus rockets and flame throwers in assault teams against Japanese-style bunkers . . . totally realistic. Then we'd take a squad of Marines, with satchel charges, flame throwers, rockets and bazookas, and we'd tell the squad leader: 'You take that bunker!' These small unit commanders knew the lives of their men were at stake—captured documents had given us an indication of the heavy fortifications we'd face at Peleliu—and they really went at it."

The training was dangerous. Lieutenant R. Bruce Watkins had a close call. "One day I was giving instruction in firing rifle grenades. The very first one I fired traveled only about 50 feet and exploded. Everyone hit the deck as if one man. Fortunately, no one was hit. There is nothing like shrapnel whizzing close overhead to get one's attention."

Not every one thought that realistic training was necessary. Ray Davis experienced it firsthand. "When a lieutenant colonel arrived from Quantico and became commanding officer, I dropped down to become the second in command. I took him out to observe training. He walked up to it and immediately started yelling, 'Stop it, stop it, somebody is going to get killed. You can't do that.' He had just come from teaching tactics, with extensive safety rules, and didn't understand that realistic training was just the ticket because we were going into a pretty dangerous situation." Davis described the guy as "a nut." Another officer was not so polite. "Everyone I knew disliked him . . . [W]e were anticipating the worst under this idiot." At one point the officer decided to visit another island where there were nurses—"Our commander joined the Nurse Corps," Davis related humorously, "and did not return for some time. Puller found out and fired him." Puller told Davis, "He's no longer CO of the 1st Battalion; you are!" and reduced the miscreant to his permanent grade of first lieutenant.

Sledge put the dangerous training into perspective. "The Japanese fought to win. It was a savage, brutal, inhumane, exhausting, and dirty business. Our commanders knew that if we were to win and survive, we must be trained realistically for it whether we like it or not."

Despite the difficulties, the division slowly regained its sharp combat edge. The level of training became increasingly difficult, graduating from squad to platoon, to company, to battalion and finally, complex regimental landing exercises off-island using amphibian tractors. There was a sense that something big was in the offing. Information started trickling down. Gordon Gayle remembered "being quite concerned that this was going to be a very difficult one . . . so I developed a training program that emphasized physical fitness and small unit control . . . fire team and squad leaders . . . of troops in assault formations using hand and arm signals."

The division held a rehearsal landing on Guadalcanal. O. P. Smith watched the 1st Marines come ashore. "I found that 'Lewie' Puller had his CP established in advance of the CP's of his two assault battalions. Lewie told me that he operated that way. He said that, 'If I'm not up front, the troops would ask, "Where the hell is Puller?" ' " *Newsweek* Correspondent Bill Hipple commented that "[Puller] wasn't ever satisfied to just sit back and command the action; he wanted to be as close as he could to it—and lend a personal hand, even firing a few shots himself, at the slightest opportunity. He wasn't content to have his CP a few hundred feet behind the front. He wanted to be right at the front."

Russ Honsowetz, who knew Puller as well as anyone, said that when Chesty "got to be a regimental commander, he didn't like the idea of being so far to the rear and out of it. He would take a small communication section and all of the regimental command post that he needed and go forward. Sometimes a little too far and get pinned down. But the troops loved him for it. They'd see him up there poking around where he shouldn't have been. 'Hell,' they'd say, 'Goddamn, the old man's up here, let's go!'" Puller's radio operator, William E. Atchison, was more circumspect. "Being that close to my all-time hero was indeed hazardous to my health! It was his brand of leadership to let himself be exposed. He was lucky. He carried a little lead in him, but he never got a mortal wound." Honsowetz related how an army regimental commander came up to the front lines. "Where's your CP?" he asked Puller. "Right here," Chesty responded. The soldier seemed puzzled. "No, I mean your CP. This must be your OP [observation post]." "No," Puller retorted, "This is my CP." The army commander turned to his adjutant and ordered, "Put my CP back down the road about 3,000 yards!"

O. P. Smith was in tactical control of a rehearsal landing because Rupertus' injury would not allow him to get in a boat—and he "seemed unconcerned about our training problems." Smith took the troops ashore and set up a command post. "General Geiger came up the beach and talked to me and said, 'Where is Rupertus?' And I told him, and that's when he said, 'If I had known, I'd have relieved him.'" Smith assured Geiger that "in the remaining two weeks before the landing, I felt General Rupertus' ankle would mend sufficiently to permit him to carry on. But, as D-day approached, I began to worry. I went to the division surgeon and said, 'Look doctor, frankly, is the general going to be able to make it for Peleliu?' He told me he thought he would, but would have to use a cane. I said okay."

The 1st Division was not so isolated that the famous comedian Bob Hope could not find it. Hope was on a USO–sponsored trip to Banika, a short plane hop from Pavuvu, when he heard about the Marines next door. Hope prodded the navy into allowing his troupe to do a morning performance. According to one Marine, "The fact that they'd come to a godforsaken place like Pavuvu really lifted our spirits. It made us feel like we weren't totally forgotten." O. P. Smith remembered that, "Because of their tight schedule, we brought the troupe over in eight small Cub planes. About 15,000 men were assembled in the open space back of the docks. The planes made their approach to a landing by flying low over the heads of the crowd." The irrepressible Hope said that circling over the heads of his audience was one of the highlights of his Pacific tour. A makeshift runway doubled as a road. It was a tricky landing according to one of the Marine pilots. "You had to make a steep bank around a large grove of palms and then line up, come down, and hit the middle of the road. It had a high crown, and if you didn't hit it just right you'd ground-loop into the ditch."

Hope's troupe put on an unforgettable ninety-minute show that had the troops laughing, cheering, whistling and applauding. The highlight of the performance was scantily clad dancer Patti Thomas. Straight-laced O. P. Smith reminisced smilingly, "First Patti did different types of dances in pantomime and after each dance, men near the stage were asked to name the dance. Successful guessers were brought up on the stage to dance with Patti." The skit brought the house down. Bob Hope closed the performance with his theme song, "Thanks for the Memories." One Marine said, "Man, what a show! One of them every day and we could fight this damned war with a smile!" George McMillan thought "it was one of the most pleasant memories of Pavuvu the men retained."

The division's training was completed in the middle of August. A final dress rehearsal to test the landing plan was held on August 29 in the Cape Esperance area of Guadalcanal. O. P. Smith thought the rehearsal "went off very smoothly, despite the danger of unexploded rockets in the beach area." A critique was held the next day, which was attended by all the "brass" of the operation. "There was nothing particularly constructive about it," Smith recalled, "everyone was pleased with everyone else. The critique did, however, give all hands an opportunity to get acquainted." In typical Puller fashion, he addressed the men of the regiment. "In about a week we're going up to attack a place called Peleleleo [one officer mentioned that he habitually mispronounced names]. The navy and air force will be shelling and bombing it for five days, so there shouldn't be much for us to do but go in and police up the area with a bayonet!" The men cheered wildly. He continued. "Still, I wouldn't mind having some insurance policies on some of you men." The men cheered even louder.

Bruce Watkins remembered that Puller "called all the officers together one day for a pep talk. He assured us that there were plenty of medals between here and Tokyo. This was not what we particularly wanted to hear. However, we took great pride in Chesty, as he was already a legend. Sometimes, he would unobtrusively step into an enlisted chow line and strike up a conversation with any private at hand, much to their

■ A final rehearsal to test the landing plan was held on Guadalcanal. It included live fire from LCI(G) gunboats and LVT(A)s. There was no maneuver ashore, but it did allow the troops to stretch their legs and get used to traveling in the amtracs and DUKWs, which are shown in this photo. *The Old Breed: A History of the 1st Marine Division in World War II*

■ A critique was held after the final rehearsal which, as O. P. Smith related, was nothing more than noting that "everyone was pleased with everyone else." Here the division chief of staff, Col. John T. Selden, goes over his notes. Seated in the front row from left to right are O. P. Smith, Rupertus and U.S. Navy Capt. T. D. Britton, commander of the transport group. *The Old Breed: A History of the 1st Marine Division in World War II*

awe and delight. He was tough on officers and very friendly to enlisted men." Emil Buff recalled how Puller berated one of the old timers. "I hear you're getting anxious to go stateside," he said gruffly. "Anybody who wants to go back before this war is over is a yellow S.O.B.!" The gaunt, Atabrine-colored infantryman responded, "Colonel, do you know how many yellow S.O.B.s you have in this regiment?"

Just before leaving the island, Rupertus stopped by Puller's tent. "Lewie, you should make general on Peleliu. It's tailored for you. Your performance of duty should bring you another Navy Cross and brigadier's star, too."

CHAPTER 8

MOUNTING OUT

L ess than a week after Puller's meeting, thirty Landing Ship Tanks (LSTs), the slowest ships of the convoy, sailed for the Palaus. They started four days ahead of the transports because of the speed differential—7.7 knots versus 12.1. The two assault battalions of the 1st Marines went aboard the LSTs, called "large slow targets" by irreverent crewmembers. On September 8, the assault transports and escort ships sailed. O. P. Smith wrote that there were over 800 ships in the task force. "Battleships to bombard the beaches; destroyers and destroyer escorts to guard the convoys; mine sweepers to clear known mine fields; sub-chasers to act as control and guide vessels; command ships to carry top commanders and their staffs; survey ships; hospital ships; net laying ships; oilers for refueling; repair ships; salvage vessels; tugs; gunboats—ships of every description and type." In addition to the hundreds of support ships, there were 770 landing craft—amphibian tractors, armored amphibians, DUKWs and LCVP (landing craft vehicle and personnel) to carry the assault troops to the beachhead.

■ The ship in the foreground with bow doors open is an LST. Second and Third battalions of the 1st Marines were embarked on this type of ship, along with the amtracs that would carry them to their landing beaches. The ships on the right are LCTs, which were designed to carry tanks and large vehicles. Combat assault loading is almost an art form. Everything has to be stowed so it is available when needed and in the right amount. *The Old Breed: A History of the 1st Marine Division in World War II*

Ray Davis' battalion, 1,478 men of Landing Team 1-1, was embarked aboard the USS *Warren* (APA 53), one of ten specially constructed assault transports. Lightly armed with one 5-inch 38-caliber gun and 20mm and 40mm anti-aircraft mounts for defense, the APA carried seventeen assorted landing craft. As the reserve, 1-1 would use the ship's wooden landing craft to get to the transfer line, where they would climb aboard amtracs for the final swim over the reef to the beach. The evolution started with the troops climbing down cargo nets to board the ship's boats. The carefully choreographed maneuver involved each boat team lined up on deck in four or five ranks. On signal that the landing craft was in position, the front rank straddled the rail and stepped down on a horizontal strand, grasping the verticals and then working their way down to the boat. As one set cleared the rail another rank started down. The maneuver seemed fairly simple, but in a heavy sea, carrying a weapon, full pack and ammunition, accidents were bound to happen. More than one man lost his grip and fell between ship and landing craft. The men were trained to keep their helmet chin straps buckled—to keep the two-pound steel pot from braining someone—and to unbuckle their cartridge belt in case they went into the drink and had to ditch it. Unfortunately the pack, heavy boondockers and waterlogged clothing were not so easy to shrug out of.

An observer noted, "The warships, including two ageing battleships, several cruisers and destroyers, joined us along with a hospital ship and, outlined against a red-gold tropic sunset, we sailed away." The convoy steered a course northwest through the Solomon Islands, across the Equator, on an approach generally parallel to the northern coast of New Guinea to the Palaus, a journey of approximately 2,100 miles.

O. P. Smith boarded the USS *Elmore*, which had been modified to serve as an auxiliary command vessel. Smith found the ship's captain and crew to be "very pleasant and accommodating. All officers and men were indoctrinated with the idea that their mission was to serve and support the embarked troops." This was not always the case. When Smith was aboard the USS *Fuller* just before the war, he found the "crew green, the food poor and we were continually harassed by peacetime ideas of 'spit and polish.'" Silverthorn was not happy with the accommodations aboard the command ship USS *Mount McKinley*. The quarters were cramped and he had to sleep on a transom, while Julian Smith used a folding bunk that had been welded to a bulkhead and Geiger was forced to share his head and living area.

Captain George P. Hunt and his company were aboard the LST 227 as it made its way slowly across the seemingly endless expanse of ocean.

■ The LSTs were crammed with supplies, equipment and men. There was not enough room below decks to billet the troops so they found room topside to spread their shelters—between vehicles, on top of supplies, anywhere there was space. Fortunately the weather was good and, if truth were told, most would rather not be in the smelly holds. *Marine Corps History Division*

"Flat-bottomed and broad of beam, she seemed motionless except for the thin curl of foam at her waterline. Dirty green and black camouflage had been smeared on her sides, and rust spread toward the top of her blunt bow. Her main deck was the forward two-thirds of her length . . . [O]n the remaining third aft rose a stubby superstructure with a boat deck, a wheel house and a canvas-covered conn where the skipper sat on a high stool with a speaking tube and a compass in front of him." The LST's tank and main deck were crammed with cargo, vehicles and equipment, leaving very little space for the men. "We had the usual

108

■ LVT(A)s headed for the beach. They preceded the troop-carrying LVTs to provide last-minute gunfire against the Japanese beach defenses. They were armed with .30- or .50-caliber machine guns and either a 37mm or 75mm anti-tank gun in the turret. In this view, the LVT(A) mounts a .50-caliber and the 75mm gun. Sandbags along the side provide protection from Japanese magnetic mines. *Marine Corps History Division*

difficulty of crowding ourselves into the limited space the navy provided us," Hunt groused. "The sleeping compartments down below accommodated only 77 and since there were 235 in my company, the others spilled over the main deck, finding what living space they could in the confusion of trucks and jeeps and water trailers and drums and piles of crates."

Among the many vehicles jammed into the tank deck of LST 227 were twenty LVT(A)s of Company "B," 3rd Armored Amphibian Tractor Battalion. Known as "alligators," the vehicles were armed with both .50- and .30-caliber machine guns and either a 75mm howitzer or a 37mm anti-tank gun. They were designed to precede the troop-carrying LVTs to the beach and provide gunfire support in the first few minutes of the landing. The division operations plan stated that "en route to Beaches White 1 and 2 . . . neutralize shore defenses by fire with particular attention to flanks. After passing through the water line beach defenses . . . render immediate fire support for assault waves." Seventy-five of the armored amphibians were assigned to lead six waves of 182 troop-carrying alligators to the beach. The 1st Regiment's assault battalions would have twenty-six of the armored vehicles in support as they landed over White Beach 1 and 2.

■ A battleship unleashing her main battery. Each ship was assigned specific targets to destroy. The command ship maintained a master target list that tracked each target and its status. Unfortunately, U.S. intelligence was unable to detect many of the enemy's fortifications, so the target list was drastically incomplete. After two days, Admiral Oldendorf ordered the ships to cease fire because they had destroyed all the targets on the master list. *Marine Corps History Division*

PRE-ASSAULT PREPARATIONS

Before dawn on September 12, D – 3, as the huge invasion armada plodded steadily toward the objective, Adm. Jesse Oldendorf's Fire Support Group—four old battleships (OBB), three heavy cruisers (CL), one light cruiser (CL), seventeen destroyers (DD), eighteen Landing Craft Infantry Gunboats (LCI[G]), four Landing Craft Infantry Mortar (LCI[M]), and four Landing Craft Infantry (LCI[L]) and the first echelon of the Escort Carrier Group—arrived off the island to begin the pre-assault bombardment. Oldendorf's fire support plan divided the island into numbered squares that were assigned to a specific ship. Every target

■ Underwater demolition teams were transported to the beach by Higgins boat. At a designated point, the boat, traveling at high speed to avoid Japanese fire, would turn parallel to the beach; the frogmen would roll over the side into a rubber boat and enter the water. Their mission was to precede the landing to locate anti-boat obstacles and mines and wire the obstacles with explosives for later detonation. *Marine Corps History Division*

■ Frogmen coating their bodies with grease before the swim. Some mixed it with silver camouflage grease to give it a shimmering look, making them more difficult to see in the water. The men's only garb were swim trunks, face masks, swim fins, and a sheath knife. *Marine Corps History Division*

was numbered and indexed with specific information. The master target list was maintained aboard the command ship, USS *Pennsylvania* (BB-38), and was continually updated during the bombardment.

Jeter Isley and Philip Crowl's *The U.S. Marines and Amphibious War, Its Theory and Its Practice in the Pacific*, explained that "Specific targets were kept track of individually, and when destroyed or partially damaged a notation was made of that fact. The plan was to employ both armor-piercing and variously fused high-capacity ammunition, to wreck the greatest number of enemy defenses in a given time, and to prevent wasting projectiles on a target already obliterated."

At 0530, the ships opened fire, blasting away at the Japanese defenses. Flame and smoke billowed upward, obscuring the beaches. Two hours later the ships temporarily ceased fire to allow carrier planes to bomb and strafe. This pattern continued for the next two days until the island's surface was turned into "a barren wasteland" according to an extract taken from an unidentified Japanese soldier's diary. His diary also noted that, "[I] could feel the blood pounding in my veins throughout my body" at the sight of the warships that were firing with impunity. Colonel Nakagawa had forbidden his hidden batteries to open fire. Despite the terrific bombardment, only one man in the soldier's cannon company was slightly injured, which was true for most of the garrison who were safe in their underground bombproofs.

By mid-morning, with the bombardment well along, two high-speed transports, USS *Stringham* (APD-6) and USS *Clemson* (APD-31), lowered their Higgins boats, with frogmen from Underwater Demolition Team 6 and 7 aboard. Their mission was to clear the beach approaches of underwater obstacles and make pathways through the coral reef for the shallow draft landing craft. Most of the men were experienced veterans from the Saipan operation and knew what to expect as they got closer to the beach. Japanese snipers and machine gunners opened up on them as they reached shallow water. A pesky sniper in a palm tree targeted one of the frogmen until a 40mm shell from a covering gunboat blew the tormentor out of the tree. "It was a very comforting sight," the swimmer reported, tongue in cheek.

Team 7 found the 1st Regiment's beaches sown with a thicket of rusty tetrahedrons and a double row of wooden posts that jutted out of the water 75 feet from shore. Alert swimmers spotted rock-filled log cribs, concrete cubes, a fire trench and an anti-tank ditch along the shore line, beyond their reach. They would have to be dealt with by Marine demolition experts. The swimmers reported one bit of good news—the reef was flat and smooth and would not pose any problem for the LVTs.

After dark on D – 1, two ten-man teams returned to destroy the obstacles with demolition charges. Nerves were stretched tight as they slipped through the inky darkness, armed only with a sheath knife. "You'd be surprised at the number of drifting logs that were stabbed that night," one remarked upon returning safely to the *Stringham.*

It took Team 6 two days to accomplish their mission because another team lost its gear after its ship was sunk in an accident. Their after-action report noted that "The operation was accomplished under heavy machine gun and sniper fire." Their report indicated that the beach approaches were strewn with large coral boulders that would prevent the passage of tanks, DUKWs and other vehicular equipment. Furthermore, the enemy had erected lines of heavily braced posts near the shore abreast of the beaches. On the following two days, although constantly exposed to enemy fire, the operating platoons blasted the large coral boulders off the beaches. On the second night, eight handpicked units proceeded to within fifty yards of the enemy's rifle pits and machine guns to place over one thousand demolition charges, which successfully cleaned out the obstacles on the beaches. A fortuitous combination of good fire support, coolness and battle-wisdom and good luck enabled the team to accomplish this whole operation without a casualty.

The Japanese maintained their fire discipline, except in one instance when an overeager coastal gun fired at the heavy cruiser *Portland.* The ship's gunnery officer spotted the gun as it was dragged from its hiding place to fire and hauled back to cover. *Portland* blasted it with five salvos of 8-inch gunfire, only to have the Japanese fire again. The frustrated officer swore, "You can put all the steel in Pittsburgh on that thing and still not get it." Oldendorf was also concerned with the lack of enemy response and ordered an aerial reconnaissance. The photos showed "an immense broken graveyard" of above-ground buildings and emplacements that were leveled and a heavily pockmarked landscape—the once green island was barren of foliage. Nevertheless, the ships steamed back in to their bombardment stations and opened fire. By early afternoon, the master target list was complete, and Oldendorf reported, "We have

■ The obstacles were blown after recovery of the teams. Here a huge geyser erupts after the explosives were triggered. Hundreds of pounds of military explosives were transported, wired and placed on the obstacles without loss of a single man—a unique achievement. *Marine Corps History Division*

run out of targets, the best that can be done is to blast away at suspected positions and hope for the best." After conferring with his staff that evening, he cancelled the next day's bombardment.

Oldendorf's decision set off a firestorm of criticism. "How he [Oldendorf] can say he ran out of targets I never understood," Gordon Gayle retorted angrily. "There were targets that had been printed on the maps that we had weeks before back in the Russells that were still intact and fighting when we got there. How he could say he ran out of targets I could never understand." Jeff Fields backed Gayle. "When we landed, some of those emplacements which we knew were there and had been targets of naval gunfire were still there untouched—all hell hit us when we landed." After D-day, Oldendorf remarked, "The pre-landing gunfire

■ Aerial view of the damage caused by the naval and air bombardment. It destroyed or heavily damaged the concrete reinforced buildings of the airfield complex. However, the Japanese had counted on this heavy pre-assault bombardment and prepared their primary defenses in the growth-covered Umurbrogol ridges where photoreconnaissance was ineffective. After viewing the post-bombardment photos, Admiral Oldendorf could not see any reason for continuing naval gunfire. *Marine Corps History Division*

support was, I thought, superior to anything which had been put on heretofore. My surprise and chagrin when concealed batteries opened up on the LVTs can be imagined." Isley and Crowl concluded "that preliminary naval gunfire on Peleliu was inadequate . . . Peleliu, like Tarawa and to a lesser extent Saipan, demonstrated that the only substitute for such prolonged bombardment was costly expenditure of the lives of the assault troops."

OBJECTIVE AREA

As the ships neared the objective area, the troops went through their last-minute preparations. Sledge remembered his mortar squad sitting on their racks in the troop compartment cleaning weapons and checking combat packs. His haversack contained "a folding poncho, one pair of socks, a couple of boxes of K rations, salt tablets, extra carbine ammo [twenty rounds], two hand grenades, a fountain pen, a small bottle of ink, writing paper in a waterproof wrapper, a toothbrush, a small tube of toothpaste, some photos of my folks along with some letters and a dungaree cap." Many wrote a last letter home. Jim Johnston dropped a note to his parents. "We are aboard ship going to a place you'll probably hear about before (if ever) you get this letter. Quite a lot of us have been in it before so we know what is coming. Now do not worry because when you get this it will all be over and everything happens for the best. As I write, I realize well that this may be my last letter . . . I am not afraid and I am happy for I know that some greater day, whether here or on the other side, we shall meet again."

Bruce Watkins found a moment on deck.

I remember leaning on the ship's rail, alone for once, my thoughts on my much-loved wife of fourteen months. I knew she was praying for me, although she could not know the hour of our peril. Brought up in a Christian home, it was natural for me to turn to God and ask for His help. I asked for sharpness of mind to make the right decisions quickly for those who depended on me. Somehow I felt it was wrong to ask for my personal safety, but I asked for strength to fight no matter how badly I might be wounded. And so the last hours passed. Soon there would be no time for reflection.

On D – 1, the troop commanders and newsmen opened the sealed envelopes that were given them by the division commander:

Headquarters, First Marine Division

Fleet Marine Force

C/O Fleet Post Office, San Francisco, Calif.

Memorandum to: All officers and men of the First Marine Division

MEN OF THE FIRST DIVISION:

Once again the eyes of the Marine Corps will be focused on you. In a few days you will prove that your selection to spearhead another and deeper thrust into enemy territory is an honor which you richly deserve.

At Guadalcanal, Cape Gloucester and Talasea, you demonstrated that you were superior to the best troops the enemy could place in the field. YOU ARE STILL SUPERIOR.

You will land after intensive naval bombardment and air bombing to meet the enemy with one idea uppermost in your minds—to carry out the mission entrusted to you.

Within 48 hours from the time that the first Marine puts foot on enemy soil, our country should have still another base from which to continue the march to Tokyo.

That each and everyone will do his duty is well known. I am proud to command such a body of men and to be with you in your victory.

■ Sailors study a map of their objective. They will be responsible for bringing in the follow-on waves of troops, supplies and equipment. On Peleliu only the first six waves would go ashore in amtracs, leaving the bulk of the assault force to be transported by these men. *Marine Corps History Division*

Good luck and God be with you.

William H. Rupertus
Major General, U.S. Marine Corps
Commanding

The message upset battalion commander Gayle. "I think it had a very negative effect because some people believed it, and if you were in my position you couldn't discredit the division commander's statement, but neither could you believe it." The division personnel officer, Lt. Col. W. E. Benedict, recalled, "I doubt that anyone with the possible exception of the chief of staff was consulted before the letter was written and distributed . . . I was given a rough draft of the letter and merely supervised its reproduction." The letter had a profound effect among the newsmen. Many of the thirty-six accredited correspondents did not go ashore at all because they thought the operation would be a pushover. Only six reporters stayed through the early stages of the fighting. The Marine Corps Peleliu monograph noted that "News coverage of the operation was sketchy, often misleading, and, when quick conquest failed to materialize, tinged with biting criticism."

Throughout the invasion force, officers and NCOs called their men together for last-minute instructions. Private First Class Sledge remembered his platoon commander: "His brow was knit, his face drawn, and he looked worried. 'Men, as you probably know, tomorrow is D-day. General Rupertus says the fighting will be extremely tough but short. It will be over in four days, maybe three. Remember what you've been taught. Keep your heads down going in on the amtracs . . . Get off the beach fast . . . The Japs will plaster it with everything they've got . . . They may meet us at the beach . . . so come out of the amtracs ready for anything. Reveille will be shortly before daylight, and H-hour will be at 0830. Hit the sack early. You will need the rest. Good luck and carry on.' "

CHAPTER 9

D-DAY

"There are amtracs burning on the reef.
"Repeat: There are amtracs burning on the beach."

Aerial Observer, H-Hour

F or those able to sleep, the sudden racket topside was startling. "The thumping of running feet on the deck above my head, the creaking of davits and pulleys" woke George Hunt from a sound sleep. "It was not before I had thoroughly rubbed my eyes that I knew where I was and what an important day in my life this one was likely to be. I realized that within a few hours darkness might surround me forever."

Life magazine artist-correspondent Tom Lea was aboard one of the transports:

> My watch said 0340 when I woke up on the blacked-out weather deck below the bridge. Barefooted and in my skivvies, I got off my cot and stood by the rail, rubbing grit from my eyes. Dead ahead, framed between the forward kingposts, there was flickering light on the black horizon. Sick yellow balls of fire flashed low in the clouds like heat lighting, but continuous. It was the

navy shelling Peleliu with the final punch before we landed. The black silhouette of a seaman on watch by the rail turned to me and said, "Them Japs are catching hell for breakfast." A Marine standing in the shadows echoed his sentiments. "Hell, I'm going ashore, find a tin can and make me some joe. There won't be any Japs when the Navy finishes.

Compartment lights flipped on. "Reveille, Reveille," shouted the keyed-up NCOs. "Hit the deck!" Half-asleep men crawled from their racks and stumbled to the overcrowded heads, only to find long lines and desperate patrons. In the crowded compartments, men struggled to dress in the narrow aisles, amidst piles of equipment and weapons. Most headed for the mess hall and the fabled "steak and egg" pre-invasion breakfast. On some ships chow consisted of black coffee, dry toast and an orange. When one disappointed Leatherneck complained, a wizened NCO chided him. "It's better not to have much in your stomach in case you get hit." Sergeant Donald A. Hallman, a combat correspondent, noted that "Only the hardiest took more than a few bites . . . A couple of slices of toast washed down by steaming black coffee filled the appetites of virtually every Marine." However, one private thought it was "Good chow, the best I ever had overseas. Steak and eggs . . . it didn't sit very well in my stomach and I was awful weak in the knees."

Fred Fox and his buddy Bill Elderton "stood on deck and looked at the flashes in the black night miles ahead. The noise from the guns was beyond our hearing. We wondered what was going on." It was the navy's four old battleships—*Mississippi, Idaho, Pennsylvania* and *Maryland*—blasting the interior of the island, in accordance with the carefully choreographed gunfire support plan. The schedule and control of naval gunfire followed a pre-landing pattern that had become standard. On the morning of D-day, gunfire support was conducted in three phases:

Phase I. Prearranged neutralization and counter-battery fires were delivered mainly by heavy ships at moderately long range until the first wave of LVTs was one thousand yards from the beach. At that point they shifted five hundred to one thousand yards inland. One old battleship and one cruiser were assigned to each of the White and Orange beaches and were to commence firing at H − 30 minutes. They were allotted 80 fourteen-inch, 120 eight-inch and 320 five-inch shells per beach.

Phase II. Close support fires were provided mainly by cruisers and destroyers at close range just before H-hour. They shifted their fire to the flanks when the first wave was three hundred yards from the beach. Their anti-aircraft guns fired air bursts behind the beaches to kill snipers and troops in the open. White phosphorous shells, which created a white smoke, were used to blind enemy observers on the high ground north of the airport. Eighteen LCI(G) gunboats led the first waves in. At the transfer line they opened fire with 20mm and 40mm guns, and then fired 4.5-inch rockets approximately one thousand yards from the beach. Four LCI(M) mortar boats with 4.2-inch mortars were stationed off the northern flank of White Beach 1. Finally, forty-eight fighters strafed the landing beaches at H - 5 minutes, in a last-minute effort to keep the defenders' heads down. O. P. Smith said proudly that "All ships were encouraged to close the range and take under-fire and visible targets."

Phase III. After the troops were ashore, fires were to be "on call" to blast targets of opportunity. Specially trained naval gunfire spotters and liaison officers were attached to the division and to each battalion and regiment. Their mission was to request gunfire support, observe the fall of the shot and adjust its fire.

Tom Lea had an eye for detail. "Dawn came dim with low overcast. In the first gray light I saw the sea filled with an awe-inspiring company of strangers to our troop ships. Out to the horizon in every direction were lean men-of-war, fat transports, stubby landing craft, gathered around us like magic in the growing light. It was D-day." Aboard LST 227 the ship's PA system blared, "Now all Marines stand by to disembark!" George Hunt watched as his "men put on their belts and packs and helmets and picked up their weapons. I looked at them for the last time as a company, and I felt very proud."

After chow, Fred Fox made his way back to the main deck and shrugged into his gear. "I folded my poncho flat and then folded it over my cartridge belt, flopping it over my first aid packet. On the left side of my belt hung a razor sharp USMC K-Bar . . . on my right side was a holster with my .45-caliber Colt automatic pistol . . . [T]wo white phosphorous smoke grenades were in one dungaree jacket pocket and two regular pineapple grenades were in the other . . . then, over the belt was a two tube CO2 inflatable life belt. This entire load was topped off with our camouflaged cloth covered steel helmet." His load weighed in at between thirty and forty pounds. Others carried even more weight. Gunners of crew-served weapons—flamethrowers, machine guns, mortars—had to add the weight of the gun and its ammunition, often seventy pounds or more.

Chesty Puller worked his way to the bridge to thank the ship's commander for his treatment of the Marines. The naval officer was looking at the bombardment. "Puller," he said, "You won't find anything to stop you over there. Nothing could have lived through that hammering." Puller looked at him skeptically and replied, "Well, sir, all I can see is dust. I doubt if you've cleaned it out. I know they have underground oil dumps for that airfield. We haven't seen that blow. I've been boning over those maps for weeks and I believe they'll have pillbox stuff, fortifications like we've never seen before." Puller turned to leave and the officer blurted out optimistically, "Good luck, Puller. We'll expect you for dinner this evening." Puller responded darkly, "If we get out of this one, you'll be back in Hawaii long before we're through with this job." Lieutenant Frank C. Shepherd, Puller's personnel officer, related that the old man told him, "We'll catch hell is my guess. One of these days we're going to be . . . driven into the sea."

Suddenly the ship's PA came to life. "Now all Marines lay to your debarkation stations!" Fred Fox shouldered his bulky seventy-pound flamethrower, squeezed through a narrow passageway and down a steep ladder to the tank deck and climbed aboard his designated amtrac. "The three-man tractor crew was down there already," he reminisced. "This particular amtrac had two machine guns on the front, on swivel bases.

One of them was a .50-caliber air-cooled machine gun, on the left, and there was a .30-caliber air-cooled gun on the right." By the time George Hunt reached the tank deck, the amtracs had started their engines. "When I swung open the heavy steel hatch, I was slapped by the deafening roar of Alligator engines and the blue, swirling exhaust which began to clog my lungs and make my eyes water. The exhaust fumes poured over us . . . beads of sweat broke out on our faces, and our jackets were already soggy wet and clinging to us."

Merle Turner, a gunner on an armored amphibian, admitted that "deep doubts gripped me until the press of activity, getting ready to leave the LST, left little time for entertaining doubts. The trick was to stay

■ An amtrac can be seen leaving the bow doors of LST 689 in the foreground. A cruiser's stern can be seen on the left, while a two-stack destroyer is on the right. Smoke from the pre-assault bombardment billows up from the island. *Marine Corps History Division*

calm and reassuring to the men in the platoon." Eugene Sledge got a sinking feeling when he looked at his ride to the beach. "My knees got weak when I saw that it wasn't the newer model [LVT] with the tailgate ramp for troop exit in which we had practiced. This meant that once the amtrac was on the beach, we'd have to jump over the high sides, exposed much more to enemy fire." A horn sounded and the LST's bow doors opened. The first amtracs clattered toward the opening.

Many of the men were apprehensive as to whether the steel amphibians would float in the open sea. First Lieutenant James R. Clark said, "It was not uncommon to see crews sitting on top of the tank [LVT(A)] as it left the mother ship, just in case it sank." Bruce Watkins "could see the steep angle of the bow ramp and held his breath as the track hit the water. It seemed we would surely submerge, but we soon righted ourselves." Fred Fox saw a DUKW (amphibious truck) come off the ramp. "It just splashed into the sea with a 105 howitzer, people, everything and didn't come up."

The LST gun crews watched the amtracs launch. "As soon as we were in the water," George McMillan wrote, "I looked up and I saw those sailors standing up on the bow and I cursed myself for not joining the navy." Tom Lea remembered a lighthearted, gallows humor–type note that was posted on the bulletin board of the ship's wardroom:

A Message of Thanks
From: Marines aboard USS *Repulsive*
To: Officers and men aboard USS *Repulsive*

1. It gives us great pleasure at this time to extend our sincere thanks to all members of the crew for their kind and considerate treatment of Marines during this cruise.

2. We non-combatants realize that the brave and stalwart members of the crew are winning the war in the Pacific. You Navy people even go within ten miles

of a Japanese island, thereby risking your precious lives. Oh how courageous you are! Oh how our piles bleed for you.

3. Because of your actions during the voyage it is our heartfelt wish that:

a. The USS *Repulsive* receives a Jap torpedo immediately after debarkation of all troops.

b. The crew of the USS *Repulsive* is stranded on Beach Orange Three where Marine units which sailed aboard the ship may repay in some measure the good

■ An excellent shot of the first wave headed into the beach. The on-line formation enables them to land the maximum number of troops at the same time. Note the wave control boats in the foreground. The ships closest to shore are the LCI(G) gunboats laying down suppressive fire with their 20mm and 40mm guns and rockets. *Marine Corps History Division*

fellowship extended by the crew and officers during the trip.

4. In conclusion we Marines wish to say to all you dear, dear boys in the Navy: "Bugger you, you bloody bastards!"

Russell Davis, 2nd Battalion scout, peered over the side of the tractor. "The sea was full of small craft and there were oil slicks on the water. The air overhead hummed with fire. Planes screamed and dived all along the transport line . . . The ships of the line put out their tongues of fire toward the island. Shell bursts blew gaping mouths in the smoke,

■ LVT(A) headed for the beach, leading the first assault wave. Upon reaching shore, they were to prepare to support the infantry with close-in fire from their 75mm or 37mm anti-tank gun. On Peleliu they performed extremely well, giving vital support throughout the campaign. *Marine Corps History Division*

and the dark and rotted teeth of the island ridge showed through. There were flashes against the ridge as the barrage lifted from the beach and rolled in on the high ground."

Lieutenant Robert W. Fisher was initially enthralled by the aerial bombardment but then saddened when, "In the midst of a fascinating display of aerial might, one of our Hellcats suddenly burst into flame and disappeared beyond the distant horizon. The effect of this tragedy on all of us was immediately apparent, and the most frequently heard comment was 'He never knew what hit him.' We later learned that this was the only plane lost in the initial bombardment."

George Hunt was momentarily stunned by the ship's gun blasts. "We were rocked by the concussions; our tractor shook in the water; and at times we were so near to the guns that we felt the heat of the flame which belched from the muzzles. The huge warships . . . reeled under the recoil of their own fire. I looked toward the beach. It was smothered in black vapor and flying spray and sand. I saw the dive-bombers plunging toward the earth. Flame and smoke shot up when their bombs hit the mark." Merwin Silverthorn remarked soberly that "the island looked like Dante's inferno."

The amphibious tractors circled until a snub-nosed Higgins boat flying a numbered pennant swung in front of the lead amtrac. An officer signaled with his arms and the circle straightened out, heading for the line of departure—an imaginary line parallel to and four thousand yards from the beach that served as a reference to ensure the assault waves hit the beach on time. Eugene Sledge recalled the moment vividly, feeling that he had

> never experienced any more supremely agonizing suspense than the excruciating torture of those moments before we received the signal to begin the assault on Peleliu. I broke out in a cold sweat as the tension mounted with the intensity of the bombardment. My stomach was tied in knots. I had a lump in my throat and swallowed only with great difficulty. My knees

■ LCI(G) gunboat armed with 20mm and 40mm automatic guns and 4.5-inch rockets. This photo shows the gun crews at their general quarters station, guns manned and ready. The white rows amidships are the rockets stacked in their launchers. The ship has been painted with stripes to reduce its visibility when operating close to shore. These little gunboats proved their worth throughout the Pacific. *Marine Corps History Division*

■ At least four and possibly five amtracs are burning in this photo. They are so close together that it might have been the same gun that got all of them. There appear to be four or five more damaged or destroyed machines on the beach on the right, at the water line. One appears to be turned on its side. The amtracs caught hell going in. *Marine Corps History Division*

nearly buckled, so I clung weakly to the side of the tractor. Finally, with a sense of fatalistic relief mixed with a flash of anger at the navy officer who was our wave commander, I saw him wave his flag toward the beach. Our driver revved the engine. The treads churned up the water, and we started in . . .

Fred Fox was in the first wave. "We were the number two tractor counting from the extreme left. The amphibious tanks with the gun turret were about 50 to 75 yards ahead of our wave." Platoon Sergeant Albert Blaisdell in tank B-16 "looked back seaward and I could see all of our landing craft lined up abreast and following us." As Blaisdell's armored amphibian reached the transfer control line—a control feature parallel to and 2,000 yards from the beach that was designed to control speed and direction—an LCI(G) gunboat opened fire with 20mm and 40mm and a barrage of 4.5-inch rockets, "an awesome noise with clouds of smoke. Dust, flame, debris, tree limbs, etc., was hurled into the air in front of us."

From his position on Patrol Craft 1230, O. P. Smith watched the gun boats "loose terrific rocket barrages against the rugged ground south of Orange Beach 3. The red back blast was visible . . . and the rate of fire was so rapid that several streaks were visible at the same time. The

■ LVT showing the effects of a large-caliber Japanese shell hit. It appears that the shell hit the left rear of the machine, opening it up like a can opener. Unless the embarked troops got off before the shell hit, it is difficult to imagine anyone surviving the blast. *Marine Corps History Division*

rget was instantaneous and vicious . . . blanketing

attalions reached the zone between the transfer
suddenly Japanese anti-boat guns opened up with
.... "As the leading waves of amphibian tractors approached
the edge of the reef," O. P. Smith recalled, "they came under Japanese
mortar fire . . . [C]asualties were severe from the fire of large caliber
automatic weapons located on the headlands north and south of beach.
The enfilade fire from these weapons caused heavy casualties among the
amphibian tractors."

First Lieutenant Wilson T. Bristol's armored track churned toward
the beach, and he "observed a nearby tank bogged down on a treacherous
reef and under a devastating concentration of enemy fire. Defying
almost certain death, he promptly brought his vehicle alongside and,
dismounting amidst a hail of shells and mortar projectiles, expeditiously
connected a steel cable to the disabled craft and towed it from the
untenable position," according to his posthumous Navy Cross citation.

One particularly effective 47mm anti-boat gun that played havoc
with the first waves was sited to fire the entire length of White Beach 1.
It was located in a point of high ground, which projected about twenty-
five yards to seaward just beyond 3/1's left boundary. The reinforced
concrete casemate was built into the coral near the base of a cliff and was
protected by four pillboxes mounting heavy machine guns, surrounded
by a series of trenches and spider traps containing dozens of diehard
Japanese infantry. The expertly camouflaged emplacements had not
even been scratched by the pre-landing bombardment.

SPITFIRE TWO (HONSOWETZ)

Russell Davis "saw the amphibious tractor in front of us go up in a shell
burst. The amtrac flamed, spread gas on the water, and wallowed in a
puddle of fire. Men spilled from it." One Marine grimly noted that they
could see dead Marines in the burned-out vehicles "black as toast," fused
upright, still holding their weapons. Sergeant James Moll's track came

under fire. "I could hear machine gun bullets hitting the armor plate in front of me. As we got closer, my heart was beating like a jackhammer." Sledge saw "a large shell explode with a terrific concussion, and a huge geyser rose up just to our right front. It barely missed us. The front of the tractor lurched to the left and bumped hard against the rear of another amtrac that was either stalled or hit. Japanese shells were screaming into the area and exploding all around us." The amtrac Fred Fox was in "hit

■ As soon as Marines hit the beach, officers and NCOs are shouting, "Get off the beach!" It would not be long before the Japanese gunners started pounding the beach with heavy artillery and mortars.

■ Marines move quickly off the beach, which would soon be littered with the dead, the wounded, and wrecked equipment. *Marine Corps History Division*

■ Machine gun team pushing inland past an abandoned amtrac that never breached the seawall. Marine in foreground is either badly wounded or dead. *Marine Corps History Division*

the reef, jumped, jerked, stalled, shifted its gears and began climbing up and over the reef, continuing to move in, bouncing across the reef." The vehicle's machine gunner, Pvt. Charles L. Wise, stood behind a .50-caliber machine gun spraying the beach when, as described in his Navy Cross citation, "an enemy shell struck his vehicle, severely wounding him in the leg. He stood on one foot and continued to fire his weapon until the vehicle reached shore and he was forcibly removed from his gun."

Corporal Harlan Murray described the drill in his LVT as it neared the beach. "We're goin' in, goin' in. And then they say, 'Okay, get ready.' And you have to turn around and face the back. And you have to stoop down. And you have to fix bayonets. The guy behind you had to pull your bayonet out of your pack and they stick it on your rifle because it's so damned cramped . . . [A]ll of a sudden there's a big explosion just behind us and another one nearer." Sergeant "Swede" Hanson remembered his landing approach clearly:

> Thirty yards from the beach we were actually catch-
> ing small arms fire. Machine guns, pistol fire, rifle fire . . .

132

> [T]he executive officer had his head up looking to see
> where we were going to come ashore, and we went down
> into a dip on this coral reef and a 40mm shell went right
> over his head. If he had a piece of fuzz on his helmet, it
> woulda knocked it off. I don't think there can be any-
> body that ever came closer to getting a 40mm in the head
> than he did. Well, he came down in a flash, and I thought
> sure that it had got part of him, but it didn't.

At 0832, the armored amphibians clambered out of the water and started firing. Henry B. Harris, a gunner on A-2, recalled, "We came into White Beach 2 . . . and went inland about 30 to 40 yards. All of a sudden, our tank went up in the air. We had crossed a Japanese anti-tank ditch and had gotten hung up on a four-foot stump, the prettiest tank trap you had ever seen and there we sat!" One minute later 2/1 stormed ashore. "I rushed forward with the others," Honsowetz recalled, "dashing, dodging, and jumping over logs and bushes. We must have moved in a hundred yards or so when we came to a swamp. I fell flat on my face and pushed my nose deep into the moist jungle floor, waiting for more fire from the Japs; maybe I could spot them. I started to wade into the swamp when the Nips again opened fire, burst after burst, and some did find the mark." One of whom was his adjutant. "[The Japanese] had these spider holes on the beach and my adjutant fell. He was right beside me and this Jap, he was in one of these holes, as we ran past he up and shot, but he shot the adjutant, not me.

Private First Class Joseph Moskalczak was in the first wave. "It was my first and last time in an amtrac," he said with relief.

> When it stopped on the beach, the rear ramp slammed
> down and I scampered out and ran to the left and
> jumped into a large shell hole about fifty yards inland.
> Then I looked to my right and saw no one. I looked to
> my left and saw a lone figure behind me on a dead run.

He joined me in the hole and soon several other Marines were with us. No one knew what to do next, so we just hugged the sides of the hole and waited for something to happen. About this time my sergeant, a BAR [Browning automatic rifle] man named Frank Minkewicz, crawled into the shell hole. "Let's go!" He yelled, and we ran up the sandy incline of the beach. Near the top we hit the deck, because I heard the crack of machine gun bullets overhead. Reaching the top of the slope, we saw eight or nine Japs. They were pulling and pushing a large cannon, one of the old-fashioned kind, with wooden spokes and three-foot wheels. A line formed on my right, but I saw no one on my left. We opened up on the Japs and killed 'em all.

Sergeant James Moll crouched down behind the LVT's side, as bullets peppered the armor just in front of him, near the bow. The amtrac lurched out of the water and stopped suddenly, its momentum throwing its occupants forward, in a jumble of arms, legs and equipment. Moll recovered and was the first man over the starboard side. His leggings caught on the metal fender, and he pitched head first into the water, submerging his submachine gun. Streaming water, he leaped to his feet and ran inland about twenty yards before hitting the deck in a shell hole. Winded from the sprint, he took a few moments to catch his breath and look around. The noise from explosions, small arms fire and vehicle engines was deafening. His eye caught a gun flash from a mound of sand just ten feet away. It took him a moment to realize it was a heavily camouflaged Japanese machine gun emplacement. He slithered out of the hole along folds in the ground that gave him cover toward the blind side of the emplacement. Taking a deep breath he stuck the barrel of the Tommy gun in the firing slit and pressed the trigger—nothing happened!—its bolt jammed with sand from the dunking. Falling back, he grabbed a hand grenade, pulled the pin, and jammed it through the firing slit. The explosion rocked the emplacement, dense smoke curling out of the firing slit. Scratch one Japanese fighting position.

An NCO from the 2nd Battalion wrote, "I rushed forward with the others—dashing, dodging and jumping over logs and bushes. We must have moved in a hundred yards or so when we came to a swamp. The man next to me fell forward streaming blood from his leg, thigh and shoulder. I fell flat on my face and pushed my nose deep into the moist jungle floor; waiting for more fire from the Japs . . . [W]e were pinned down." He was not alone. Hundreds of men scrambled to find shelter from the incessant Japanese fire. The beach was covered with Marines who were not fast enough or lucky enough to find a shell hole, bomb crater or fold in the earth. NCOs and officers were among the first to fall trying to lead their men off the beach. "Lieutenant Myers was hit by a sniper," a Marine reported sadly. "The lieutenant fell out of reach of the Marines unless they were to expose themselves. Several boys started out after him . . . but the lieutenant drew his pistol and said, 'Stay back. Stay back or I'll shoot'—and he died soon after."

Honsowetz was all over, braving the fire, driving his men forward, off the beach toward the airfield. Company G, initially pinned down by heavy machine gun fire from coral-hardened bunkers, sent its assault squads against them, while riflemen and machine gunners gave them cover. Russell Davis was one of the riflemen. "I wiggled away toward the bunker. The assault men had it in its last

■ Stretcher bearers carry wounded Marine to aid station through shattered undergrowth. Although the bearers appear to be unarmed, the man in the front right is armed with a carbine. *Marine Corps History Division*

stages. Riflemen worked all around it and some of them were close to the wall, stuffing hand grenades through the fire ports. A flamethrower man was trying to get the nozzle of his hose unplugged . . . while a demolition man wriggled forward with his shaped charge [demolition]. Somebody yelled, 'Fire in the hole!' There was a smashing sound and a tower of debris squirted up over our heads."

Bruce Watkins led his men to a "rise in the ground of about ten feet on the southwest edge of the airfield"—the hundred yards sprint off the beach had cost him six men, and he never saw a single enemy soldier. He carefully peered over the embankment and saw a "line of trenches about 100 feet forward." He passed the word to his men to rush them. "Sprinting across this flat open stretch, we received heavy machine gun fire from our left flank, the bullets whistling and ricocheting off the coral deck. We dived into the trenches and consolidated a front line." Suddenly he heard one of his men cry out. "Lieutenant, help me—I can't move." Watkins left cover and "sprinted back to where Alick lay in the open stretch . . . shot through the thumb and thigh." Watkins "scooped him up" and carried him to safety. He came upon another man, "Sergeant Stasiak on his back, holding his stomach, with blood all over himself . . . [A] bullet had torn through flesh and muscle clear across at hip height and it looked real bad. I told him it looked worse than it was, counting on his toughness to keep him going." Watkins had both men placed on stretchers and evacuated.

Russell Davis was dug in at the end of the airfield. His platoon leader sought him out and ordered him to report their location to Colonel Honsowetz. Davis found him with the battalion OP group, "running and ducking into holes" because of enemy snipers. Later, Davis was ordered by Honsowetz to "Go back to the beach and bring up any tanks that have landed." Twenty minutes after the first wave hit the beach, the regiment's fifteen Sherman tanks from "A" company, 1st Tank Battalion, arrived at the edge of the reef and slowly began to make their way through gaps in the coral, courtesy of the underwater demolition teams. They were immediately taken under intense mortar and artillery

■ Hundreds of Marines were stranded on the water's edge by the failure of the assault waves to push farther inland because of overwhelming Japanese fire. The men in the foreground appear to be a communications unit, identifiable by the rolls of wire and waterproof radios they are carrying. Three destroyed amtracs burn in the background. *Marine Corps History Division*

fire. According to official records, "over half of the tanks received from one to four hits during the ten minute crossing." Fortunately only three were knocked out, primarily because two to four feet of water protected their suspension systems and lower hulls. That was not to last however, for in the next few hours six more Shermans were knocked out.

"When the command tank in which he was leading his platoon across a section of beach received a hit from a concealed enemy 75mm field gun, 1st Lt. George E. Jerue remained exposed to heavy enemy mortar fire while directing an advance of about three hundred yards along the mine-strewn beach to enable his lead tank to fire and destroy the enemy gun and crew," his Navy Cross citation stated.

The 2nd Battalion continued to advance against "moderate" resistance and by 0945 had reached the O-1 phase line, about 350 yards inland, where they held up waiting for orders.

SPITFIRE SIX (PULLER)

The White Beaches were a scene of devastation. "Our amtrac was among the first assault waves," a veteran recalled bitterly, "yet the beach was already a litter of burning, blackened amphibian tractors, of dead and wounded, a mortal garden of exploding mortar shells. Holes had been scraped in the white sand or had been blasted out by the shells; the beach was pocked with holes—all filled with green-clad helmeted Marines." Chesty Puller was among the first to hit the beach. As his LVT grounded, he shouted, "Get the hell off the beach, we'll be a big target!" Despite his gimpy leg—a shrapnel wound from Guadalcanal— Puller recalled,

> [I] went up and over that side as fast as I could scramble and ran like hell at least twenty-five yards before I hit the beach, flat down. When I looked back to the amtrac I saw four or five shells hit it all at once. A few men were killed, getting out too slow, but most of them were saved, because they got out before we stopped moving. We lost our communications officer; his leg was blown off and he couldn't be saved. I looked down the beach and saw a mess—every damned amtrac in our wave had been destroyed in the water . . . or shot to pieces the minute it landed.

Most of Puller's communications equipment and operators were lost when the amtracs carrying them were shot up crossing the reef, leaving him out of contact with O. P. Smith for several hours.

Sixteen-year-old Charles H. Owen went over the side of his amtrac.

    It was a long jump . . . like falling into hell. The beach was being hit by heavy small-arms fire and mortars and artillery. There were bodies and parts of bodies all around. I was terrified. We had always been told to get off the beach. It was the most dangerous place to be. But many troops were still there and not moving. Out of nowhere came a major I never saw before or again. He ignored all the torrent of enemy fire, and was busy kicking asses and screaming at us. All I could think of

■ The price of freedom. A squad leader checks on one of his men who did not make it off the beach. *Marine Corps History Division*

was to get off the beach before the crazy son of a bitch shot me.

Tom Lea described the scene. "Jagged holes in the scattered stone and dirty sand, splintered trees and tangled vines made a churned, burned wilderness. Strewn through this chaos were the remnants and remainders of the Marines' advance . . . Scattered everywhere were discarded packs, helmets, rifles, boxes, clothes, rubber lifebelts—the rubbish of battle. Lying on the seared leaves and hot sand were dead bodies yet ungathered by burial parties."

Swede Hanson sprinted for cover. "All of a sudden I'm running by a little fellow who is sitting gook style. He's got a pipe in his mouth, and my God, it's our regimental commander, Chesty Puller," Hanson chuckled remembering the incident. "And I can't believe that man is up so close to the front lines observing everything. And as I ran by him, he says, 'Give 'em hell, Marine.' It was so damn hot . . . I threw off my gas mask. That I knew I wouldn't need. The sun was going to get me before gas did." Japanese fire from the left flank was taking a terrible toll. Puller "tried to get a line set up for defense. Every platoon leader was trying to form a line of his own, just as I was. Runners were going up and down the beach, as we tried to get organized. That big promontory on my left hadn't been touched by the ship's guns and planes, and we got a whirlwind of machine gun and anti-tank fire."

SPITFIRE THREE (SABOL)

Lieutenant Colonel Stephen Sabol's third battalion touched down on White Beach 1 exactly at 0830 and immediately pushed forward against heavy small arms, machine gun, artillery and mortar fire. A particularly galling fire was coming from a pitted ridge that jutted out from the island. George Hunt, "K" Company's commander described it. "The point, rising thirty feet above the water's edge, was of solid, jagged coral, a rocky mass of sharp pinnacles, deep crevasses, tremendous boulders. Pillboxes, reinforced with steel and concrete, had been dug or blasted in the base of the perpendicular drop to the beach. Others, with coral and concrete piled six feet on top were constructed above, and spider holes were blasted around them for protecting infantry. It surpassed by far anything we had conceived of when we studied the aerial photographs." Colonel Nakagawa had emplaced an anti-boat gun in position to enfilade White Beach. It was a particularly nasty Type 41 (M-41) 47mm gun that wreaked havoc from its camouflaged position in a waterline, casemated pillbox. It was untouched by the pre-assault bombardment. The battalion-after-action report noted that it destroyed six amtracs.

■ A Japanese sniper takes aim at his target. On Peleliu, snipers firing from concealed emplacements took a heavy toll of the advancing Marines. *Marine Corps History Division*

Hunt's reinforced company was assigned to take the heavily defended Point to secure the left flank of the division. Hunt said that Puller personally chose him for the assignment. "[Puller] gave me the toughest job of taking the left flank because he had developed a respect for my company." Hunt's company of 228 men and 7 officers comprised three rifle platoons, a mortar section (three 60mm mortars), a three-section machine gun platoon (six .30-caliber Browning machine guns) and a small headquarters platoon. Hunt and many of his men were combat veterans of Guadalcanal and Cape Gloucester. They were confident in themselves and their company, but they would soon learn that Peleliu was a different sort of operation.

Before leaving Pavuvu, Hunt was given aerial photographs of his objective. They "showed anti-boat obstacles on the coral reef in front of the beach, entrenchments on the beach and two pillboxes on the Point." After carefully studying them he decided that after landing, the company would perform a gate-like maneuver by "pivoting 90 degrees to the north with our left flank anchored on the beach" and fight our way to the first day's objective. He assigned the 3rd Platoon to clear the Point, while the 2nd Platoon assaulted the right half of the company objective. The 1st Platoon was to follow behind the 3rd Platoon. He attached one machine gun section to each of the two assault platoons and kept the third section in support, along with the 60mm mortars, sometimes called the company commander's artillery. The company practiced the maneuver over and over again until "every man in the company knew what to do in relation to the man next to him." Hunt was well aware of the awesome responsibility. "Should we fail to capture and hold the Point the entire regimental beach would be exposed to heavy fire from the flank. We were proud of our responsibility, and every man in the company was determined to fulfill it."

CHAPTER 10

THE POINT

Hunt braced himself as "the nose of the amtrac shot upward, hung in mid-air; the tracks took hold, and we leveled off and jerked to a halt." He shouted to his men to get out and followed them by rolling over the side. "The impact of the eight-foot jump jarred my legs and momentarily upset my balance. Regaining it, I raced across the beach." Hunt ran for about seventy-five yards before going to ground out of breath. "My lips and tongue [were] as dry as sandpaper. Black vapor and the pungent odor of gunpowder which was seeping from the earth helped to clog my throat. Sweat was running off the end of my nose." His two runners, first sergeant, radio operator and the machine-gun platoon commander, Lt. Raymond G. Stramel, took cover around him. His radio operator immediately tried to establish communications with the platoons but no one answered his repeated calls. Suddenly, mortar fire erupted to the right and to the left, bracketing the small group. Small-arms fire snapped overhead. Men were falling—and the plaintive cry "Corpsman!" rose above the din—it was pandemonium on the beach.

■ Captain George Hunt's initial scheme of maneuver. Second Platoon was assigned to assault straight ahead, while the Third Platoon with First Platoon in support would swing left to take the Point. *Marine Corps History Division*

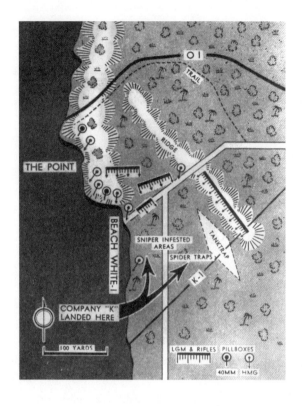

Hunt struggled to get a clear picture of the situation. "I had to know what they were doing . . . [T]he uncertainty became agonizing." The heavy fire kept him close to the ground—it was worth a man's life to stand up—and no one was answering the radio. He sent out runners to contact his platoon commanders to gain information, but they had not reported back. The situation, as far as Hunt knew, was very grim. To make matters worse, a wounded man stumbled into the command post exclaiming, "There are K Company guys dead and wounded lyin' all around." Suddenly another man cried out. "Blackburn was wounded in the arm," Hunt remembered. "His young face turned very white, and his lips curled up with the pain." Something had to be done—and quickly. Hunt rolled out of the shell hole, yelling for his radio operator to follow, and headed for the Point.

As Hunt ran along the shell-blasted sand, he was shocked to see the full extent of the Japanese fire. "I saw a ghastly mixture of bandages, bloody and mutilated skin; Marines gritting their teeth resigned to their

■ Marines taking cover behind an embankment while awaiting orders to move out. It appears that one of the men in the center background has been hit and is being treated. All of them are careful about keeping below the berm. *Marine Corps History Division*

■ A wounded Marine receiving first aid from a navy corpsman. The injured man is from a machine-gun squad that got caught in the open. The corpsman is risking his own life to treat the casualty in the exposed position. *Marine Corps History Division*

wounds; men groaning and writhing in their agonies; men outstretched or twisted or grotesquely transfixed in the attitudes of death; men with their entrails exposed or whole chunks of body ripped out of them." He took cover as the winded radio operator continued to call, "Hello One, Hello Two, Hello Three, do you read me, over," but there was no answer—silence. Then through the static, "I heard the call I had been waiting for," Hunt exclaimed thankfully. "It came in slurred and crackling at first, then clear as a bell." It

■ A destroyed bunker containing a Japanese Model 41 (1908) 75mm mountain gun. The extent of the damage suggests it was hit with a large-caliber shell, most likely naval gunfire. Four of its crew lie dead in the foreground. *Marine Corps History Division*

was 1st Platoon's Lt. William L. Willis with a brief status report. "I'm up behind the third platoon . . . they've had a hell of a lot of casualties and need stretcher bearers badly."

Hunt discovered that the 3rd Platoon had landed a hundred yards too far to the right. They tried to assault the Point but lost heavily and were pinned down about fifty yards from the Point. During its hard-fought assault, the platoon had knocked out one 40mm gun, two heavy machine guns and numerous light machine guns, but the gains had been at the cost of the platoon's leadership. The platoon commander and platoon guide were badly wounded and put out of the fight. Fred Fox and

146

his assistant flamethrower operator stumbled onto the officer. "I saw Lieutenant Estey sitting in the brush with a big gash in his left arm above the elbow." Fox traded his .45-caliber pistol for the lieutenant's Tommy gun, thinking he would need the extra fire power.

Platoon Sergeant John Koval "unhesitatingly assumed command and, despite a wound sustained while leading an assault against enemy pillboxes and infantrymen entrenched in spider holes along the beach, tenaciously continued pressing the attack toward a Japanese anti-boat gun emplacement which was inflicting heavy damage on our landing craft," his posthumous Navy Cross citation read. "Although wounded a second time and in a dying condition, he courageously directed the final assault and was responsible in a large measure for the destruction of the enemy gun."

Hunt also learned that the 2nd Platoon commander had been killed on the beach by a sniper and the platoon sergeant wounded. Private First Class Joe Dariano braved the enemy fire. "Our guys were dropping all around me. We were totally unorganized—without officers or squad leaders, and completely cut off from the rest of the company and battalion. Out of the forty-five guys in my platoon, nineteen were killed and twenty-one were wounded."

The leaderless men fought their way through seventy-five yards of rifle and machine gun fire to a ten-foot-deep tank trap where they were pinned down by extremely heavy fire from a coral ridge directly ahead of them. The boulder-strewn, tree blasted high ground rose about thirty to forty feet high and was studded with heavily camouflaged Japanese machine gun positions. Minutes after crawling out of the tank trap, Dariano was hit in the head and shoulder. The platoon corpsman dressed his wounds and told him, "You'll be okay, so just hang on. We'll get you evacuated as soon as possible, but we've got a lot of dead and wounded guys, and the Japs have us pretty well hemmed in; looks like we may have to stay in this ditch for a while." The remnants of the 2nd Platoon were trapped, cut off from any help and unable to maintain contact with the 3rd Platoon. It created a gap in the lines, which was quickly filled by Japanese.

■ Japanese pillboxes were often constructed of concrete two or three feet thick and heavily camouflaged. This photo, taken from its rear entrance, clearly shows the thickness of the concrete and its vegetation cover. *Marine Corps History Division*

Hunt ordered Lieutenant Willis to "push through and take the Point." Willis quickly gathered his men and the remnants of the 3rd Platoon and carefully worked around the base of the Point. The Japanese were concentrating on the beach and did not see the Marines until a deadly fire hit them from the flank. In a bitter fight, the enemy riflemen in trenches and spider holes were killed, but five pillboxes remained—four mounting heavy machine guns and the fifth a 47mm anti-tank gun. The pillboxes

■ The inside of an emplacement showing a destroyed Japanese 47mm gun. The number of expended shells indicates that this gun was used heavily until knocked out. *Marine Corps History Division*

were constructed of reinforced concrete surmounted by five feet of coral rock and manned by six to twelve enemy soldiers. However, as formidable as they were, without protecting infantry they were vulnerable to attack from their blind side. His Navy Cross citation described how Willis, with grenades and small-arms fire, "led his men forward in a daring and skillful assault. During the fierce hand-to-hand conflict, which reached a high pitch of intensity when he and his men had penetrated the Japanese ring of infantrymen and were assaulting the pillboxes themselves," Marines worked their way close to the pillbox and stuffed hand grenades in the embrasure, knocking them out one by one.

Fred Fox came face to face with one of the emplacements. A Japanese soldier ran right by him, only a few yards away, and disappeared into a dugout.

> We couldn't see an embrasure . . . but there was a stairway cut into the coral going down into the ground. I threw a white phosphorus and two regular hand grenades down there, but nobody came out. So, I took a couple of steps down to where I could see clearly. A Japanese officer, with cloth cap and black rimmed glasses lay at the bottom of the steps. His left arm was burnt black but he was leaning on his elbow with a Nambu pistol in his hand aimed at me. I pressed the trigger on the lieutenant's Tommy gun and fired four or five rounds into him. I went on down the steps and into the middle of the 12x15 foot room. There was another officer with a sword stuck in his belly, sticking up in the air. There were several other Jap bodies in the back corner.

Photograph by Fabian Bachrach

Fox beat a hasty retreat after relieving the body on the stairs of its pistol.

Willis led the attack on the last concrete and steel

■ Captain George P. Hunt's "K" Company was responsible for taking the Point on the left flank of the landing beaches. Hunt was awarded the Navy Cross for heroism while leading his men. *Coral Comes High*, Harper & Brothers

THE POINT

NAVY CROSS CITATION, CAPT. GEORGE P. HUNT
The Navy Cross is presented to George P. Hunt, Captain, United States Marine Corps (Reserve), for extraordinary heroism as Commanding Officer, Company K, Third Battalion, First Marines, First Marine Division, in action against enemy forces during the assault on enemy-held Peleliu, Palau Islands, from 15 to 17 September 1944. A bold and aggressive leader, Captain Hunt led his men in a daring assault against the enemy who were firing from concrete pillboxes on a coral point. Knowing the great danger the seizure of this point would incur, but realizing the immediate necessity for its capture, he quickly and skillfully maneuvered his company and, with two platoons, captured the point after a fierce struggle during which five hostile concrete pillboxes, numerous coral pillboxes and lighter emplacements were destroyed and over one hundred of the enemy were killed. Isolated from the rest of his Battalion for a period of twenty-six hours with only thirty-four men remaining, Captain Hunt expertly organized a defensive perimeter and, successfully defending his position against three hostile counterattacks, repulsed all three of them and annihilated four hundred and twenty-two Japanese. By his outstanding leadership and cool judgment in the face of grave danger, Captain Hunt contributed materially to the success of our forces during this critical period, and his gallant conduct throughout was in keeping with the highest traditions of the United States Naval Service.

emplacement. "I figured out a plan. A squad covered the rear exit of the pillbox, while Anderson, one of my corporals, sneaked part way down the rocks about twenty yards in front of the embrasure, while I crawled to a cut in the cliff where I could heave a grenade without being shot." Willis, according to his Navy Cross citation, "maneuvered himself to an advantageous but precarious position, hurled white phosphorous grenades at the embrasure, thereby enabling his comrade to encircle the pillbox." Anderson aimed a rifle grenade at the firing aperture and pulled the trigger. "The grenade launched perfectly and smacked the gun on the barrel," Willis recalled. "It ignited something flammable, and after a big explosion the pillbox burst into flame. Black smoke poured out of the embrasure and the exit. I heard the Japs screaming and their ammunition spitting and snapping as the heat exploded it. Three Japs, with bullets popping in their

■ A wounded man is helped off the lines. The Marine in the foreground has pulled his camouflage cover over his neck to protect it from the boiling sun. Another is bare chested. The heat on the island often soared into triple digits . . . and coupled with little water brought many Marines to their knees. *Marine Corps History Division*

belts and flames clinging to their legs, raced from the exit waving their arms and letting out yells of pain. The squad I had placed there finished them off."

Hunt reached the Point minutes after the last pillbox fell, gathered the survivors and established a hasty defense. Fox noted that "each [man] had spread out and kind of picked a place to pile rocks up to get behind. I moved on down to the left and found a place about ten feet from the edge of the cliff by the water's edge where I could get behind something and started to dig a shallow foxhole in the coral rock." Fox figured that, "out of perhaps ninety in the two platoons, we had only thirty men in fighting condition on top of the point." Hunt counted 110 dead Japanese in and around the blasted hilltop but estimated that nearly two thirds of his company was casualties, including "most of my machine gun platoon that had been mowed down on the beach." It was a huge price to pay, but the division's left flank was secure—for the moment.

While "K" Company fought to clear the Point, the battalion's 81mm mortar platoon rushed inland about thirty yards and started to dig in. In that short distance, they lost three men to shrapnel and seventeen missing. Corporal Albert William Mikel related, "There were about twelve of us from the 3rd and 4th gun squads. We had two mortars but no ammunition, and most of us were armed with only a .45-caliber pistol." The men were scared because there were dead Marines all around "who had K-3-1 stenciled on the back of their jackets." They didn't know what to do until suddenly, Lt. James J. Haggerty appeared behind them wearing a blue New York Yankees baseball cap on his head, with his hands on his hips, and legs apart. "He spoke very calmly and with complete confidence. He said, 'You people pick up those mortars and follow me.' Having given that order, he turned and walked toward the ocean. One by one, we crawled out of the safety of our foxholes and followed him.

About one hundred yards ahead of the mortar position, "I" Company was making slow progress fighting through a swamp. "I waded into the mucky water, at one time up to my belt," a bedraggled rifleman griped. "I threw away my pack and leggings as they seemed so very heavy . . . and fought on. We eliminated several Japs at this spot and I had my first chance to fire at a live one. Sambo dashed from behind one boulder for another but we caught him about halfway in between and almost clipped his body in two." His unit took several casualties but pushed on. "We received orders to move up another hundred yards and hold our ground. We charged forward dodging from shell hole to shell hole and under barbed wire . . . I jumped into a very small shell hole with a very large Jap—he was dead and just sitting there with his eyes open; at first I sucked in my breath and gasped. I didn't lose much time in finding another hole!"

Not only did the men have to brave enemy fire, but the fierce heat was almost unbearable. Albert Blaisdell watched "as our infantry came struggling through the morass of swamp, up to their hips in slime and gooey mud and climbing over blasted logs. Most of them were exhausted

■ With burning amtracs as a backdrop, these Marines are sheltering behind another that was stopped on the beach. By stopping, they are providing a lucrative target for Japanese gunners. The watch word for men in the assault waves was "get off the beach!" *Marine Corps History Division*

and without water and suffering from the 105-degree heat." Blaisdell's armored amphibian had "three or four five-gallon jerry cans of water, which we found to be tainted by paint inside the can. This we shared with those who needed it. It was terrible, but it was wet!" Dozens of men succumbed to dehydration and were temporarily out of action, further reducing the line company's foxhole strength.

The harsh terrain and Japanese fire were making it extremely difficult to maintain contact, and within a few minutes of landing "I" Company lost touch with "K" Company on their left flank. Lieutenant Colonel Sabol recognized the danger and ordered "L" Company to close the gap. Two platoons rushed forward but were almost immediately pinned down by Japanese entrenched in the same coral ridge that had stopped "K" Company's 2nd Platoon. "Five Marines were killed right in front of me before they got this one lousy Jap in a hole in the ground," a dismounted tanker lamented. "It was like opening a can with a can opener to try to get each of them out." Another Marine groused about the coral. "Around this place there's nothin' but sharp coral. I mean, you get down on your hands and knees, you're getting cut. And grenades are going off. And each time this coral is shattering in small bits and it peppers you. I guess it would be as if somebody turned a sandblaster on you. It stung you all over."

Shortly after 1500, "I" Company was counter-attacked but it was beaten off by a combination of artillery fire, close air support and naval gunfire. The battalion reported that "This fire covered an area from 200 to 2,000 yards in front of the lines. The firing was intense . . . keeping the enemy from bringing up reinforcements . . . and launching extensive counter-attacks through the gaps in our over-extended lines." It also reported that "Company 'K' was separated into three parts. The remnants of the 1st and 3rd Platoons and the OP [observation post] group were in an isolated position on the Point. The CP group and the 60mm mortar platoon were pinned down about 300 yards south of the Point and the remnants of the 2nd Platoon were still pinned down in the tank trap." An estimated 150 Japanese infiltrated into a gap left by

A graves-registration team goes through the grisly task of preparing the dead for temporary burial. They must first identify the remains, note the cause of death and complete the casualty card. In the heat, bodies decomposed quickly, adding to their morbid assignment. It was important to bury them as soon as possible. *Marine Corps History Division*

"K" Company. It had been a tough day—of Hunt's original 235 men, only 78 were left at daylight. Over 400 Japanese were found in and around the Point. Third Battalion had lost 251 men killed, wounded and missing in action.

SPITFIRE ONE (DAVIS)

At 0910 1st Battalion, the regimental reserve, started in to the beach. J. R. Murray wrote rather tongue in cheek that "Mortar shells began falling around all the LVTs; the Japs had apparently sited their heavy weapons to cover the area between the reef and the shore, and were making the situation uncomfortable." Three of the tractors in his wave were hit going in, their ammo exploded and scattered burning debris over the water. "When we came in," Capt. Everett P. Pope recalled, "I could see

■ "The Price" by Artist Tom Lea. *Life* magazine artist Lea went ashore with one of the first waves "to set down in sketches and words what the men did in battle and what the battle did to them." *U.S. Army Center for Military History, Washington, D.C.*

aircraft strafing the beach. I could count twelve individual fires . . . and I thought this was going to be OK until I realized they were amtracs and then I knew we were in for difficult times—and we were!"

Ray Davis and several members of his CP group were in a "free boat"—an LVT that had not been assigned a specific wave. As he peered over the side of the lurching amtrac, he saw a scene of utter destruction. Oily black smoke rose into the sky, marking the funeral pyre of more than twenty burning tractors off White Beach 1 and 2. The bright flashes of exploding mortar and artillery fire marked the landing beaches that were wreathed in a heavy pall of dust and smoke. Japanese anti-boat obstacles, posts strung with barbed wire, formed irregular patterns in the shallow water. They also planted small flags as artillery and mortar registration points.

As the heavy vehicle slammed into the edge of the coral reef, Davis was knocked off his feet. The driver gunned the engine, and the powerful machine easily lifted itself up and over the coral. Splashes from Japanese artillery and mortar fire erupted to the right and left. Three tractors were hit, with great loss of life. The ammo that was aboard exploded . . . One of the tractors blew up, scattering burning debris over the beach. Dead Marines floated lifelessly in the water, the suction of the passing LVT drawing them in its wake. There was no stopping to pick them up. Many of the dead drifted out to sea and were never recovered. They were listed as missing in action. Other remains were not identified and buried as Unknowns. Specially trained graves-registration teams had to wait until after the fighting moved inland to gather the dead. Theirs was a grisly task—decomposition, ghastly wounds and traumatic amputations complicated the job of identifying remains. As an example, one of Bruce Watkins' men stepped on a bomb. "He completely disappeared, the only trace of him being a long piece of scalp, recognizable by his very black hair."

Davis' vehicle ground to a stop, the aft ramp came down fast, and he scrambled out into the maelstrom. Tom Lea described the scene on the beach: "I fell flat on my face just as I heard the *whishh* of a mortar I knew was too close. About fifteen yards away, on the upper edge of the beach,

■ A command group setting up a temporary CP in a shell hole. An amtrac provides shelter from small-arms fire . . . but may attract Japanese artillery and mortar fire. *Marine Corps History Division*

it smashed down four men from our boat. I saw a wounded man near me, staggering in the direction of the LVTs. His face was half-bloody pulp, and the mangled shreds of what was left of an arm hung down like a stick, as he bent over in his stumbling, shock crazy walk. He fell behind me, in a red puddle on the white sand."

Davis was scheduled to land an hour after the initial landing. "My battalion landed in reserve, which was meaningless, because the Japanese defenses were so thick and so sturdy that when I got off the amphibian tractor on the beach, my run for cover was not quick enough, and I got a fragment from a mortar shell through my left knee. It wasn't serious—I just put tape over it and got to work." Sledge described the pandemonium. "Up and down the beach and out on the reef, a number of amtracs and DUKWs were burning. Japanese machine gun bursts made long splashes in the water as though flaying it with some giant whip. The geysers belched up relentlessly where the mortar and artillery shells hit. I caught a fleeting glimpse of a group of Marines leaving a smoking amtrac on the reef. Some fell as bullets and fragments splashed among them. Their buddies tried to help them as they struggled in the knee-deep water."

Tom Lea remembered turning his head seaward, where he saw a direct center hit on an LVT: "Pieces of iron and men seemed to sail slow-motion into the air. As I looked over my shoulder a burst smashed into a file of Marines wading toward our beach from a smoking LVT. Jap machine guns lashed into the reef while lines of Marines fell with bloody splashes into the green water. The survivors seemed so slow and small and patient coming in, out there." Bill Hipple wrote a firsthand account of the landing in the September 20 issue of *Newsweek*:

> A heavy mortar shell splashed fifty yards away . . . I was packed in so tightly with twenty Marines, weapons and gear that both of my legs were asleep and I wondered whether I could jump over the top at the propitious moment . . . We couldn't see anything, but we heard the continuous 'whoomp-whoomp' of enemy mortars and artillery . . . We clumped on the beach and halted. My sleeping feet needed no urging. I vaulted 6 feet to the beach and flung myself into a large shell hole. Snipers bullets and mortars kept coming and an officer yelled, "Spread out, everybody!" Some of us pushed into the underbrush—a onetime forest now a mass of tangled foliage, stumps and holes.

Lisle Shoemaker of *United Press* was in the same boat as Hipple. He recorded the scene: "Several of us started down the beach, crouching

■ A heavily camouflaged and revetted coconut pillbox. The firing embrasure is difficult to see in the heavy brush and is part of a mutually supporting complex of machine-gun and rifle pits. *Marine Corps History Division*

low like groundhogs looking for a convenient rock to hide under. We keep glancing around like race track touts, dodging booby-trap land mines and hoping we do not see a Jap pillbox, with its snoot sticking out our way." He came upon Gene Sherman of the *Los Angeles Times*. "A *zzzzzz* sound whizzes right between us. 'Jesus Christ Shoe, that was a bullet, or a shell, I think.'" The adrenalin rush and all the running got to him. "I crawl up under a scrubby tree and collapse. I can't move an inch and I am not carrying loads like the Marines. I am only toting my typewriter . . . I remember thinking I really don't care if I am captured or wounded . . . it is no matter so long as I am not killed."

Davis' battalion had to fight its way off the beach. It suffered heavy casualties from the murderous Japanese fire. Lieutenant Mueller, of "C"

Company, was shot through the head as he stepped ashore; Lieutenant Buss, of "A" Company, was wounded in the chest by a sniper and died. The cries, "Corpsman" and "Stretcher bearers," were nerve-wracking. "The beachhead was extremely shallow and the Japs were pouring in small arms fire from our front and flanks," the battalion after-action reported. "About 70 yards in from the shore was a low coral cliff which was offering protection to individual enemy riflemen; mortars and artillery were shelling the beach." To make matters worse, a steel-reinforced blockhouse in "C" Company's sector was giving them fits until an assault squad knocked it out.

Ray Davis had a hard time gathering his battalion after hitting the beach. Robert Fisher, one of his Marines, explained why. "There were several factors which prevented us from quickly reorganizing. The terrific pounding . . . had leveled everything along the beach. Landmarks had disappeared. In addition, some of the troops had landed several hundred yards from where they had been briefed . . . and consequently they were temporarily lost. Finally, we could not go into our assembly area—300 yards inland—because the assault battalions were pinned down on the beach." Fisher found out the hard way when he walked toward the designated assembly area. A Marine yelled out, "Hey, Mac, you'd better get down; this is the front line." By 1100, the battalion was digging in just behind the regimental command post.

Fisher estimated that it took "about an hour . . . to collect most of the battalion in one area along the beach. Major Davis ordered us to dig in. The sand made digging easy, and we soon had our command post, switchboard and all, set up immediately in the rear of the front lines." Major Nikolai S. Stevenson was responsible for the rear CP: "As executive officer it was my job to be sure that communications kept us in touch with the rifle companies struggling to advance. Also involved was the need to keep food and ammunition flowing forward and to evacuate the wounded." Major Stevenson was also there in case Ray Davis was incapacitated. On D-day, the forward CP "was a little more than a hundred yards in front of the rear command post, which had barely cleared the water line." The two remained separate so that one shell did not get them both.

Puller was trying to piece together what little information was getting through to him. The loss of his radio operators and their precious equipment forced him to depend on the less reliable method of using runners, which slowed the flow of information when many of them were killed, wounded or pinned down. To make matters worse, a mortar shell hit his CP, taking out even more communicators. Sometime in early afternoon, Puller learned of "K" Company's desperate straits. He ordered Ray Davis to commit one of his companies to help out. " 'A' Company moved into positions trying to take advantage of a Jap anti-tank ditch," the battalion after-action report stated, "but snipers and automatic weapons sited down this ditch, taking 'A' Company with damaging enfilade fire from their left flank while they were facing east toward the ridge." The company was stopped cold; casualties were severe. Davis recalled that "The enemy had tunneled back under the coral ridge lines, sometimes 100 to 200 feet, and they would lay a machine gun to shoot out of a distant hole, with deadly crossfire from well dug-in and fight-to-the-death defensive positions."

The Japanese counterattacked and cut off a squad. "Sergeant Riley noticed two amphibious tractors and a Sherman tank that had been knocked out on his left," read the after-action report. "He ordered his men to form a skirmish line to the right of the tank, . . . took its machine gun and brought fire to bear, inflicting heavy casualties on the enemy and pinning them down." The squad was rescued when the company executive officer sent out another tank. Upon Riley's return, he was elevated to platoon commander after all its leaders had either been killed or wounded. Riley was later wounded and the platoon was turned over to the ranking Marine, Pfc. G. E. Hogan.

With "A" Company pinned down, "B" Company was committed to the attack but suffered the same fate. Corporal Herbert B. Goff "boldly faced the withering barrage in a determined effort to outflank the Japanese opposing troops and, skillfully disposing his men for maximum effectiveness, fearlessly led them in a determined attack," as recounted

■ Aerial view of the landing beaches. The smoke in the upper right of the photo is from at least five burning amphibious vehicles. A plume of white smoke in the middle center is from a phosphorus shell. *Marine Corps History Division*

in his posthumous Navy Cross citation. "Aware that the fire of his squad was insufficient to neutralize the heavily fortified emplacement, he pressed forward alone and, armed only with grenades and a submachine gun, succeeded in silencing the hostile weapon and annihilating the crew before he was fatally struck down by enemy fire." His effort was not enough, and "B" Company was forced to go to ground.

Davis threw in "C" Company, his last fresh infantry, and led them in a vicious, no-holds-barred slugfest. However, Japanese small-arms, mortar and artillery fire was just too great. The advance was stalled, leaving a dangerous gap in the lines. If the Japanese exploited the hole by attacking in force, the entire beachhead could be in jeopardy. "It was possible," according to the 1st Marines report, "that a coordinated counterattack in force along the corridor between the coral ridge and the sea could roll up the line and sweep down on the beaches." All three of Puller's battalions were heavily committed. The situation looked bad. One of Puller's men observed after the battle that "the fact that we were, for all practical purposes, cut off from the rest of the division didn't bother the Old Man at all. In thinking back, it was a made-to-order situation for Chesty. He liked nothing better than to do things his own way, without the brass breathing down his neck."

Puller, recognizing the danger, gathered a scratch force of headquarters personnel and one hundred men from the 1st Engineer Battalion to build up a second line behind the north flank. The situation was desperate, but it seemed that Puller still did not recognize the extent of his regiment's losses. Late in the afternoon, a communications team from division managed to run a phone line to Puller's CP. "I got Lewie on the telephone and asked him how he was coming," Smith recalled. "All right," Puller replied. "Do you need any help?" Smith asked. "No, I can manage," Puller responded in typical fashion. "What about casualties?" "Maybe as many as forty killed and wounded," was Puller's response. "[I] thought Puller seemed confident that he could hold his own," Smith wrote. "He'd been taking a beating all day, but that's Lewie; he wouldn't ask for help. He had as yet no very definite idea as to the number of casualties he had suffered." Jeff Fields echoed his comment. "It wasn't till later that we really knew they were taking a beating. Puller is such a fighter, he can carry the ball. I might add that never once did he ever scream for help." After reviewing the situation, Smith was sure that "the regimental commander was not fully cognizant of the situation of all elements of his regiment for several hours after landing."

Puller's estimate of casualties was grossly underestimated. At the time of his conversation with Smith, hundreds had been lost. "When the tide went out that night," one man reported, "you could have walked 300 yards across the beach on the bodies of dead Marines." Third Battalion alone suffered 251 casualties. Much later, as Puller learned more about the situation, he sent a message to division. "Enemy well dug in. Opposition strong. Little damage done by our preliminary fire. A hard fight ahead. Casualties over 20 percent. I've ordered no man to be evacuated unless from bullet or shell wounds. Request further supply fresh water. Ours still undrinkable; men retching."

As Davis' utterly spent battalion dug in for the night, urgently needed supplies were brought forward and the wounded evacuated. The after-action report noted, "A colored Seabee unit landed in our area in the afternoon and immediately began doing valuable work, carrying stretchers loaded with ammunition and taking the wounded out." The battalion daily situation report included a footnote, "One unarmed Seabee was credited with killing a Jap sniper with his bare hands."

As darkness fell, exhausted Marines peered out into a nightmare no-man's-land of shattered trees and blasted coral rock. Parachute flares turned this broken landscape into an eerie patchwork of green light and shadow. Japanese infiltrators skillfully exploited the cover to advance toward the American positions. Suddenly, the Marine lines were blanketed with grenades and mortar fire. Japanese infantry rose out of

■ A command group opens for business in a Japanese anti-tank ditch. The trench was designed to prevent tanks from proceeding inland. They could also be a trap, since the Japanese often targeted them for artillery and mortar attack. *Marine Corps History Division*

the darkness. With screaming battle cries—*banzai, banzai*—they ran forward—to be met by the concentrated fire of automatic weapons and small-arms fire. The fighting became hand-to-hand, and the Japanese attack faltered, beaten back by superior firepower. A few managed to infiltrate behind the lines but were killed the next morning.

PLAYMATE FORWARD (SMITH)

Conditions ashore were chaotic throughout the day. Japanese fire had cut down many unit leaders, disrupting the normal flow of information up the chain of command. Those leaders still alive were trying to get the decimated assault units off the beach and to stay alive in the hurricane of fire. Reporting information was not a priority. What few reports that got through were sketchy and did not present a clear picture of conditions on the beach. "Spider," an aerial observer, painted a dismal picture as he observed the battlefield from three thousand feet.

> "Playmate, this is Spider. Resistance moderate to heavy, I'd say. Over."
>
> "Spider, this is Playmate. Where are our front lines? Over."
>
> "Playmate, this is Spider. Lines well inland on the right and center, but left of Spitfire is still on Beach White 1. They seemed to be pinned down. Over."
>
> "Spider, this is Playmate. Can you see what's holding them up? Over."
>
> "Playmate this is Spider. There's heavy fire from the point just north of White 1. They seem to have both beaches enfiladed. More amtracs are burning on the beach. . . ."

General Rupertus, call sign Playmate, was desperate to get information. All he could do was monitor the radio nets aboard the USS *DuPage*, his floating headquarters. Fragments of the chaotic conditions ashore came across the command radios, which were scattered around him. They did not present a clear picture, which only increased his apprehension. He was dependent on Smith for an on-scene report.

O. P. Smith and his small command section left the USS *Elmore* at 0830 and proceeded to a Transfer Control Vessel off Orange Beach 3. "Finding a given Control Vessel is not as easy as it would appear," Smith recalled. "When you are eight miles out in a small boat it is difficult to see much." After hailing several ships to get directions, the party reached their destination. "From the Control Vessel, the beach was only 2,000 yards distant and with glasses it was possible to take in most of the details. The LCI gunboats periodically loosed terrific rocket barrages. Columns of smoke were coming up from the area hit by the rockets and naval gunfire, and unfortunately from some of our own burning amphibian tractors. There were splashes from Japanese mortar or artillery shells in the water over the reef and a few scattered splashes to seaward. Periodically another amphibian tractor would go up in flames."

Initially Smith planned to go ashore in a DUKW but, "after seeing all the burning amphibian tractors and all the mortar fire coming down inside the reef, I decided I'd rather go in on an LVT that wouldn't waste any time going across the reef." An aide hailed an empty tractor, and the party scrambled aboard. They headed for Orange Beach 2. In the midst of the turmoil Smith recalled a humorous incident: "There was no surf breaking on the edge of the reef and the driver hit it in stride, knocking most of us flat. One of the clerks was carrying a thermos of coffee and it was knocked over the side." Japanese mortar and artillery fire splashed all around the vehicle—near the small flags they had planted as registration points—and a sniper took a shot, causing the driver to "pull his helmet tighter on his head." A formidable-looking barbed wire fence emerged out of the smoke, but the thirty-thousand pound LVT easily crushed it.

The driver continued to head toward the north end of the beach, until Smith finally said, "Look, you are going to run out of beach here pretty quickly, and we've got to move in." With that encouragement, the driver headed in and pulled up under a coral ledge at the north end of Orange Beach 1. He dropped the ramp, and the command group rushed out to find cover. Smith and the main party holed up under a bank, while three men scouted the area for a more permanent site. One of the scouts had a narrow escape. "A Japanese popped up from out of the sand and took a shot at Benedict," Smith related. "Benedict shot back; both missed. The matter was quickly settled when the other Marine bumped off the Jap with a submachine gun."

The scouting party found an anti-tank ditch just behind Orange Beach 2, to which the command group lost no time in relocating. "The move down the beach was without incident," Smith recounted matter-of-factly, "except for being pinned down by sniper fire" . . . and finding the beach "sown with mines, part of the aerial torpedo and part of the horned variety." The mines were designed as anti-boat and anti-vehicle and required considerable pressure to set them off. Nevertheless Smith said, rather tongue in cheek, "One has an understandable aversion of stepping on one!" In some cases, the minefield was over one hundred yards in depth, but fortunately, many of them were not armed. Smith related how, "On Orange 3, a young tank lieutenant, on landing with his tanks, had dismounted and, under fire, had marked a passage through the mine field by unrolling toilet paper to mark a safe path." The mines in the CP area were finally disposed of by the division engineer, who wanted to move in. Smith told him, "Look, Frank, I'll be glad to have you if the first thing you do is take those darn mines and dump them in the ocean." There was also one other housekeeping chore that had to be done. "Three Japanese had been buried in the sand at the end of the draw . . . and had not been buried too deeply," Smith related. "To kill the odor, we thoroughly sprayed the place with DDT and threw more sand over the bodies."

Bruce Watkins was haunted by the specter of the dead:

As soon as possible they were laid out at company or battalion command posts. Covered with ponchos to keep off the flies, they were a constant reminder of our mortality. In the heat of Peleliu, decomposition was rapid and the smell of death was constant, particularly at night when we were stationary. Our Graves Registration troops worked valiantly to remove our dead, while the Japanese were left where they fell . . . and they could be buried in mass graves. Most of our dead for the first three days were buried at sea because enemy fire didn't allow a designated burial site. No one who has been in combat will ever forget the smell of death.

Smith's communicators "immediately set up the radio and tied in the field telephone with the Shore Party line." He reported his position to division and made contact via landline with the 5th and 7th Marines yet had difficulty establishing communications with Puller's 1st Marines. The 5th Marines reported that they were taking heavy fire but had a firm foothold on the beach. The 7th Marines reported that the situation was "confused" and that all was not going well. Furious enemy resistance was making it difficult for Hanneken to get a clear picture of the fight. Smith radioed the command ship with the information at hand.

The sketchy report only served to make Rupertus more anxious. "[Rupertus] planned to land as fast as he could and not later than H plus 4 hours," Smith related, "by which time, he assumed that all of the south end of the island and the airfield would be ours." Aboard the command ship, Seldon was being pressured by Rupertus. "[A]s the situation progressed, [Rupertus] became more obsessed with the idea of an early landing. It was all I could do to keep him from going in immediately." Rupertus kept pestering his assistant. "He tried to get me to tell him to come ashore," Smith said. "I knew he shouldn't . . . because he had this tremendous headquarters, and to move [it] would have taken a lot of amphibian tractors and we just didn't have them."

Rupertus kept working on his chief of staff, but Seldon reasoned with him. "I told him, 'General, if you go ashore, you'll know less than you do now.'" The logic of his argument got to Rupertus and he backed off for awhile. "I knew he was anxious to come ashore," Smith recalled, "and in the late afternoon, against my better judgment, I radioed him that the situation appeared favorable enough. Fortunately there was a shortage of LVTs which prevented the CP from moving ashore." Smith noted that "the general had to spend the night on the ship, and he was not very happy about it."

In the late morning, a grim report from the 7th Marines—"Heavy casualties. Need ammo, reinforcements"—caused Rupertus to make two controversial decisions. He ordered the Division Reconnaissance Company and 2/7, the division reserve, to reinforce the 7th Marines. Smith, ever the tactician, knew that "This was an improper use of the Reconnaissance Company, as there later developed several opportunities for [their] employment." Rupertus also knew that committing his only major reserve was chancy. "All right," he told Seldon, "go ahead, but I've shot my bolt when they go in." The commander of 3/7, Maj. Hunter Hurst, did not think much of the decision. "We at no time requested reinforcement, and, in fact, recommended against it, since the beachhead was already over-crowded." As it turned out, 2/7 did not land because of the onset of darkness and the lack of LVTs to get them over the beach. "The beachmaster stated that he could not and would not attempt a further landing." At 2015, the battalion was ordered back aboard their ship, but in the darkness and general confusion in the transport area, "the landing team became separated and reported back throughout the night." Others spent the hours of darkness bobbing about in small boats, trying to stay out of the way of patrolling destroyers. A small number of headquarters personnel actually landed and spent a restless night under Japanese mortar fire.

An hour after landing, Smith was surprised when Roy Geiger slid over the bank of the ditch to the accompaniment of mortar shells. Smith said, "Look General, according to the book, you're not supposed to be here at this time." To which he replied, "Well, I wanted to see why those amtracs were burning, and I'd also like to see the airfield." Smith pointed and said, "That's simple, all you have to do is just climb up this bank and there it is." Geiger scrambled up to look when "the Japanese sent over a couple of their 150mm mortar shells that made a horrible screech, sounding like they were just clearing your head." Startled, he hastily slid down the bank, having seen all the runway that he cared to see. Geiger also wanted to visit Puller's CP, but Smith talked him out of it. "Now look, General, there is a gap of 800 yards above here, and we don't know who's in there. You just shouldn't go up there." After quite a bit of jaw boning, Smith was able to talk Geiger out of it.

The two officers compared notes to come up with an estimate of casualties. They thought the division had suffered approximately 250, which was well short of the official count of 1,111. It was later determined that the 1st Marines alone had suffered over 500 killed, wounded and missing.

Shortly after Geiger's visit, a frenzied runner stumbled into the CP. "He was out of breath," Smith related, "and his story was not exactly reassuring. He had run into a Japanese tank which had broken through to the beach and was shooting up the Shore Party." His story was confirmed by an alert aerial observer (AO) who radioed excitedly "Jap tanks in the open, coming your way!"

CHAPTER 11

COUNTERATTACK

A cry went up from the 1st Marines' frontline infantry. "Tanks!" The electrifying shout instantly brought the exhausted men out of their lethargy. "I saw a cloud of dust with the ugly snout of a Nippon tank at the head of it," one NCO wrote. "Then came another, then another from behind a bunker, another from here and one from there . . . Jap tanks pouring out of their hiding places dodging and swirling crazily about." Matthew Stevenson was close to the edge of the airfield: "I saw to my horror, three Japanese tanks moving directly toward the center of our line. We had never encountered these in our previous campaigns; I wanted desperately to stop them."

What the Marines were seeing was an attempt by Colonel Nakagawa to throw them back into the sea. This counterattack force, consisting of an estimated thirteen to fifteen light tanks, supported by several hundred infantry, had been cleverly hidden behind the ridges north of the airfield. The tanks advanced, as one officer observed, "in what can best be described as two echelon formations . . . headed for the center of the

■ The light Japanese tanks were no match for the Marine defenders, who threw an amazing amount of ordnance at them as they advanced across the open area. Many of the machines were so thoroughly demolished that it was almost impossible to determine how many tanks were in the assault. *Marine Corps History Division*

1st Battalion[, 5th Marines]. About half of the enemy tanks had from eight to a dozen Japanese soldiers riding [tied] on the outside of the tanks." This formation passed diagonally across 2/1's lines and struck at the junction between the 1st and 5th Regiment.

Major Gordon D. Gayle's 2nd Battalion, 5th Marines, was advancing across the southern edge of the airfield as "the Japanese tanks came roaring in on us. Very fortunately, I had my tank platoon right at hand— a matter of fifty yards or so away from where I was—and sent them into the fray at the critical time. The Japanese tanks were no match for our tanks . . . and didn't last long, although they did get into our front line, mostly right at the boundary between the 2nd Battalion and the 1st Battalion on the left. Everybody, of course, on the airfield claimed credit for knocking out the tanks because everybody was shooting at them."

Robert Fisher reported that Major Stevenson "immediately set up a tank defense, which employed the full list of anti-tank weapons—37mm gun, bazookas, rifle grenades and a Sherman tank with its 75mm gun." Private First Class Robert L. Bungard rushed forward with his bazooka. "[He] coolly took a position directly in the face of a tank and destroyed the vehicle with his launcher," according to his Navy Cross citation. "When two more Japanese tanks came crashing through the lines several minutes later, he again fired his launcher from an exposed position . . . and destroyed the onrushing vehicles."

Lieutenant Colonel Lewis W. Walt, executive officer, 5th Marines, reported that "at the time the enemy tanks were approximately half way across the airfield, four Sherman tanks came onto the field in the 2/5 zone of action and opened fire immediately." The smoke and dust cut visibility. Bruce Watkins watched as "one of the Japs got behind one of ours and was blazing away at the back of the Sherman. I remember screaming at our tank to look back . . . when suddenly the Sherman's turret swiveled 180 degrees and let loose a 75mm round that blew the turret right off the Jap tank. It continued to run for a ways like a beheaded chicken." One alert tank gunner saw his anti-armor round pass completely through a Japanese tank and quickly switched to high explosive shells, which knocked the enemy vehicles to shreds. Platoon Sergeant James D. Miller "maneuvered his tank into the hostile formation and engaged them in action," his Navy Cross citation records. "Then, courageously exposed himself to intense enemy mortar, artillery and small-arms fire to deliver more accurate fire orders to his crew from the turret of his tank."

At the height of the attack, a navy dive-bomber dropped a five-hundred-pound bomb in the midst of a mass of Japanese, obliterating many and scattering the rest.

Eugene Sledge and his mortar section were set up in an open area when he "looked out across the open airfield toward the southern extremities of the coral ridge . . . and saw vehicles of some sort moving amid

■ Two dead crewmen lie behind the knocked-out Japanese light tank. The Japanese counterattack was a good tactical decision but did not achieve anything except the destruction of their tank company. *Marine Corps History Division*

swirling clouds of dust. 'Hey," he yelled, 'what are those amtracs doing all the way across the airfield.' Someone yelled out, 'Them ain't amtracs, they're Nip tanks!'" Hundreds of Marines "opened fire with machine guns, automatic rifles, small arms and bazookas." Stevenson watched entranced as one of his men aimed a bazooka. "One missile hit the first tank, which burst into flame. The hatch flew open and as the crew struggled to escape, rifle shots picked them off like bugs. One bazooka misfired, but an intrepid Marine leapt forward and placed a hand grenade on the tank's tread. The explosion caused the tank to lurch helplessly sideways, its motor roaring like a chorus of bulls." As described in his Navy Cross citation, Pfc. Dale C. Lyth "picked up his light machine gun and two belts of ammunition and, moving directly into the path of an attacking tank, deliberately exposed himself to its fire while he delivered accurate fire into the vision slot of the vehicle, killing its operator and stalling the tank within thirty feet of his gun. When the remainder of the tank crew attempted to escape, he annihilated them with hand grenades."

Private Dan Toledo "heard this rumbling sound and felt the ground shaking. I spun around and there was a Japanese tank bearing down on me. It was so close I could plainly see Japanese strapped to the side. They were dead. I pointed my submachine gun, pulled the trigger . . . but click, it didn't work! I then grabbed a nearby grenade launcher and pointed it at the tank . . . but it didn't work or I was too scared and nervous to operate it properly . . . I don't know which." The tank was so close it filled the young infantryman's vision. "I dove down into the tiny chink I'd created in the ground and scrunched my body into a tight little ball. The tank treads rolled directly over me." The hard coral sides held, keeping him from being crushed. "The tank then wheeled back around with the barrel aimed directly at me. Just at that moment when I should have died, the hatch opened and one of the tank crew popped his head out to look around. That was just enough time for a Marine nearby to drop a grenade through the hatch."

Bruce Watkins fixed an anti-tank grenade on his M-1 rifle and fired at a tank only sixty feet away. "I aimed high. It formed a nice arc over the top of the tank." He tried again and "was able to hit the right tread, stalling the tank. The platoon then poured everything we had at point-blank range, killing the occupants as they tried to exit the turret."

Rifleman Russell Davis was hunkered down in the dirt on top of a bank beside a bullet-riddled scrub palm. As the attack came closer, he brought his M-1 rifle to bear and cut loose. "I fired on, and all thought of incoming fire had gone from my mind. There were pitching, bucking, wheeling shapes in the smoke and I wanted to hit them, and when one of them flamed up in the gray and rolled on its nose I had a feeling of deep pleasure, and I was sure I had stopped it with my own fire. Later I realized that was unlikely; but then I believed it, and hundreds of other riflemen believed the same thing."

The tanks quickly outpaced the accompanying infantry. "They lit out for the American lines like so many of the proverbial bats from hell," one observer reported, "too fast to support their assault troops or for those troops to support them." The Marines were wild with excitement.

■ A Marine cautiously inspects the remnants of the foiled Japanese tank attack. *Marine Corps History Division*

As Davis watched, "two bazooka men posed on the lip of the bank like circus performers getting ready for a high-wire balancing act . . . [T]he front man aimed and triggered [a shot and] the tank stopped and toppled over. One of the bazooka men cheered like a little boy: 'Yay! Yay! That's us!'"

The action was fast, furious and often confused. A Marine described the destruction of a tank only ten yards from him:

> A tank rushed for the machine gun on my right . . . [I]t was not ten feet away when it burst into flame, leaving a trailing fire as it still rolled forward. The lower half of a twisted and burnt Jap body fell not a pace from me. The machine gunners jumped to safety just in time as the tank came crashing over their position. A Marine rushed up to give the tank a squirt with his flamethrower, but the turret gun caught him square in the chest. One Jap raised his head above the turret to have a look and was immediately shot to death. Another was killed as he tried to escape through the bottom hatch. Still another inside the tank raised a bloody and dirty white flag, and got his hand shot off. Then hand grenades were tossed into the tank.

Smith and the men in his command post prepared to "repel boarders!" "One tank got about 200 to 330 feet from my CP . . . [O]ur people let go with everything they had . . . [T]he noise built up to a crescendo [until] . . . the artillery, which was just behind us, destroyed it with point blank fire." As this was going on, an out-of-breath runner came into the CP and shouted, "There's a Japanese tank on the beach shooting up the Shore Party men!" To top it off, a shell landed just short of the ditch's protecting bank and wounded a Marine. The man slid down the bank and landed on Smith. "He had a small shell fragment in the back of his head," Smith described calmly. "Hankins did an excellent job of first aid, first stopping the flow of blood, then applying sulfa powder and a bandage. The boy was not badly hurt and was talkative. To him the wound was a ticket home."

Within minutes, the Japanese tank attack was stopped dead in its tracks; the counterattack failed. After the firing died down, Robert Fisher inspected one of the disabled tanks. "[We] were amazed at its small size

and lack of effective armor. It was considerably smaller than our own light tanks and certainly no match for a Sherman." Lieutenant Colonel Arthur J. Stuart, CO 1st Tank Battalion, reported that "the Japanese tanks were actually only light reconnaissance vehicles . . . with only one quarter inch to three eights inch armor . . . and were never intended for frontal action against heavy weapons." His after-action report stated, "This tank attack was in keeping with the usual Japanese *banzai* spirit, but [was] very poor tank tactics." After the battle, the division attempted to count the number of tanks in the attack. An accurate number could never be satisfactorily made because many of the tanks had been so thoroughly demolished that it was impossible to tell which parts belonged to which vehicle.

■ Remnants of the destroyed Japanese tank attack were strewn around the southern end of the airfield. The light tanks were no match for Marine Sherman tanks, bazookas and rifle grenades. *Marine Corps History Division*

OPTIMISTIC ASSESSMENT

Unknown to the Marines, there was an underwater telephone line from Peleliu to General Inoue's command post on Koror. On D-day evening, Colonel Nakagawa gloated that "by 1000 hours, our forces successfully put the enemy to rout . . . At 1420 hours, the enemy again attempted to make the perilous landing on the southwestern part of our coastline. The unit in that sector repulsed the daring counter-attack, and put the enemy to rout once more. However, in another sector of the coastline near Ayame [Orange Beach 3] the enemy with the aid of several tanks were successful in landing, although they were encountering heavy losses inflicted by our forces . . . Our tank unit attacked the enemy with such a cat-like spring at dusk, that they were able to inflict heavy damage on the enemy."

While Colonel Nakagawa's report was pure hyperbole, the landing had been costly. The carnage on the beach was incredible. Wrecked amtracs sat half-submerged and still burning in the shallow water, abandoned vehicles of every description littered the shoreline. Discarded packs, helmets, rifles, boxes and supplies of every description lay abandoned on the cratered sand. "Two dead bodies and five wrecked LVTs were our closest company," Tom Lea observed as he crouched in a shell hole. "I stared at the sand bank above my head and saw against the smoking sky the tangled, broken wrecks of coco palms and tropical trees with their big leaves hanging burnt and dead." A line of dead Marines covered with camouflaged ponchos waited for burial. Further inland, rifles thrust muzzle-first into the sand marked the location of more uncollected bodies. Still others bobbed lifelessly in the shallow water, "the flesh bluish grey as the pitiless sun began to bring the peculiar and intolerable stench of human dead," wrote Lea several hours after the landing.

As tough as the landing had been, the Marines now held a beachhead 3,000 yards long, averaging 500 yards in depth, with one maximum penetration of 1,500 yards. "What General Rupertus had hoped to accomplish on D-day was to seize Objective 0-1 and 0-2," O. P. Smith related. "0-1 was a coordinating objective which included 300 yards

of beachhead behind the landing beaches and that part of the island
south of the airfield. Objective 0-2 included Objective 0-1 plus the entire
airfield. What we actually captured was approximately Objective 0-1
north of Orange 3 and a wedge across the island east of Orange 3." The

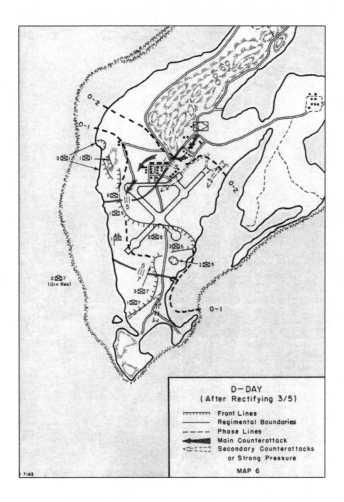

■ D-day front lines showing that the 5th and 7th Marines were pretty well tied
in. The 1st Marines in the north had gaps in their defensive line, which the
Japanese used to infiltrate snipers and launch limited counterattacks. *The
Assault on Peleliu, Marine Corps Monograph*

181

effort had been very costly, Smith noted. "Until several days later, when we got the complete casualty reports from the transports, we did not realize what this shallow beachhead had cost. The toll was 92 killed in action, 1146 wounded in action, and 58 missing in action. These were very heavy losses and could not have been sustained for very many days without destroying the combat efficiency of the division."

Amphibian vehicles, the work horse of the landing, had also suffered heavy losses. A combat correspondent wrote that "only about half of those that came ashore at H-Hour are still operational. A large number of those carrying assault waves got direct hits and burned. Many had their bottoms torn out on the reef . . . and, as the infantry moved inland, they were blasted by mortar fire. Five amtracs were knocked out on the airfield, as they zig-zagged across at high speed. The drivers named this route 'Purple Heart Run.'" During the afternoon tank battle, he reported that "two of the tracks lay claim to a Jap tank. The enemy tank, seeing one of the amtracs coming across the strip, turned into it and rammed the American vehicle. Another amtrac came to the rescue and butted the Jap tank from the rear. Caught between the two, the Jap three-man crew bolted out of the turret one by one. As they showed themselves, the amtrac crew killed them with carbines."

O. P. Smith was very concerned about the loss of so many of the valuable machines: "We had hoped that all the divisional artillery would be ashore and registered before nightfall." The loss of so many vehicles kept it from happening. "Actually," Smith noted, "by nightfall [only] 1 1/2 battalions of 75mm pack howitzers and 1 1/3 battalions of 105mm howitzers were ashore and registered." In addition, "supply had been somewhat slowed down by Japanese mortar and artillery fire. There was a shortage of water and ammunition, but the floating dumps on the pontoon barges off the reef were used to replenish supplies."

CHAPTER 12

TERROR IN THE NIGHT

A s dusk approached, there was furious activity all along the Marine lines. Russell Davis noticed worried-looking NCOs and officers scurrying about encouraging the men to "Dig in, dig deep. Get the wire out." Machine guns were brought forward and carefully positioned to provide overlapping fields of fire. Company and battalion mortar squads registered their weapons on likely approaches to the front lines. Artillery and naval gunfire observers memorized target numbers so they could call for fire in the darkness. Everyone knew the Japanese were coming and dreaded to hear them screech *"banzai"* as they launched human wave assaults. "Dusk had come and visibility was closed down to a few dozen feet," Russell Davis remembered; "The smoke, settling in the hollows behind the bank, helped to make it darker." George McMillan wrote: "The hours of tension and danger did not stop with dusk; every man lay taut in his shallow foxhole through the night, beseeching the sun to hurry, to restore to the battlefield its bright, accustomed focus."

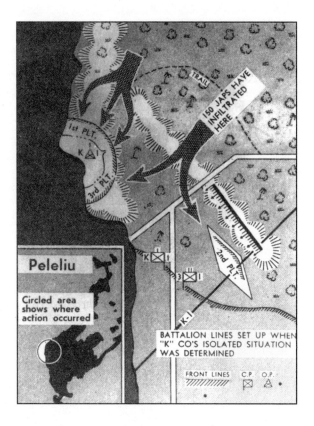

■ The perimeter of the 1st and 3rd Platoons, "K" Company. The Japanese launched counterattacks from the ridges in an attempt to throw the surviving Marines into the sea. The 2nd Platoon of the company was severely cut up in the tank trap farther east. *Marine Corps History Division*

Nowhere was it more tense than on the Point. All afternoon the Japanese had staged scattered infantry and mortar attacks on "K" Company. The Marines held, although more and more men were lost. All the company's machine guns had been knocked out, and Hunt had resorted to using a captured Japanese heavy machine gun on the lines. Fred Fox had "liberated" it from its dead crew. "I found the air-cooled Hotchkiss in a small clearing; two dead Jap bodies lay alongside it." He was amazed to find that the two Japanese soldiers were dressed in spotless

184

khaki summer uniforms with wrap leggings and split-toed shoes. They had rank insignia on their collar. "We carried the gun up to the Point," Fox explained, "and gave it to [Cpl. Robert Anderson] from the machine gun platoon who said, 'O.K., I'll take it.' I had no desire to keep carrying that damn thing anyway."

The gunners found a large supply of ammunition and kept it shooting for the next thirty-six hours. Just before dark, an LVT snuck in with badly needed supplies of ammunition, barbed wire, C rations—and water. Even with this bonanza, Fred Fox was not happy. "The water was brought up in a 55 gallon drum, but the drum had not been cleaned and the water tasted awful, sickening. It was oil and water and no way could we drink it. So, when you got the chance you went out, found some dead Jap bodies and took their canteens."

Fox tried to scrape out a hole in the coral but it was impossible. He piled up rocks for protection and carefully laid out grenades and ammunition so he could find them in the dark and then hunkered down—waiting. "I guess we all knew that something unpleasant was going to happen . . . [T]his was the Japanese's time . . . this was their time to fight."

Hunt made a last tour of the lines. "As blackness crept up and completely enveloped us, we were subdued to an eerie silence. Even the clicking sounds of a rock, probably brushed off by the sweep of a man's elbow, seemed a harsh disturbance. Though there was no moon, the sky . . . was just light enough to reveal the weird and grotesque silhouettes of knotted trees and stumps." Jagged, pinnacled rocks melded with the gnarled tree remains, providing cover for Japanese infiltrators. Their odd shapes played tricks on the defenders' imaginations, transforming them into Japanese attackers in the darkness. "The Jap loves the night and he loves to sneak," Hunt philosophized. "He is an animal who prowls noiselessly with padded, two-toed shoes on his feet. When he attacks . . . out of the night . . . with bayonet and knife, he is dangerous and clever."

Fred Fox had picked up a buddy and now the two of them shared a foxhole. They lay on their backs facing the Japanese. "Some time between eleven and twelve," Fox related, "we heard movement out in front. You got the feeling something was going to happen." Swede Hanson was close by. "You could hear movement going about, and your ears got bigger and bigger because you're wondering, is it a Marine or is it a Jap? And you didn't want to take a chance . . . so I start throwing hand grenades out there in front. And then I waited. Then, *brrrrr*, that Nambu machine gun. So I threw a couple more hand grenades out there and I heard *brrrrr*, but it took a little longer to get that one in."

Hunt requested illumination. "Flares swished up from the rear. I prayed they wouldn't break over our own position and light us up . . . but they burst well in front of us, flooding the area with light." Someone shouted "There they are!" and the fight was on. "A machine gun fired a burst," Hunt exclaimed. "Another one—it opened up with a vibrating

■ Japanese combat art depicting a night attack. *Marine Corps History Division*

■ A hastily positioned Browning water-cooled .30-caliber machine gun. This automatic weapon could fire four hundred to six hundred rounds per minute from a cloth belt. *Marine Corps History Division*

roar, BARs and rifles . . . Hand grenades were bursting in rapid succession. The explosions were muffled in the woods, where there were gullies and ridges. Then much louder bursts—approaching our lines— closer—and I heard the cry 'Corpsman!' Jap mortars, big stuff, were pounding in the middle of us. Shrapnel was clinking across the rocks."

Corporal Bob Anderson sat behind the captured machine gun. "Whenever someone heard the Japs jabbering, they would call for a star shell and when it would go off, we could see Japs running out to our front. Then I would open up with the machine gun at the running Japs. I don't know if I hit any or not, but I used up a lot of ammunition."

Hunt recounted how when it was dark, "white muzzle flashes spit into the black." He said, "The noise increased as the Japs answered and their bullets spattered on the rocks and ricocheted in every direction. Their mortar shells thundered into the coral raising the stink of gunpowder."

Suddenly the Japanese mortar fire stopped—then "things began to slow down a little bit." Fox recalled that "every once in a while, there would be another burst of gunfire—but the fight was over—flares revealed nothing." At first light, the ground in front of the lines was strewn with enemy dead. A Marine told Anderson, "I never saw so many dead Japs in one place in all my life."

Elsewhere along the lines, the Japanese infiltrators were at work. At one point, 2nd Battalion's Russell Davis was startled by a voice calling out, "Amelicans, Amelicans. Pigs . . . dogs. Amelican pigs and dogs." He knew it was a Japanese trick, so he held his fire. "Amelican pig," the enemy taunted. "You die. You die. You die." The Japanese threw fire crackers in an attempt to get the Marines to open fire and give away their positions "but were unsuccessful as the men were seasoned troops by this time and fired only when distinct targets were available."

The frontline infantry knew that to move outside one's foxhole was extremely dangerous. Russell Davis related how, "John, 'the loner,' had grown restless in the night. He had moved out of his hole and the other man had been trigger-happy and poured a whole clip into John, without challenging him, without giving him a chance. It seemed very unfair." Nighttime passwords were issued that contained the letter "L," because most Japanese had trouble pronouncing it. Multiple Ls were especially effective, though when placed together, the danger of slurring over the difficult consonants is lessened. The Japs were able to produce a word similar to 'jolly' with 'jorry,' but they floundered conspicuously saying "Honolulu." In the stress of combat, men often forgot the password. A dog handler failed to give the correct password when challenged and was bayoneted by a frightened sentry. Fortunately he was not badly injured.

"Shortly before midnight a terrible scream erupted from one of the foxholes," Tech. Sgt. Donald Hallman wrote in a press release: "Another voice yelled frantically, 'Jap! Jap! He got my buddy!" A crouching figure dodged among the foxholes. A dozen men fired at the shadowy form but missed; the infiltrator escaped. He left behind a dead Marine and a badly wounded one. A doctor and a Corpsman braved the darkness and crawled to the wounded man's side to administer first aid."

A radio operator made a frenzied call and flares suddenly blossomed over no man's land. All along the line, tense scared men peered into the greenish-tinged landscape. Shadows played on their imaginations—a bush appeared to be a crouching enemy soldier; a boulder took on a human form. Gunfire erupted and explosions quickly followed as the defenders' nerves reached the breaking point. Flashes outlined the front lines as rifle and machine gun fire lashed out into the darkness.

■ The remains of a Japanese soldier killed while trying to infiltrate Marine lines. The Japanese did a considerable amount of night training and were particularly adept at infiltration techniques. *Marine Corps History Division*

Gradually, officers and NCOs restored order. The firing died down and then stopped.

In another press release, Hallman wrote, "an hour later, there was a single shot. 'It's the lieutenant,' was the cry. 'The lieutenant has been killed in his foxhole.' Later there were more shots. Someone yelled, 'I'll teach you, you son-of-a-bitch!' You could hear the sound of blows, of men fighting. . . ." Further back toward the beach, Hallman reported an instance of hand-to-hand combat. "Three Japs crept to within ten feet of the artillery command post. A Marine spotted them. He fired and killed one, and then another as the other two charged towards him. The third, bayonet raised for the kill, kept coming. The Marine's buddy grabbed the Jap's rifle, broke it over his foe's head, strangled him, and then threw the

■ The poncho-covered remains await identification before burial in the division cemetery. Specially trained graves-registration teams performed the task. *Marine Corps History Division*

190

body into the rocks." The Japanese infiltrators had achieved their mission. They killed and wounded several Marines—and, just as importantly, they were wearing down the American's combat efficiency by denying them sleep. First Battalion reported the night's activity in their sector. "Sporadic firing most of the night as localized counter-attacks and Jap individuals were eliminated. A few enemy managed to infiltrate during the night and were killed behind our lines the next morning."

Sometime around 0200, a Japanese artillery battery opened up, "walking" its fire up and down the beach area, probing for troops and supply dumps. The crowded beachhead suffered a terrifying bombardment; explosions rocked the darkness. "All night long came repeated cries for stretcher bearers. Exhausted as they were, I sent them forward again and again," Nikolai Stevenson recounted. "The stretchers lay near the water's edge, the cries of the wounded haunting us as the surgeon and the medical corpsmen struggled in the dark to relieve their agony."

Robert Fisher was hunkered down with him in the CP. It was relatively quiet, he noted, except "snipers made life unpleasant by firing over our heads throughout the night. There is something about sniper fire in the still of the night that makes it seem more dangerous than it actually is. The bullets crack so loudly as they pass over you that they seem to be fired from just outside your hole, whereas they were probably fired from several hundred yards away."

The battalion reported, "During the night our artillery laid down an almost continuous barrage. We were subject to intermittent machine gun, mortar and rifle fire. All companies report some casualties."

PLAYMATE FORWARD (SMITH)

O. P. Smith's CP was not immune to enemy fire. "A Japanese mortar shell landed in the ditch about fifty yards south of us," Smith reported.

> It landed directly on a group, including a doctor, killed three and wounded several others. Spent fragments landed in our group. Later in the night the Japanese

started moving about in the vicinity of the CP. There was a flurry of shooting a short way down the trench and we hit the dirt. (In the morning we buried three freshly killed Japanese.) At 0330, a small counter-attack developed against the right of the 7th Marines. As the Japanese attacked they gave their characteristic *banzai* shout, which carried to the CP. It was soon drowned out by our return fire, which finally ceased. We knew the counter-attack had been repulsed. Just as it was getting fully light—0600—the Japanese launched a fairly heavy attack against the 5th Marines, directly in front of the CP. It was a fairly noisy affair, but it did not last long. Later I found a knocked-out Japanese tank 100 yards in front of the CP. It had been destroyed by point-blank fire from one of our artillery pieces.

The massive human wave *banzai* attack on D-day never happened. Where was the main Japanese force?

CHAPTER 13

D + 1

THEY WILL DIE,
THEY WILL DEFEND

The pattern of the attack for each day was set. Usually the attack jumped off at 0700, preceded by an artillery, air and naval gunfire preparation. Normally, the fighting was broken off at 1700 and the troops dug in for the night.

After a harrowing, sleepless night, Bob Fisher expressed that "it was with a feeling of great relief that we saw the first streaks of dawn the next morning. We knew we could beat the Japs in the daytime, but they were an awful nuisance at night." He would soon change his mind. Japanese spotters on the high ground picked out the Marine positions and brought down a merciless rain of artillery and mortar fire. Men huddled in makeshift shelters absorbed the punishment. Counter-battery fire from cruisers and destroyers off-shore and artillery on the beach tried to range in on the hidden enemy guns but with little success. The Japanese were too well dug in—and their positions were located in terrain that the flat-trajectory naval guns could not reach. Marine 75mm and 105mm howitzers were too light to penetrate

■ A battery of 75mm pack howitzers fire at the Japanese. The light eight-pound projectile could not penetrate the enemy's hardened positions, but it could be used effectively against troops in the open. *Marine Corps History Division*

the coral and concrete reinforced positions, unless they scored a lucky hit.

Explosions ranged all along the front lines and in the rear areas in a cacophony of noise that numbed the senses. "The sounds rushed upon each other as the tremendous traffic of steel and powder broke, ceased, parted, rent the air overhead," George McMillan explained. "The freight-car rumble of naval shells could be marked at once. Smaller shells were distinguished by their pitch—the higher the whistle, the smaller the shell, down to the almost inaudible whisper of the feared mortar shell. No man on Peleliu will ever forget the sound of an incoming mortar shell, with its whisshhh-shh-shh, whisshhh-shh-shh, insistent, intimate, as if each bore a secret that could not wait to be told." The shelling

RADIO TOKYO

An American intercept station picked up Radio Tokyo's September 16, 1944, morning broadcast. "Our glorious forces have again slaughtered thousands of blood-thirsty American Marines in a stupid invasion attempt, this time in the Palau Islands. Commanded by valiant and brilliant Col. Kunio Nakagawa, superb and valorous Japanese troops bravely frustrated the daring landing by 1000 hours, putting the screaming enemy hordes to flight. At 1400 hours, the ill-fated butchers attempted again to make a landing on the southwest tip of our coastline. This frantic and disorganized counterattack was also repulsed and the fiendish Yankees were put to rout once more, with the sea red with their blood."

brought on a feeling of helplessness. "I hugged the pillbox wall until my fingers were stiff," Russell Davis described. "Then I let go and clubbed at my legs with my clenched fists. But they were useless. I knew then what 'paralyzed with fear' meant."

Suddenly, without explanation, the Japanese fire lifted. With a feeling of immense relief, the shaken survivors cautiously emerged from their shelters. Only twenty-four hours had elapsed from the time they had landed and already ferocious Japanese resistance, sleep deprivation, little water and the terrible heat and humidity had worn them down. Foxhole strength in the rifle companies had been reduced by a third. Many of the best NCOs and officers were gone, creating a leadership vacuum that was filled by less experienced men.

Yet, bleary eyed, battered and bruised, Puller's Marines were prepared to carry out his orders. During the evening, Puller passed the word to his battalion commanders to resume the attack, following a heavy thirty-minute naval and air bombardment. The regiment was aligned west to east with 3/1 on the left, 1/1 in the center and 2/1 on the right, adjacent to the 5th Marines.

Honsowetz was assigned to "swing his east-facing 2/1 leftward and to capture and clear the built-up area between the airfield and the ridges." He had two companies on line, "E" Company on the left and "F" Company on the right, alongside a company of the 5th Marines. At 0800 the attack kicked

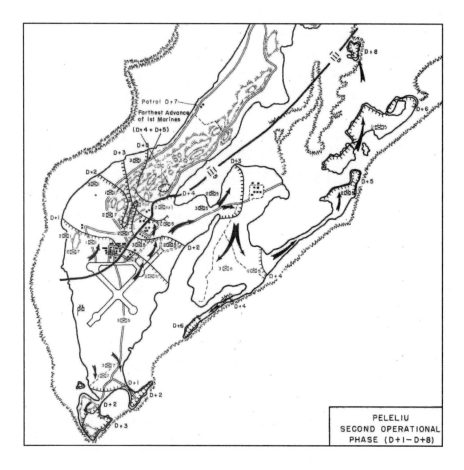

PELELIU
SECOND OPERATIONAL
PHASE (D+1—D+8)

■ First Marines arrayed from left to right on D + 1—3/1, 1/1 and 2/1, adjacent to the 5th Marines. The virtually impregnable outpost line of the Japanese Umurbrogol Mountain defenses lie a hard day's fighting away. *The Assault on Peleliu, Marine Corps Monograph*

off. The battalion made good progress, crossing the west turning circle of the runway within half an hour. Russell Davis was with "F" Company, which had to cross the flat runway, absolutely devoid of cover. "When I got to the edge of the field I made two starts at running out, but both times I turned back and hugged the side of a pillbox. The field was still swept with fire . . . [T]here were shell bursts all over the field, but men still ran

■ The rubble left by naval and air bombardment of the airfield's buildings often provided cover and concealment to Japanese snipers, who had to be cleared out by close combat . . . as shown by the three riflemen laying down suppressive fire. *Marine Corps History Division*

■ Two Marines cautiously advance through the debris of a vehicle park on the northern edge of the airfield. The shattered vegetation makes it extremely difficult to see. *Marine Corps History Division*

through them." First Lieutenant Joseph A. L. Fournier led a patrol across the airfield and, as succinctly told in his Navy Cross citation, "located an automatic gun battery delivering enfilade fire and knocked out the deeply entrenched fortification, killing twenty Japanese." Davis finally made it across the airfield and reported to Colonel Honsowetz, who had worked his way over with his OP group. In the confusion of the attack, Honsowetz had lost touch with his assault companies. "I showed him on the map and on the ground where we were," Davis reported. "I estimated we had the survivors of two companies across the airfield. The colonel called the good news back to Regiment."

"F" Company fought their way across "through the clutter of the north end of the airfield, a Japanese barracks area, and pushed on into the debris of a demolished village." The battalion reported, " 'F' Company is entering the building area [and] has extremely heavy casualties." Thirty-six minutes later it reported, " 'F' Company has passed the blockhouse area [and] there is heavy resistance."

Russell Davis was with a Marine who had been hit.

> I was sitting in the lee of a smashed blockhouse, my back against the steaming concrete that seemed ready to crack in the heat. Beside me was a big Polish man with half his dungarees cut away—his left arm wasn't there at all, and his white chest and shoulders above the stump were beginning to burn under the sun. The stump oozed but did not bleed and he was so strong that he still could speak. He said—and the shock and pain could not make him any less the man he was—"Look at that! Not much blood at all. No blood that I can see. Maybe just a little."
> I waited with him for a Corpsman who never came—at least while he was still alive.

Bruce Watkins, with "E" Company on the left flank, advanced through the wooded edge of the airfield. "We approached a barracks area where we were stopped by heavy fire from a large round concrete bunker approximately fifty feet in diameter," he explained. "We tried anti-tank grenades to no avail." One of his sergeants stuffed a grenade in a firing slit, but the enemy gun continued to fire. A Sherman tank tried, firing two shells, when suddenly "we heard the whine of a navy dive bomber coming directly at us." Watkins and his men hugged the ground. "He released the bomb, probably a 500 pounder, and we all watched as it headed toward us in a slight arc. Miraculously, the bomb hit dead center on the bunker, collapsing it and killing all the Japanese within. The concussion stunned us and covered us with white coral dust. We got shakily to our feet, like so many ghosts, in great wonder at being alive. No one had been hit."

Second Battalion continued pushing until it reached a point just short of phase line 0-2, the West Road, a gain of as much as 1,500 yards. Heavy enemy fire forced it to dig in for the night. The other two battalions were not able to match Honsowetz's gains.

SPITFIRE ONE (DAVIS)

Ray Davis' 1st Battalion attacked straight into the teeth of the enemy defenses. "We jumped off early . . . got off in good order and went across the edge of the airfield, heading north. Our mission was to go through the lead battalion to seize the regimental

■ The Japanese emplacements included concrete-reinforced bunkers that were almost impervious to everything but heavy ordnance . . . or direct infantry assault with explosives or flamethrowers. This emplacement shows the damage caused by naval gunfire. *Marine Corps History Division*

objective, some coral ridges. We went some 200 to 300 yards and ran into the beginnings of a fortified area . . . right into the heart of it. We couldn't move without getting shot at from two to three directions." "B" and "C" Companies continued the attack, taking heavy casualties as they mopped up Japanese emplacements. The battalion report singled out one NCO. "Sergeant Monarch, with the 'C' Company assault team, took and destroyed numerous dug-outs constructed in the coral ridge." Four months later the Indiana native was formally recognized in his Navy Cross citation: "When the advance of his unit was held up by a deep zone of strong enemy emplacements consisting of a series of concealed concrete pillboxes and rifle pits, and the cross-firing of heavy weapons swept the front of his company, Sergeant Monarch skillfully maneuvered his men into advantageous positions to deliver accurate covering flamethrower and rifle fire against the Japanese strong point . . . [He] personally placed heavy explosive charges into the embrasures . . . destroying ten of the strongholds."

■ The body of a Marine lies where he fell, waiting for a graves-registration team to take it for burial. Note the empty K-Bar sheath and the shattered rifle. *Marine Corps History Division*

"B" Company fought its way through the Japanese defenses and made contact with Hunt's beleaguered remnants. "I'm guessing about 4:00 in the afternoon," a very relieved Fred Fox recounted. "I don't know where it came from, but the word was being passed that 'B' Company had broken through the Japanese counterattack lines and were now tied in with us." "C" Company managed to fight its way alongside and tied in. The battalion report stated that, "The area through which 'B' and 'C' Companies worked [was] rutted with anti-tank ditches and a network of camouflaged pillboxes connected by trenches on the low and flat ground. The coral ridge was honeycombed with rifle pits and machine gun nests. In particular, a pillbox with a pair of twin-mounted .80-caliber machine guns gave us a great deal of difficulty."

The battalion OP group moved up behind the assault units. "We passed near a deep anti-tank ditch," Davis reported. "Dead Marines from the preceding day lay scattered about. It was apparent that the Japs had sited anti-tank weapons from the left flank and mortars from the ridges to the front to cover this ditch well." A battalion report noted that "The few dead [Japanese] up to this point were all clean, well fed and equipped and rather large in stature—most were 6 feet in height. One of those killed had a dog tag indicating that he was a member of the 9th Company, 2nd Infantry Regiment of the 14th Infantry Division. Later intelligence identified members of the 3rd and 7th Companies, indicating that at least two battalions of enemy confronted the Marines. The report also noted that, "The Japs we fought were not the wild, attacking hordes of the early stages of the war. These Japs were from a Manchurian Division, well equipped, well fed, well trained and well disciplined."

An exhausted, weaponless NCO was captured by a patrol after it discovered him hiding in a cave that had been bypassed. One of only half a dozen Japanese soldiers captured during the battle, he verified the 2nd Infantry Regiment as the main enemy unit on the island. He freely admitted to a Japanese-speaking Nisei (a Japanese American) that he was a message center chief in the 2nd Regiment's 6th Company. On D + 1, his company had been overrun and only he and three others escaped. During an attempt to locate Colonel Nakagawa's headquarters, his three companions were killed, and he had been trapped in the cave. So far as he knew, he was the only survivor of the 6th Company. Shown a captured sketch map, he traced the defensive positions of the regiment and pointed out the location of sixty to seventy holdouts. He estimated that the preliminary bombardment killed one-half of the 2nd Battalion; the remainder fought on. Those who were wounded and couldn't walk committed suicide with hand grenades. Throughout the interrogation, he vehemently opposed the release of his name to the Red Cross because it would shame his family.

■ A frontline Marine fixes a "K" ration meal while his buddy keeps watch. One of the heavy waxed paper rations lies at his feet. He is pouring water from his canteen into a "field expedient" cup . . . half a grenade container. *Marine Corps History Division*

Davis compared the Japanese his battalion was fighting against the ones on New Britain. "Those of us who followed the Matusda Division on Cape Gloucester as they floundered through the jungles of New Britain in abject defeat were unaccustomed to the ferocious and wily foe in front of us . . . [T]hey were too cautious and tactical to waste their efforts in a few *banzai* charges." The Japanese were disciplined fighters, and when forced to withdraw, retired in good order, taking their dead and wounded with them. This frustrated the Marines because "it was not possible to make an estimate of enemy casualties when the only ones to be found were the few snipers that infiltrated the lines."

At 1700, the battalion dug in for the night. Sporadic mortar and small-arms fire continued to plague the exhausted men, but they were cheered when the battalion S-4 (logistics officer) was able to bring up ammunition, chow and something to drink other than the foul-tasting water. "This was the first day that the men found fruit and tomato juice in the front lines," it was reported. "A great many stomachs are constricted because of effort, fear, and battle fatigue; it is of great value to be able to derive nourishment and energy from a drink which does not demand the amount of effort from the stomach for digestion that the heavy, solid, or greasy foods do." The men were also supplied with "C" rations, which they considered "the equivalent of a steak dinner" after trying to wolf down Australian rations that were "too greasy and unappetizing for a stomach that has contracted from shell blast and fear." The battalion's losses for the day were fourteen men killed in action, eighty-one wounded and two missing.

SPITFIRE THREE (SABOL)

Sabol's 3rd Battalion kicked off the attack on time, but "L" Company was immediately stopped by heavy enemy fire emanating from the

■ Sweat-soaked stretcher bearers struggle to bring in a casualty. The grimace on the face of the bearer speaks volumes about the difficulty of retrieving the wounded in the island's rough terrain . . . often under fire. *Marine Corps History Division*

ridge to their front. A tank was brought up and blasted it with high explosive rounds. Artillery was also called in and, after about an hour, "slight progress was made and the south end of the ridge was finally taken. The attack then progressed along the ridge in the face of heavy small arms fire and occasional mortar fire," the battalion after-action report noted. "I" Company on the right encountered the same fierce resistance but maintained its advance while keeping contact with Honsowetz's left flank company. Sabol was able to maintain a continuous line along his battalion front, as the entire regiment pivoted to the west. Several resupply LVTs were able to get to "K" Company shortly after first light. "Tractors rolled up to us all day along the reef," George Hunt recalled. "They brought my mortar section from up the beach . . . with clover leaf after clover leaf of shells. They brought up Lieutenant Klopf with his artillery observation team and a radio to communicate to his gun batteries—and the remaining ten men from my second platoon."

With the resupply and reinforcement, Hunt allowed that "It would be our turn to throw the heavy stuff: mortars and artillery. We had seven machine guns on the line and thirty more men. Radios were working, and there were two telephone lines to battalion. For the first time since we landed I felt secure." He felt secure enough to send out a reinforced reconnaissance patrol. "Sergeant Hahn and five or six men went forward several hundred yards to scout the Jap lines," Fox recalled. "A firefight started." Hunt watched helplessly as the Japanese opened up on the small patrol. "We could not fire . . . for fear of hitting our own men. Japs were bobbing in and out of the rocks—I could see their flat, brown helmets." One of the wounded made it back and reported, "There's a mess of 'em in the caves—take a hell of a lot of men to rout 'em out." Hunt decided that he could not commit more troops in a pitched battle where the Japanese had the advantage. All he could do was cover the patrol's withdrawal. "Hahn got back with one killed and two wounded," Fox recalled. Hunt reported that the patrol had been attacked by an estimated forty Japanese.

Hunt called Lieutenant Colonel Sabol to brief him on the fierce action. "Colonel, still plenty of Japs up front of us—seem to be gathering for something—maybe a night attack. . . ." His prediction was right on the money. "About midnight the Japs really started the action," Fox related. "They began with mortars and then followed up with everything else, almost a *banzai* charge! It was rifles, machine guns and hand grenades—everything that was available." O. P. Smith received a report indicating that, "At 2200, 'K' and 'B' companies were hit with an estimated 500 troops and a heavy mortar and grenade barrage, accompanied by a small flanking action along the water's edge."

Fred Fox's position was closest to the water.

> I heard somebody speaking Japanese out in the water in front of me. I eased down the cliff to where I could walk back to Hunt's command post . . . about 30 to 40 yards in front of one of the captured Jap bunkers. I guess I took one step, maybe two, when I heard a step behind me . . . I turned around as fast as I could. In turning, I hit a bayonet that had started into my chest and knocked it out of the way. It cut through my jacket and left a four-inch by one-half-inch gash through the flesh of my left chest. I had a pistol in my hand; it was cocked and loaded but I didn't shoot the man. I hit him in the face with it . . . as hard as I could. He immediately dropped the rifle, which I took and bayoneted him. I pulled it out and started yelling "Nips! Nips!"

One of the men in a nearby position rushed back to the CP. "What's the matter?" a startled Hunt demanded. The scared Marine replied, "We've been hearin' voices just in front of our position, and a kind of squirming and gagging as though someone was being stabbed. We think the Japs grabbed a guy who went out to see what the score was." Taken aback by the report, Hunt decided to take a look. "We wound through the rocks about ten yards and entered the coral basin . . . Stretched out on the coral were dead men who had stiffened in rigid positions. Dark liquid, which I knew was blood, lay in pools around them. There was a stirring to my left, and I saw an arm thrown forward, heard the snap of the grenade pin and then the explosion. The noises were more distinct now—whispered gibberish and low squeals of pain."

■ A ridge-top fighting position manned by two Marines. The man in the foreground is armed with a Browning Automatic Rifle (BAR), while his buddy carries an M-1 rifle. The hastily scraped together position of logs and piled rocks is typical in the hard-scrabble coral terrain. *Marine Corps History Division*

Fox was in serious trouble, caught between the enemy and his own men. "In a second or two there were another two or three Japs starting after me. Then there was an explosion, and I went down . . . hit along the left side with five chunks of steel in my left leg and left arm. Then there was another Jap! He started to bayonet me and I started rolling out into the water . . . but he got me two times, once in the neck and once more across the back." A flare lit the scene. One of Fox's buddies saw the fight and opened up with a rifle. "As soon as he started firing, the Japs left me alone and started trying to climb the cliff to get him," Fox recounted. "What happened to me then, I'm not sure. I lay quiet in the water. At certain times I would look out of the corner of my eye . . . and I could see wrap leggings and split toed shoes . . . I looked to the right and I could see the shoulder of a Jap uniform laying in the water with me."

Back on the Point, there was the sudden cry of "There they are! They're comin' in on us!" Hunt found himself "bellowing until I thought my lungs would crack. 'Give 'em hell! Kill every one of the bastards!' The

Japs were assaulting us with stampeding fury, wave after wave, charging blindly into our lines . . . [A]bove the uproar I heard their devilish screams, 'banzai, banzai!'"

Sabol reported that "it was the obvious intention of the enemy to retake the Point regardless of cost. They charged directly into the fire of our automatic weapons and hand grenades." A heavy artillery barrage was immediately called in to within 250 yards. Hunt's own 60mm mortars landed within thirty yards, and his men covered the remaining distance to the lines with their own hand grenades.

Despite this firepower, about thirty Japanese managed to penetrate the lines. In the light of parachute flares, figures could be seen in deadly hand-to-hand struggles. Hunt watched transfixed as "two figures, dim and queerly distorted in the battle fog, fought against each other on the crest of the cliff. Their arms were swinging wildly, their heads

■ A typical frontline battalion aid station, where lifesaving measures were taken to stabilize the casualty until he could be evacuated to the rear. Here a head-wound case is being treated by navy corpsmen. *Marine Corps History Division*

lowered and legs intertwined. The largest figure seemed to heave forward with his entire right side. The knees of the other bent back, he turned sideways and losing his balance tumbled off the cliff."

The Japanese attempted to go around the left flank through the water's edge just below the cliff. Sabol reported that "those advancing in the crevices in the coral were killed by Tommy guns and burned out with thermite grenades. Those in the water were machine gunned." Barely conscious, Fox lay bleeding as automatic weapons fire snapped

■ A bare-chested Col. Lewis B. Puller in a lighter moment during the battle. Puller was hampered by a bum leg, the result of a wound suffered on Guadalcanal. The gathering of officers suggests his CP was well behind the lines . . . uncharacteristic of Puller, as he was always well forward. *Marine Corps History Division*

over his head. "The guns fired across the water over me and against the cliff," he said. "This went on until sometime just before daylight when I began to get water in my mouth. The tide was coming in." He yelled for help and was rewarded when a Marine answered. "I found out it was Andy Byrnes, the machine gunner who had been firing all night."

The rescuer left the cover of his machine gun position and worked his way down to the water's edge. As Byrnes stooped over to lift Fox onto his shoulder, Japanese snipers opened fire. "He did a hell of a brave thing to come out in the open to pick me up," Fox related gratefully. Miraculously, Byrnes was able to bring the unconscious man ashore without being hit. Fox regained consciousness. "I guess it was about ten o'clock in the morning and it was getting hot. I was lying on a stretcher in the sun with my head on my arms. I felt a hand check my pulse and I jerked my head up, scaring him. He jumped about a foot."

Fox was loaded on an LVT and taken to a transport that had been converted to a hospital ship. "They took me into the operating room where a doctor asked, 'Where are you hurt?' I said, 'Well, on my leg and my back and neck.' He decided to pull off the bandages the Corpsman had put on . . . [I]t was the shock of my life because they were stuck to my neck with dried blood." Fox made it back to the States and spent eight months in various hospitals before being discharged.

PLAYMATE (RUPERTUS)

At 0950 on D + 1, General Rupertus hobbled down the ramp of an amtrac and assumed command ashore. His game leg still bothered him, and he leaned heavily on a Malacca cane. O. P. Smith quickly brought him up to speed on the tactical situation and then reverted to his usual subordinate role. Rupertus, who had followed the action from the command ship, was not happy with the progress of the attack on the Umurbrogol. He picked up a field telephone and angrily called Puller. "Can't they move any faster?" he snapped. "Goddammit, Lewie, you've gotta kick ass to get results. You know that, goddamnit!" The 1st Marines had already suffered a thousand casualties and had now hit the Japanese main line of resistance. Rupertus just did not fully understand what the regiment was up against.

With Rupertus ashore, Smith was free to visit the division's commanders.

> To visit "Lewie" Puller and the 1st Marines was always an adventure. Puller believed in keeping his CP well forward. The first time I visited him I followed the wire lines. We crawled through a swamp and found Puller in an abandoned quarry north of the airfield. It was a hot day and Puller was stripped to the waist. He was smoking his battered pipe; characteristically he held the pipe between his incisors and talked out of the side of his mouth. Puller's main gripe at the moment was that the 5th Marines were calling artillery fires where he already had troops. It is understandable that there could

■ Major General Roy Geiger on the left being briefed by Col. Harold D. Harris. Major General William H. Rupertus looks on. Geiger became increasingly frustrated with Rupertus, who refused to employ army troops to relieve the battered 1st Marines. *Marine Corps History Division*

be confusion as to the exact location of troops, as the map of the rugged area north of the airfield was far from being a true representation of the ground.

Smith's second visit was a little more exciting.

> A day or so later I visited Puller again and this time his CP was located up the west road . . . where the bluffs to the east of the road come very close to the road. His CP installations were scattered along the base of the bluff. This defilade was necessary because the Japanese were laying down considerable mortar fire in the area and considerable small arms fire was passing overhead. I kidded Lewie about his position, but that's the way he operates. While at the CP some Japanese snipers worked down to a position north of the CP where they could fire into it. Puller organized a patrol and sent it out to get the snipers. In a few minutes there were a few bursts of fire and shortly after that the patrol returned with the report that it had liquidated two snipers. I was able to replenish Puller's supply of pipe tobacco from a supply which Captain Graham had very kindly sent in from the *Mt. McKinley.*

Just after Rupertus came ashore, General Geiger appeared at the division command post on one of his daily inspection visits. "General Geiger spent nearly every day at the front lines," Merwin Silverthorn proudly recalled, "and when I say front lines, he went all the way out to battalion commanders positions, if not company commander positions . . . a great compliment for a man in his late 50s." Geiger took Rupertus aside and the two engaged in a heated discussion. Bill Ross quoted Geiger's aide. "The argument was over the crucial matter of when Rupertus intended to call in the Army's 81st Wildcat Division to reinforce—or possibly relieve—Chesty Puller's badly shot-up 1st Marines." Geiger was increasingly concerned about Rupertus' stubborn unwillingness to call on the army for relief of the 1st Marines.

O. P. Smith talked to Geiger two days later on board the command ship. "I met General Geiger and found he was contemplating committing one regiment of the 81st Division . . . I suggested to use the 5th Marines, which had just about completed its mission on the east coast, but he was adamant." However, Rupertus was dead set against using army reinforcements and would not willingly agree to use them.

Rupertus wasn't the only commander that was jealous of his command prerogatives. Omar Pfeiffer observed a discussion between Rupertus and Puller:

> The 1st Regiment was having very, very heavy going and had suffered such heavy casualties that it was a question of whether it had lost its combat effectiveness. General Rupertus asked Puller whether the 7th Marines, who had accomplished its initial mission, should relieve his battered regiment. Puller shot back, "Send reinforcements from the 7th but they will be under my command." That was the main thing that [Puller] was interested in; he wanted to keep his regiment in there and not surrender command to another regimental commander.

Rupertus honored Puller's request and ordered the division reserve, 2nd Battalion, 7th Marines, attached to the 1st Marines. Puller could not use them right away because the battalion was some distance away, inland from Orange Beach 3. Lieutenant Colonel Spencer Berger had to reassemble his men and make his way across the beach to the 1st Marines' area.

If General Rupertus had any doubts about the tactical situation, he kept them carefully concealed. He issued what would become the standard order to the regimental commanders: "Resume attack with maximum effort in all sectors at 0800 hours."

CHAPTER 14

D + 2

BLOODY NOSE RIDGE

BLOODY NOSE RIDGE

A t the end of the second day, Puller's regiment was in somewhat better tactical shape than after the initial landing, but it had taken heavy casualties, and the toughest fight was yet to come—the jagged hill mass, nicknamed Bloody Nose Ridge. The terrain was described in the Regimental Narrative:

> The ground of Peleliu's western peninsula was the worst ever encountered by the regiment in three Pacific campaigns. Along its center, the rocky spine was heaved up in a contorted mass of decayed coral, strewn with rubble, crags, ridges and gulches thrown together in a confusing maze. There were no roads, scarcely any trails. The pock-marked surface offered no secure footing even in the few level places. It was impossible to dig in: the best the men could do was pile a little coral or wood

debris around their positions. The jagged rock slashed their shoes and clothes, and tore their bodies every time they hit the deck for safety. Casualties were higher for the simple reason it was impossible to get under the ground away from the Japanese mortar barrages. Each blast hurled chunks of coral in all directions, multiplying many times the fragmentation effect of every shell. Into this the enemy dug and tunneled like moles; and there they stayed to fight to the death.

THE BLOCKHOUSE

George McMillan wrote, "The 1st Battalion started out fine, moved with surprising ease for about an hour, but then was brought up sharp by fire from a concrete blockhouse the size of a small office building which stood directly in its path. Its reinforced walls were four feet thick, and as if that were not enough protection it was also supported by twelve pillboxes all connected by a maze of tunnels." The battalion reported "that a large concrete structure 60 feet by 60 feet and about 20 feet high with 4 feet of reinforced concrete walls lay directly in the center of the battalion's advance." E. B. Sledge was glad his battalion did not have the mission. "We pitied the 1st Marines . . . [T]hey were suffering heavy casualties." Davis reported that "it could be called a fortress because of all the pillboxes surrounding it." Admiral Oldendorf had been badly mistaken. There were plenty of targets! The bunker and pillboxes were not even scratched.

Matthew Stevenson recalled that "Dawn came and with it the fiercest fighting yet, centering around a squat concrete building with three-foot thick walls, impervious to 37mm and 75mm shells firing at point-blank range." Tom Lea scanned the area. "Looking up at the head of the trail I could see the big Jap blockhouse that commanded the height." Davis ordered the lead company, now ground down to a reinforced platoon, into the attack. The men crawled forward, using whatever cover they could find to get closer to the Japanese position. The constant crack of small-arms fire and the roar of automatic weapons and exploding grenades were deafening. Here and there a figure writhed in agony, while other crumpled figures lay still in the debris. The attack ground to a halt. Davis pulled the troops back. "I took twenty-five casualties, including three dead," he recalled sadly.

First Lieutenant N. R. K. Stanford, a naval gunfire forward observer, worked his way into a position where he could call in fire. "I was lying in the coral rubble of a shattered bunker in front of the blockhouse with the Nambu fire going high to my left and the Jap mortars bursting in the ripped and twisted coconut grove behind me." The outline of the emplacement was blurred by the haze of coral dust, which hung in the air from muzzle blasts and mortar fire. "I set up my SCR-284 [radio] nearly at the top of an abandoned bunker and crawled through the loose coral to look over a broken timber revetment at the top of the bunker." His radio operator handed him the handset, and he established contact with

■ Ray Davis' battalion ran head-on into this huge Japanese blockhouse, which was still in operation despite the navy's assurance that all targets had been destroyed. Davis lost twenty-five men trying to knock it out. *Marine Corps History Division*

■ The blockhouse showing the effects of fourteen-inch naval gunfire. Huge chunks of concrete were stripped away from the steel reinforcing rods. The Japanese inside were killed by concussion as well as shrapnel. *Marine Corps History Division*

"Ironsides," the call sign of the battleship USS *Mississippi*. "Ironsides, this is Charlie Nine. Target at . . . reinforced concrete blockhouse . . . AP [armor piercing] one round. Main battery . . . commence firing."

The 14-inch shell passed low over his head with a heart-stopping crack and landed beyond the target with a huge explosion. Stanford requested an adjustment. "Down 200, one salvo." It rumbled overhead, smashing into the blockhouse. "I was numbed from the concussion and it took my eyes a few seconds to focus, but I could see that the camouflage had been stripped away and the shape of the blockhouse altered." Tom Lea described the scene. "There were dead Japs on the ground where they had been hit . . . I saw some of the bodies were nothing more than red raw meat and blood mixed with the gravelly dust of concrete and splintered logs." The battalion reported, "The nearest body was fully 30 feet away . . . a severed Jap hand lay in the doorway . . . 15 to 20 dead Japs lay inside, not a mark on them, killed by the terrific concussion."

The battalion moved out, but heavy Japanese mortar and artillery fire opened up on the exposed Marines. Casualties mounted. Private First

Class George E. Cook was hit but "steadfastly refused to be evacuated and continued to press the attack in the face of continuing fire," according to his Navy Cross citation. "Wounded again . . . he courageously elected to remain and continue the attack. Observing a wounded comrade lying in a fire-swept area . . . [he] ran forward, picked up the wounded man and carried him back to the lines . . . [W]hile returning he sustained further wounds." Both men were carried to the captured bunker where the battalion aid station and communication center had been set up. Cook was quickly stabilized by the battalion surgeon, placed in an amtrac and evacuated to a transport that had been turned into a hospital ship. Unfortunately the Marine he tried to save died before reaching the aid station.

Lieutenant Robert Fisher took up residence in the shattered structure. He marveled at the number of men the battalion surgeon handled and evacuated from the blockhouse. Fisher saw a Marine severely wounded by a mortar round. "Suddenly a shell landed squarely beside him and mangled his left forearm so badly that it hung to the elbow by only a few tendons," Fisher recounted. "Despite the severity of the wound, he walked unaided for five hundred yards to the battalion aid station, where the doctor immediately amputated the arm and sent him to the rear. I will never forget the sight of him walking back with his mutilated arm."

A stretcher bearer told of evacuating the wounded. "We ran up the road about 400 yards or so to this blockhouse where there was a lot of wounded. We started out with four of us on a stretcher but on our first trip in, two got hit. I made four trips before I came down with heat prostration." Tom Lea described a chaplain at an aid station. "He was deeply and visibly moved by the patient suffering and death. He looked very lonely, very close to God, as he bent over the shattered men so far from home. Corpsmen put a poncho, a shirt, a rag, anything handy, over the grey faces of the dead and carried them to a line on the beach, under a tarpaulin, to await the digging of graves."

Casualties among the officers and NCOs forced Davis to halt the attack and reorganize. "A" Company had been hit so hard that two

■ The remains of several Japanese soldiers who were attempting to move a weapons cart and got caught on a trail in the open. *Author collection*

platoons were combined under a surviving lieutenant. As the unit moved through some dense brush, a Japanese officer armed with a pistol and a sword suddenly charged the veteran officer. He casually turned to the BAR man on his left and muttered, "Well, why don't you shoot him?" The Marine obliged by emptying half a magazine into the enemy officer. If that wasn't enough, a *Rikusentai* (Japanese Marine) machine-gun squad tried to set up their gun to shoot them in the back. An alert rifleman spotted the group, and the combined platoon opened fire, killing all but one, who managed to throw a hand grenade that slightly wounded one of their number. Despite the wound, the Marine sharpshooter hit the Japanese soldier in the head with a single rifle shot. The platoon continued to blaze away at the Japanese in the brush. Their heavy fire kept the enemy pinned down, making it impossible for them to escape. At the end of a short firefight, the lieutenant reported "at least 40 dead Japanese were counted along a 300 yard stretch of road."

Davis' battalion continued the attack toward the Umurbrogol's outpost hills, with two abbreviated companies on line—"C" Company on the left and "A" Company on the right. At the base of Hill 160, "The Japanese turned their fire on it," George McMillan recorded, "cutting our exposed front lines to ribbons under perfect observation. The 1st was forced to push on, to seek desperately for some of that high ground to storm the Japanese out of their emplacements on the bluff." The attack was stopped cold by a Japanese 70mm mountain gun, which opened fire at point-blank range from a concrete hardened cave on the slope of Hill 160. The deadly effective howitzer fired for almost forty-five minutes, inflicting terrible casualties on the two assault companies. The battalion reported that "three of 'A' Company's machine gunners were killed and three wounded. One whole machine gun squad and gun from 'C' Company was knocked out." Davis was in awe of "Pfc. T. W. Pattee of the 81mm mortar OP, who was hit by shrapnel which tore a six-inch piece out of his left arm. It left his hand dangling by a small piece of muscle. Although severely wounded, Pattee assisted in carrying a wounded man back to the OP—and then walked another 650 yards to the aid station."

Two Sherman tanks joined the assault. Infantry alone could not do the job. "All we did was run up to Bloody Nose Ridge and throw round after round of 75mm shells into all the holes we could see in the cave areas," Pfc. Larry Kaloian, a loader, described; "[T]he infantry was right alongside us. We were protecting them and they were protecting us from a *banzai* charge or someone who might throw a Bangalore torpedo at us." As one tank tried to bring its gun to bear on the cave, an eight-pound anti-tank round slammed into its protective armor, disabling it. The crew escaped but saw "hundreds and hundreds of nicks from bullets." Minutes later, the second tank spotted the enemy field piece as it pulled back into a tunnel. The gunner declared that "when that baby comes out again, I'm going to take a crack at it." The tank fired point-blank into the cave mouth as the gun reappeared, destroying it and killing the ten-man crew. "It was like a shootout in one of the western movies," the tank commander declared. "Thank God our gunner was a crack shot."

Suddenly another position opened fire. This time it was a six-inch naval gun that had remained hidden from the pre-invasion bombardment.

Its first shell sent the frontline infantry scrambling for cover behind a three-foot road embankment. The shell passed over them and hit fifty yards behind, directly in the battalion's support units. Men armed with bazookas worked their way forward and succeeded in knocking it out. The infantrymen continued to claw upward. "The pock-marked surface offered no secure footing even in the few level places," McMillan noted. O. P. Smith wrote, "Many men were wounded by rock fragments thrown up by the blast of the Japanese mortar and artillery shells." As the men struggled forward, yard by yard, more and more were hit, and the cry "Corpsman, Corpsman" was almost constant.

Davis' attack was frustrated by the terrain. "We would fight for hours, losing men every step of the way, along one of these ledges, only to find it ended abruptly in a sheer cliff and have to fight our way back. It was terrible!" Stevenson recalled. "All the jungle foliage had long since been blasted away; the landscape seemed like the mountains of the moon." E. B. Sledge was told by survivors that they "not only received heavy shelling from the enemy caves there but deadly accurate small-arms fire as well . . . The enemy fired on them from mutually supporting positions, pinning them down and inflicting heavy losses." O. P. Smith remembered, "There were dozens of caves and pillboxes worked into the noses of the ridges and up the ravines. It was very difficult to find blind spots as the caves and pillboxes were mutually supporting. We found out later that some of the caves consisted of galleries of more than one level with several exits." One of Davis' NCOs put it another way. "When we hit them on top, they popped out of the bottom; when we hit them in the middle, they popped out of both ends."

As the battalion scrambled forward, Stevenson worried about adjacent units:

> It became clear to me that there were no friendly troops on the right flank. It was completely open, entirely vulnerable to a Japanese counter-attack which could surge all the way to the beach. I called Colonel

Puller to warn him of the peril and the urgent need for reinforcements. When I reached him on the field telephone he was true to form. First, he confused me with Steve Sabol and when this was cleared up, his gruff voice spoke its usual formula, "Just keep pushing, old man." I stood transfixed, with my runner beside me as we heard Japanese voices and the clink of weapons on the far side of the vital road. Unbelieving, I called again. This time I got lieutenant colonel "Buddy" Ross, who instantly perceived the urgency. "Stay right there, Steve, don't move; I'm sending up a unit from the Seventh. Tie them into the line as soon as they get there." Within what seemed like minutes, they appeared and immediately took up firing positions to plug the gap. No sooner was this done when there came wild shouts of "*banzai*" as the Japanese poured across the road into the devastating but crucially effective fire of the newly arrived Marines.

■ Marines searching enemy remains for anything of intelligence value. The weapon in the foreground appears to be a Japanese light machine gun. *Marine Corps History Division*

Somewhat later, a machine gun section moved through the same area, never suspecting that many Japanese were still lurking in the heavy undergrowth and had set up an ambush. As the lead squad entered the kill zone, the Japanese killed and wounded all five in a shower of grenades. The Marines never had a chance to fire a shot. However, the squad behind heard the firing and immediately assaulted through the ambush knocking down many of the enemy. They didn't have time to mop up, as they had to keep up with the assault units. As the third squad came through, they learned that "some of the Jap officers had played 'possum,' " according to Corporal Paul A. Downs, "and gave us the works on one side, while something like fifty Japs jumped us from the other. Loaded down with gear as we were, many of us couldn't even fire a shot." Many of the Marines were cut down in the deadly melee. One of the survivors, Pfc. Jack Jean French, emptied his rifle, picked up a carbine and emptied that. Weaponless, he shouted for help. "There's wounded here! Help me get them." Sergeant A. E. Crawford, his squad leader, heard the call. "The first thing I knew, there I was on my way back to help that kid." He picked up a BAR and waded into the Japanese—'Understand I got ten Japs with it,'—until running out of ammunition. He then picked up a Tommy gun and continued the fight, expending another 250 rounds of ammunition before the Japanese withdrew. Corpsmen came forward to treat the wounded, as the survivors moved forward to support the attack.

By early afternoon, "A" Company gained the ridge. Its commander reported, "We're up here, but we're knee deep in Purple Hearts." The units on its flanks could not maintain contact, so Davis had to order him back down the hill. The withdrawal was as costly as it was to go up. "They were forced to retire under heavy small arms and grenade fire from their front and machine gun fire from the 2nd Battalion sector," the battalion reported. "It was decided that possession of Hill 160 would create a gap and stretch the lines too thin." The men of "A" Company who had struggled all day to take the hill were not comforted by the rationale in the report. Morale among the survivors reached a low point.

■ A graves-registration member fills out a casualty tag for a Marine killed in action. Great care was taken to record the casualty's name and service number for proper notification of his family. *Marine Corps History Division*

Davis reported that " 'A' Company depleted itself on the bare ridge on the right as 'C' Company became seriously overextended on the left and was faltering. Everything we had was thrown in to fill the gaps. Remnants of 'A' and 'B' Companies, engineer and pioneer units and headquarters personnel were formed into a meager reserve as darkness fell."

At 1700 the battalion dug in, while engineers demolished caves and pillboxes to prevent them from being used by Japanese infiltrators. The battalion tried to soften up the Japanese for the inevitable nighttime attack. Stevenson recalled that "a forward observer, a young ensign from the battleship *Mississippi*, appeared and declared himself ready to direct fire from its big guns on the enemy positions. For the rest of the night we called in salvo after salvo, hour after hour, on the honeycombed ridges facing the fast dwindling strength of our companies. However, as morning came the fire ceased and the Jap machine guns and mortars resumed their lethal chorus." Ray Davis and his command group—Jim Rodgers and Nikolai Stevenson—huddled together to plan the attack for the following morning. "Clearly it was to be the battalion's last throw of the dice," Stevenson reported. "If Bloody Nose Ridge could be taken, our fire from its height into the enemy-held crevices below would eventually dislodge them and Peleliu [would be] won at last." His assessment was more wishful than prophetic.

The battalion reported that it had captured or destroyed "one large blockhouse, thirty-seven pillboxes, twenty-four caves, two anti-tank 47mm guns, two 70mm mountain guns, one six-inch naval gun and numerous machine guns. Over 300 enemy dead were counted." A footnote at the end of the report stated: "At the point where the battalion OP was set up, three enemy carrier pigeons were shot and the attached messages were sent to R-2 [regimental intelligence]." Battalion casualties for the day due to enemy action were 14 killed in action, 81 evacuated and 2 missing in action. Many more were victims of the 112-degree heat and combat fatigue. The battalion total strength at this time was 18 officers and 474 enlisted men.

An officer of the battalion tried to explain the term "combat fatigue," commonly known as "shell-shock":

■ Hill 200 (left) stopped Honsowetz's 2nd Battalion in its tracks. Casualties were heavy, and yet Puller ordered him to continue the attack. Japanese on Hill 210 (right) poured a devastating fire into the Marines' flank. The terrain shows the effects of bombardment by air, artillery and naval gunfire. *Marine Corps History Division*

To those who have never seen it occur, combat fatigue is hardly understandable. But those who have experienced the constriction of the blood vessels in the stomach and the sudden whirling of the brain that occurs when a large shell bursts nearby or a friend has his eyes or entrails torn out by shrapnel can easily understand the man who cannot control his muscles and who stares wildly. It isn't fear alone that causes shock to the system. Often it is the knowledge of his impotence, his inability to help his ship-mate who is whistling through a hole in his chest, that

225

■ A Marine Corsair provides close support by dropping napalm. Note that the aircraft has not even retracted its wheels after taking off from the island's airfield. Many claimed that the missions were the shortest bombing runs of the war. *Marine Corps History Division*

momentarily snaps a man's brain. Quite often, under the stress of combat fatigue, a man will perform acts of heroism that a reasoning mind would call foolhardy.

Ray Davis recalled an instance where one of his most valuable officers succumbed to fatigue. "I noticed Lieutenant Maples was in a state bordering on war-psychosis. He led his men forward into withering fire, exposing himself to assist his men. He was suffering from fatigue and the shock of seeing his men fall—but he never relaxed and kept moving in an entranced way. Finally one day he was shot in the abdomen and died just before reaching the hospital ship. This was his third campaign and he had distinguished himself in each."

SPITFIRE TWO (HONSOWETZ)

Russ Honsowetz's battalion also ran into a buzz saw. It guided on the narrow, coral-surfaced West Road and made good time, until chaos erupted. A torrent of fire from a two-hundred-foot ridge, known as Hill 200, poured into his lead element, quickly knocking out a tank and two amtracs. A deadly Japanese 37mm mountain gun fired point-blank into them from a cleverly hidden cave. Enemy machine gunners and snipers added to the firestorm of lead. Russell Davis was with the assault company as it worked its way "across a clearing littered with stumps and coral and the scrap of war, up and down low hillocks and through a draw, and then onto the foot of the ridge. We got part way up the ridge and then the hills opened and fire poured down on our heads." Those men not bowled over in the initial burst of fire scrambled to find shelter. Davis and two others were "plastered down into a hole and there we lay while the world heaved up all around us. We could do nothing but huddle together in terror. We couldn't go ahead . . . we couldn't go back. We were witless and helpless, with nothing to do but lie and take it."

The attack slowed. But "[t]he slightest concentration of Marines brought heavy fire at once," Bruce Watkins lamented. Puller, monitoring events at his CP, was incensed at the slow progress and called Honsowetz to demand action. "Look, Honsowetz, I want the sonofabitchin' ridge before sundown . . . and I mean, goddamnit, I want it!" Honsowetz renewed his efforts to get the battalion moving. He requested additional tank and artillery support. Marine 105mm and 75mm artillery batteries swung into action from their positions south of the airport. Russell Davis crouched beside an artillery forward observer as he called in the target coordinates. "The shell came shrieking over and made a vast flame against a distant hill, beyond a deep draw," Davis recalled. "The FO shouted corrections into the phone, 'Right 50, drop 200.' [Next he shouted,] 'On the way,'" as a warning that the artillery battery had fired. Davis hunched even further down behind a large rock as "shells swished by in a steady stream and the hillside flamed and writhed under the barrage." Yard by yard, the advance continued.

Navy carrier pilots on station over the island flew in to bomb the Japanese positions that were holding up the assault. Bruce Watkins said he

> heard the whine of a dive bomber coming directly at us. To this day, I believe the pilot mistook us for Japs . . . [H]e released his bomb, probably a 500 pounder, and we all watched as it headed toward us in a slight arc. Sure that we were going to be decimated, we could only hug the ground and pray. Miraculously, the bomb hit dead center on the bunker, collapsing it and killing the Japanese within. The concussion stunned us and covered us with white coral dust. We got shakily to our feet, like so many ghosts, in great wonder at being alive. No one had been hit.

As the assault ground forward, the extreme heat and lack of water put men out of action. "The heat was terrible," Russell Davis recalled. "One big, redheaded man horribly burned and cracked around the face and lips, suddenly reared out of his hole like a wild horse. 'I can't take the heat,' he bellowed. 'I can take the war but not the heat!'" O. P. Smith noted, "The thermometer went up to 105 degrees. In the intense fighting over rugged ground the men soon exhausted their canteens. Resupply was difficult. We began to have a good many cases of heat exhaustion." Water was brought ashore in fifty-five-gallon drums, but distribution to frontline units was almost impossible. Those lucky enough to get the

■ The fighting in the mountains was brutal . . . often more vertical than horizontal. At times the Marines had to be mountaineers. This Marine struggles to climb to the top of the ridge. *Marine Corps History Division*

water found that it was almost undrinkable. The oil drums had been improperly steam-cleaned, and as a result, the water was fouled. In addition some of the barrels had rusted in the tropical heat, polluting the water. "Some stupid son-of-a-bitch sure as hell goofed," an expressive NCO groused bitterly. "God, how I'd like to get my hands on that . . . good for nothing . . . so help me, I'd kill him without a second thought."

Within an hour, two company commanders were wounded in action. Bruce Watkins was close to the "E" Company commander when he was hit. "Captain Joe Gayle dashed up the steep spine of the ridge. Just as he reached the top, a bullet struck him in the neck and he tumbled down the ridge for all the world like a Hollywood movie. Lieutenant Marc Jaffe stopped his fall and tried to hold back the bleeding with a finger on each side of his neck. How much this helped, we would never know, but Joe lived to tell the tale with only temporary paralysis and the most interesting scars—like nickels on either side of his neck." The "F" Company commander was also wounded, and his leaderless company was badly scattered.

Honsowetz ordered an injured lieutenant to "get all the 'F' Company men you are able to find and if you are not too badly wounded stand by with them for orders." Suddenly the battalion command post was bracketed by artillery fire and several men wounded, including the adjutant. Two amtracs in the CP area were knocked out by artillery fire. Just before noon, "G" Company reported eighty-seven casualties.

The battalion slowly advanced toward its objective, Hill 200. The fighting was often hand-to-hand, close-in, life-and-death struggles with knife and bayonet, the weapon of choice. Bruce Watkins remembered an incident that stuck with him:

> Just to my left was Private First Class Darden . . . As we started up the slope, a Jap officer dashed out of a cave fifty feet in front of us. With his saber raised and coming downhill . . . he headed for the startled Darden, who raised his M-1 rifle and began to fire steadily at the Japanese. I thought he had the situation well in hand

and I didn't fire. The Jap, however, still kept coming, although I could see Darden's bullets strike him. He finally made one final lunge, just reaching the unbelieving Marine's boot with the tip of his saber as the clip ejected from the M-1 signaling the last of eight rounds.

By sheer guts, the exhausted survivors fought their way to the top of the ridge just prior to twilight and tried to build protective shelters. It was impossible to dig foxholes in the granite-like coral, so they took cover in shell holes or piled up rocks. Incredible as it seemed, a communicator managed to string a telephone line to Honsowetz's CP. One of the first calls was from Puller. "How are things going?" "Not very good," Honsowetz replied. "I lost a lot of men." Puller asked, "How many did you lose?" "I don't have a good count yet, but I think I lost a couple hundred men." Puller immediately demanded, "How many Japs did you kill?" Taken off balance, Honsowetz responded, "Well, we overran one position that had twenty-five in it. We got 'em all. There were a lot of Jap bodies around, but I don't know how many. Maybe fifty." Puller responded angrily, "Jesus Christ, Honsowetz, what the hell are the American people gonna think? Losing 200 fine young Marines and killing only fifty Japs! I'm gonna put you down for 500."

The loss of the hill forced Colonel Nakagawa to move his CP. He reported that, "under the protection of heavy naval gunfire, an enemy unit composed of two tanks and approximately two companies of infantry successfully advanced to a high spot on the east side of Nakagawa."

SPITFIRE SIX (PULLER)

In his nightly report to division, Puller stated that "Front line units have been decimated." The regiment had lost 1,236 men. Puller called Col. John T. Selden, the division chief of staff, and asked for replacements.

"Johnny, half my regiment is gone. I've got to have replacements if I'm to carry out division orders tomorrow morning."

"You know we have no replacements, Lewie," Selden responded.

"I told you before we came ashore that we should have at least one regiment in reserve. We're not fighting a third of the men we brought in . . . all those damn specialists you brought."

"Anything wrong with your orders, Lewie?"

"Give me some of those 17,000 men on the beach," Puller retorted.

"You can't have them, they're not trained infantry."

"Give 'em to me and by nightfall tomorrow they'll be trained infantry," Puller replied grimly.

A staff officer at division thought that Rupertus, despite the heavy losses, still believed it would be a quick victory. "The overall feeling seemed to be that a breakthrough was imminent. Enemy resistance would collapse, or at worst, disintegrate as had happened on Saipan, Tinian, and Guam after a certain point had passed. The trouble with this reasoning was that on the other islands the collapse had occurred when U.S. troops reached favorable terrain and had been heralded by at least one suicidal *banzai* charge. But there were no *banzais* on Peleliu, and the terrain was becoming worse instead of better."

Puller hung up and stumbled through the darkness to pass the word to the battalion commanders. "We press the attack at eight o'clock in the morning. No change. Full speed. Use every man." He came back limping. His leg was beginning to swell—the old wound from Guadalcanal was acting up. Selden called back: "Puller, you got my orders?" "Yes, you needn't explain further. I just came back from my battalions. We're going to take ground tomorrow without replacements. We're willing to try, but don't forget we're just going to add ten or fifteen percent to our casualties."

O. P. Smith wrote a critical assessment. "The operations of the 1st Marines had been heartening. There had been an advance all along the line and, in the face of very stiff opposition and full scale fortifications, some of the commanding ground north of the airfield had been taken. Our hold on Hill 200 was tenuous. The Japanese still held Hill 210, but we were in firm possession of Hills 100, 180, and 150. The cost in casualties in the 1st Marines through September 17th had been 1,236. The 3rd Battalion had only 473 effectives, of whom 200 were headquarters personnel. The excessive heat was becoming an important factor in the fight. Men were beginning to drop from heat exhaustion."

SPITFIRE THREE (SABOL)
The 3rd Battalion report noted that "Our advance continued slowly through difficult terrain against light sniper fire." At 1700, the battalion brought up supplies and dug in for the night, with all three companies on the line. A swamp kept them from tying in, but the gaps were covered by 60mm and 81mm mortars. Sabol reported losing 59 men and estimated that 344 enemy had been killed in action.

CHAPTER 15

D + 3

INTO THE BREACH

In order to continue the attack, Puller put all available headquarters personnel in the front lines. "Regiment sent forward several officers and men," according to Stevenson, "a dozen or two cooks, bakers and truck drivers, converted overnight into riflemen . . . and a 37mm gun." The division also furnished one hundred men from the Shore Party battalion. More importantly, Rupertus released the division's reserve, Lt. Col. Spencer Berger's 2nd Battalion, 7th Regiment, to the 1st Marines. Upon receipt of the authorization, Puller sent a warning order to Berger to "relieve the 1st Battalion at daybreak the morning of the 18th and to be in position to attack at 0700."

Under sporadic mortar and small-arms fire, Berger and his operations officer, Maj. John F. Weber, carefully worked their way forward to the 1st Battalion's CP. Davis' number two man, Maj. Nikolai S. Stevenson, quickly briefed them on the tactical situation. Stevenson painted a pretty dim picture. There were dozens of mutually supporting caves and pillboxes housing riflemen, machine gunners, mortars,

■ A natural cave improved by the Japanese and made into a headquarters command post. Often the caves consisted of several levels, multiple exits and deep laterals, which were almost impossible to knock out. *Marine Corps History Division*

rockets and field pieces. The Japanese had carved them into the noses of the ridge and up the ravines so that it was extremely difficult to find blind spots. Many of the positions were at the base of the cliffs, others were partway up, and some were on top. Often they consisted of galleries of more than one level with several exits, with baffles to lessen the effect of direct fire and flamethrowers. He pointed out that a particularly effective Japanese tactic was to run a field piece out of a cave, fire, and then run it back inside before we could react. Finally, Stevenson gave him a summary of casualties, which were shockingly extreme—over half the battalion was gone!

After receiving the sobering brief, Berger, Weber and a 1st Battalion guide made a very hazardous reconnaissance around the lines. Berger and Weber then met Davis in his advance OP, where Berger attempted

■ Battle weary Marines work their way back from the front lines. The term "raggedy ass" Marines got its meaning from the man in the center . . . his trousers are shredded, cartridge belt is missing, helmet askew . . . but still on his feet and carrying his rifle. *Marine Corps History Division*

to get the lay of the land. He had trouble orienting himself on the ground because of the incredibly broken terrain. "There was no such thing as a continuous attacking line. Elements of the same company, even platoon, were attacking in every direction of the compass, with large gaps in between. When companies were asked for front lines they were apt to give points where the company commander knew or thought he had some men . . . There were countless little salients and counter-salients existing." At one point, Berger called for prep fires on an objective and found that "some of the target areas lay behind or squarely upon positions shown on some unit overlays as having been occupied the previous day."

The two men worked out the details of the relief—a very difficult maneuver because the entire area was under Japanese observation and fire. At 0600 the remnants of Davis' battalion started withdrawing from their exposed positions as Berger's men replaced them. "Slowly we rose, formed two files on each side of the cart track leading back," Stevenson recalled, thankful to be alive. "The relief took place in full view of the Japs atop Bloody Nose Ridge. If they had opened up, it would have been the final and apocalyptic carnage. Inexplicably, they didn't. We marched slowly away, some of the men contorted with the dry heaves, brought on by the salt tablets given to lessen the dehydration of the murderous heat." Sometime later, the Japanese "welcomed" Berger by shelling his CP for ten minutes with heavy mortar fire, causing ten casualties.

About this time Puller moved his OP to a small quarry, within easy rifle shot of Hill 210. Berger was embarrassed to find Puller "operating behind some outcropping of coral, closer to the enemy than [my] command post. In fact, it was difficult to get out an operations map and read it without exposing ourselves." Despite the enemy fire and the difficult terrain, Berger's men got into position and prepared to kick off the attack on schedule.

At 0700, the attack began after a thirty-minute bombardment that included, planes, artillery and naval gunfire. The infantry moved out, "E" Company on the left, "F" Company on the right. The Japanese immediately responded with mortars, artillery and heavy small-arms and machine-gun fire. Within minutes the two companies were taking heavy casualties and were pinned down. They requested more stretcher bearers and tank support. The battalion reported, "With the aid of the tanks, the companies were extricated and the attack moved forward." The heat was intense and, when combined with the exceedingly difficult terrain, was causing many men "to become physically exhausted and snapping mentally." It was reported that "the coral hills rising over 200 feet dropped off into steep ravines and draws running in all directions and were covered with automatic weapons placed in every conceivable position." The attack had run into a meat grinder.

Berger braved the enemy fire and went forward to check the lines and talk with his company commanders. O. P. Smith recalled somewhat humorously that "Berger had grown a black mustache of Japanese style. He wore a cap that resembled a Japanese forage hat. If you took a quick glance at him, he resembled a burly Japanese officer. It is not a good idea to look like a Japanese." Somehow Berger avoided being shot and laid

■ A flamethrowing LVT burns out a Japanese position. The jellied gasoline not only burned the occupants of the caves . . . but also sucked the air from them, smothering those further inside. *Marine Corps History Division*

plans for a continuation of the attack with his commanders. The attack continued, "moving forward slowly, with tanks . . . to knock out caves on the sides of the ridges."

During the advance, an "F" Company squad was ordered to withdraw after it was partially cut off. It came under fire from enemy positions above and from the rear. Several men took cover in a depression and exchanged hand grenades with the Japanese. "Private First Class Charles H. Roan was wounded by an enemy grenade which fell close to their position and immediately realizing the imminent peril to his comrades when another grenade landed in the midst of the group. He unhesitatingly flung himself on it, covering it with his body and absorbing the full impact of the explosion," stated his posthumous Medal of Honor citation.

A flamethrower LVT was sent up to burn out the Japanese, but accurate small-arms fire wounded two of its crew and set it ablaze. The driver of the vehicle, Pfc. Clarence O. Kelley, "steadfastly fought the blaze until ordered to abandon the vehicle by his crew chief, after which he reported that this weapon and tractor were out of action and made his way back to the conflagration under intense mortar and sniper fire," his Navy Cross citation recorded. "Ignoring the flames and exploding ammunition, he drove the burning tractor to an area where the fire was extinguished." The companies reported "heavy losses among the flamethrower and bazooka operators"—replacements were sent forward. Late in the day, the battalion halted for the night—casualties had been heavy, 26 KIA (killed in action) and 88 WIA (wounded in action), against an estimated 225 enemy dead. Berger reported, "Toward dusk Japs infiltrated around the CP in increasing numbers and we were seldom free from sniper fire." He directed artillery and his own 81mm mortars to lay down harassing fire all night long.

SPITFIRE THREE (SABOL)

Third Battalion moved out on schedule, but "our advance was very slow. Our guide was right and the resistance and bad terrain encountered by the battalion [2/7] on our right held us back," Sabol reported. The battalion stopped at 1600, after advancing for most of the day against only minor opposition. Even so, it suffered thirty-three casualties.

SPITFIRE TWO (HONSOWETZ)
HILL 200

As the battalion prepared to attack, Bruce Watkins stared at the forbidding high ground. "That hill looked tough, and if I had been frightened before, I was thoroughly frightened now. I could only imagine the hail of fire we would receive climbing that hill. However, I also knew that I had only to lead and every man in the first platoon would be right behind me." Rifleman Dan Toledo was in the attack. "Our company was the first unit to assault the high ground north of where the worst fighting would occur. The first ridge is labeled Bloody Nose Ridge . . . but that's not its real name. We named it 'Prostitute Ridge' because we climbed off and on it so many times." It was completely bare of vegetation. The undergrowth had been blown off by shell fire and bombs.

"Old Marines talk of Bloody Nose Ridge as though it were one," Russell Davis recalled, "but I remember it as a series of crags, ripped bare of all standing vegetation, peeled down to the rotted coral, rolling in smoke, crackling with heat and stinking of wounds and death. In my memory it was always dark up there, even though it must have blazed under the afternoon sun, because the temperature went up over 115 degrees, and men cracked wide open from the heat. It must have been the color of the ridge that made me remember it as always dark—the coral was stained and black, like bad teeth. Or perhaps it was because there was almost always smoke and dust and flying coral in the air."

Watkins decided to "take the first and second squads straight up the front while Monty [Sergeant Monty Montgomery] took the third up the left flank, thus hoping to give the Japs a more spread-out target." Russell Davis had a grandstand view of the assault: "[T]he riflemen were assembled at the base of the cliff. The orders were to take the cliff. It was a stupid order." In the hole next to Watkins, a Catholic Marine clutched his rosary, praying for deliverance. Watkins was inspired "to employ what I had come to call my thirty-second prayer. Mine went something like, 'Father, let me do my job and do it well. I don't ask You to save me, but help me to be a good leader. If I must be hit, give me the strength to carry on and Your will always be done.'" The attack kicked off. "The hill was pretty steep and I never felt so exposed as scrambling over the top of that ridge first. Just before we took off a mortar shell hit in Kincaid's squad leaving him only half a dozen men but they came just the same." Davis was appalled. "We had lost heavily, ever since the beach, but I had not realized how bad the losses were until our companies moved out on the cliff. Clawing and crawling up the cliff went platoons that were no more than squads, and companies that were no more than large platoons. I counted one platoon. It mustered eighteen men on that push. But they went up."

O. P. Smith noted that, "In desperate fighting progress was made on both sides . . . but the enemy continued to lay down heavy mortar and artillery barrages, accompanied by vicious counterattacks and withering small arms fire, all along the lines, particularly on the forward nose of Hill 200." Dozens of men were wounded, four of whom lay in the open under direct Japanese fire. Hospital Corpsman Russell Johnson "unhesitatingly pressed forward against the merciless barrage and succeeded in carrying three wounded men back to our lines. Observing a fourth casualty far in advance of our lines, he again risked his life to effect a rescue, but was fatally struck down by hostile fire," his posthumous Navy Cross stated.

Watkins' platoon was terribly exposed. "A concentrated shelling began and great chunks of rock were blown up as the Japs found the range. In a very few minutes, casualties were severe. It became clear that the ridge was untenable." The company commander urgently requested "all available stretcher bearers." The entire line was pinned down by mortar fire. Honsowetz called Puller and pleaded for reinforcements—"the situation was desperate." "From the base of the cliff," Davis recounted, "we could pick out each man and follow him until he got hit, went to ground, or climbed to the top. As they toiled . . . Japanese dashed out to roll grenades down on them, and sometimes to lock, body to body, in desperate wrestling matches. Knives and bayonets flashed on the hillside."

The Japanese fire was too much, and Watkins ordered his platoon off the ridge. "It was my personal code to be the last one to leave if we had to abandon a position. This was one of two times that I had to do it. As men and stretcher bearers stumbled down the steep slope, I saw a red-haired private take a direct hit. He was vaporized! One minute he was there and the next gone without a trace." Honsowetz requested smoke to mask the withdrawal. "Halfway down the hill," Watkins recounted, "a large shell landed very close and a large shard, the size of my arm, came at me with a deadly whirring sound. I was sure that it was going to take

■ Getting the casualties off the hill was a physically exhausting effort, as well as a dangerous one. Japanese snipers drew no distinction between fighters and saviors. Dozens of stretcher bearers were lost attempting to bring in a wounded man. *Marine Corps History Division*

my head off. Instead, it cut the strap of my helmet. My knees turned to water and I crumpled to the ground. It was perhaps the single most frightening moment of the war for me."

The only reinforcements at hand were the remnants of 1st Battalion. Puller called Ray Davis and ordered him to send a company to Honsowetz. It was the fate of 1st Battalion to be piecemealed into the fight. "With a heavy heart I watched them go," Stevenson remarked sadly, "knowing so well that in combat any supporting unit is always given the dirtiest, the most dangerous assignment."

An hour later, Lt. Francis D. "Bonzai" Rineer of "B" Company reported to a dugout that served as the 2nd Battalion CP. Honsowetz gave Rineer a quick brief and then personally led him to the edge of a wood, where he pointed out Hill 205, slightly forward and to the right of Hill 210. He ordered Rineer to seize it. Honsowetz promised two machine gun sections to support the attack. Rineer moved his men forward and spread them out in an attack formation, using the road as a line of departure. At his signal the company moved out and cautiously advanced up the hill. Surprisingly, there was little resistance and the company seized the high ground with only twelve casualties.

Rineer found that the captured ground was only an isolated point on a larger ridge system and decided to continue the attack. "Their charge to the top of the hill was one of the bravest and yet most disastrous acts of the campaign," according to Robert Fisher. His Navy Cross citation describes how "with only forty men left in his company, he assaulted the steep coral ridge . . . in the face of intense fire emanating from hostile machine guns entrenched in coral caves and personally remained in the midst of the furious fighting . . . until seriously wounded in both legs. Steadfastly refusing evacuation, he courageously struggled forward." Bravery alone could not overcome the overwhelming enemy fire, and Rineer was forced to withdraw his battered command, now numbering twenty-six men.

Major Frank O. Hugh wrote that the ridge system was, "The most formidable terrain obstacle yet encountered, an incredible complex of up-ended peaks and palisades which was to gain evil fame under the name of the Five Sisters." Lieutenant Rineer related that, "Mortars from behind the hill and machine guns from the ravine to our flank[,] and artillery fire from the nose itself pinned us down almost at once."

Meanwhile Watkins' platoon "reached a relatively safe area at the foot of the slope and regrouped." His platoon numbered about thirty and was badly shaken by the heavy shelling. They were also in need of food and rest. "About this time," Watkins related,

> Lt. Col. Honsowetz approached me with an order to go back up the hill. It was an emotional moment for me and the only time I ever refused to carry out an order. I told him that I would not order my men up there again until the gun that blew us off was silenced. However, I would personally go up with him if he felt that was a

■ A typical example of the terrain in the Umurbrogols. The coral limestone ridges formed jagged peaks and sharp ridges, which had to be climbed by men burdened with weapons and ammunition . . . and under fire. *Marine Corps History Division*

solution. He gave me a long look and then turned away. He knew that I spoke the truth and that going back up would have sacrificed more men needlessly . . . I realize he was under tremendous pressure from Colonel Puller.

A jubilant Nakagawa prematurely notified Lieutenant General Inoue that "Since dawn the enemy has been concentrating their forces, vainly trying to approach Higashiyama [Bloody Nose Ridge] and Kansokuyama [Hill 300] with fourteen tanks and one infantry battalion under powerful aids of air and artillery fire. However, they were again put to rout, receiving heavy losses."

Second Battalion was dying. Honsowetz phoned Puller. "I told Chesty that my situation was desperate and there was no possible way I could take Hill 210 without reinforcements. Puller repeated his orders to take the ridge, and I said, 'Christ, we can't do it, the casualties are too much and we've been fighting all day and all night.' And he said, 'You sound all right, you're there. Goddammit, you get those troops in there and you take the goddamn hill!'" Thirty-year-old Russ Honsowetz swallowed hard, gathered himself together and led his men forward. "Colonel Honsowetz showed up waving his .45 in the air and shouting for us to move up the ridge," Watkins related. "We rose up then, those pitiful remnants, by individuals and little groups and started up the ridge." They desperately "clawed up and over razorback crests, shinnying coral pinnacles, plunging down into sheer-sided gullies and ravines, dodging behind boulders, [and] by evening . . . had gained the forward slope and were firmly, if uncomfortably, established."

Watkins led his survivors back up the hill. "Kincaid and I kept moving along the ridge building up a line until we got on top of a little pinnacle of rock. It was getting darker but on that little peak we had magnificent observation of a great deal of the island. So I decided that I would spend the night there with one other man and told the boys to dig in the best they could in the coral surface." "The ground was tougher than concrete," according to one combat correspondent. Watkins said, "It was a pretty vulnerable spot as the ridge dipped and then sloped up again and we were all that would prevent an attack from sweeping down on the platoon's left flank."

Two hours later the Japanese attacked. "There must have been a couple hundred of them and we had about eighty men in the whole company; [between] my platoon and Lee Height's platoon [we had] maybe fifty men [on location]." The Japanese did not know that Watkins and

■ A 105mm howitzer just after firing. The expended brass cartridge case is just about to hit the ground. Unfortunately the eighteen-pound shell was not heavy enough to penetrate the enemy's concrete and coral reinforced positions. *Marine Corps History Division*

Kincaid were on the pinnacle because the two had been careful to only use hand grenades, which did not give their position away, as the flash of a rifle would. "We just kept still and waited; we could hear 'em down the slope about 40 feet [away] messin' around," Watkins related. Tension mounted unbearably when a knee mortar started firing over their heads.

The two Marines were on the horns of a dilemma; they had to try to knock out the mortar—and if they did, it might give their position away. "Well, we couldn't wait any longer, so by the light of the next flare, we threw grenades and used [our] Tommy guns. We knocked out the mortar . . . and then about fifty of them came down the ridge in single file." Watkins called for mortars and kept giving corrections until "finally the shells landed right in 'em." A Japanese officer spotted them and led a charge toward the two Marines. "He swung his saber on Kincaid first. Kincaid's Tommy jammed . . . but he warded if off. He included me on the next swing and we both fell flat. Kincaid grabbed his pistol and threw it in his face which gave me half a second I needed to get ole Betsy [Tommy gun] into operation. He fell backwards on the other Japs." The two men held off attack after attack until dawn. As the sun came up, they counted about forty dead Japanese around their position. During the fight, Kincaid was wounded in the forehead by a spent bullet but, as his Navy Cross citation recorded, "for fifteen minutes more continued his fierce defense of the position."

At the end of the third day, the 1st Marines had suffered 1,500 casualties, one half its total strength. Lieutenant Colonel Lewis W. Walt talked to Puller at a command conference. "He was absolutely sick over the loss of his men; he thought we were getting them killed for nothing."

CHAPTER 16

D + 4

RESUME THE ATTACK

"All infantry units will resume the attack with maximum effort in all sectors at 0830 hours on 19 September."

Rupertus attack order

SPITFIRE (PULLER)

By D plus 4, the regiment was in shambles. Rifle companies had melted away, squads disappeared, platoons combined—the old timers were all gone, replaced by inexperienced youngsters and headquarters personnel—and yet the attack continued. Puller recalled 1st Battalion's "A" Company, 65 men and 2 officers out of its normal strength of 235, and threw it into 2/1's line. It gamely advanced over a fire swept plateau, "where the heat was so terrific there were more casualties from heat exhaustion than the enemy fire." They pressed on until halted by a sheer cliff that dropped 150 feet. At 1320, its commander, Lieutenant Burke, reported that the adjacent unit, 2/7, was pinned down and could not cross the ridge." Honsowetz ordered him to "Advance at once across the ridge to relieve pressure on them." A desperate Burke responded, "We cannot move out as there is heavy machine gun fire raking the entire ridge."

An equally desperate Honsowetz bawled out the young officer, "It is necessary that you move out at all costs." He then added, "I am giving you

■ The men advanced over the rough terrain—blasted trees and coral rock—
into the heart of the enemy's stronghold. Here a BAR man accompanies
riflemen and a flamethrower team. *Marine Corps History Division*

a direct order; you will move out at once!" At that point, Honsowetz lost
contact with Burke. It can only be surmised that Burke realized it was an
impossible mission and turned off his radio. Sometime later, contact was
established and "A" Company finally received permission to withdraw in
the face of a perfect storm of Japanese fire. Only six men of the assault
force were still unwounded at the end of the day. Captain Rogers, a division staff officer said, "We came to know as a fact that Colonel Puller
distanced himself from the reality of what his regiment was up against."

Puller's depleted regiment had come up against the southern ramparts of Nakagawa's defensive pocket. The ramparts were later known as the Five Sisters. O. P. Smith described them as

> almost sheer . . . It was not possible to work from Sister to Sister as there were precipitous drops between peaks. On the east side . . . was a series of rugged peaks, later called The Five Brothers, also generally sheer. Closing the north end of the pocket was Baldy Ridge . . . [T]he west side of the pocket was closed by what was known as the China Wall. This rugged pinnacle defied scaling except with alpine equipment. The bulk of the Japanese were housed in caves around the interior face of the pocket. On the peaks . . . the Japanese maintained relays of snipers and machine gunners, which were reached by ladders, prepared paths, or shafts from caves below. The approaches to the positions were so few and so exposed that a minimum number of men could stop a much larger force. Thousands of rounds of artillery, mortars and bombs had poured in and around the pocket . . . but the Japanese inside the caves were untouched.

Colonel Harold D. "Bucky" Harris, commanding officer of the 5th Marines, commandeered a flight in an observation plane to get a close-up view of the terrain. "I was appalled at the sight of those ridges from the air. Sheer coral walls with caves everywhere, box canyons, crevices, rock-strewn cliffs, and all defended by well-hidden Japs. I knew then that there would be no breakthrough." After returning from the flight, he briefed Rupertus and Puller. "I told them what I had seen, and suggested they fly over and see for themselves. They just smiled and said they had maps." Harris lamented, "I knew then we were in for a bloody siege." A 1st Regiment survivor of the first attack told a buddy in the 5th Marines,

■ A destroyed Japanese six-inch gun, with the grisly remains of one of its crewmen draped over the breach. Many of these heavy guns remained intact during the naval bombardment and caused heavy casualties after the landing. *Marine Corps History Division*

"They got them poor boys makin' frontal attacks with fixed bayonets on that damn ridge and they can't even see the Nips that are shootin' at 'em. One poor kid was really depressed; don't see no way he can come out alive."

At 0630, "B" Company was pounded with a heavy barrage of mortar, artillery and automatic weapons fire, suffering fifteen more casualties, one of whom was Pfc. Merle E. Manahan. "While firing a support mission and, without orders, Manahan displaced his gun forward and advanced in the face of heavy hostile mortar, machine gun and rifle fire until he found an exposed position from which he could observe the Japanese automatic weapon," his Navy Cross citation states. "When [his] gun crew became casualties, Manahan manned his gun alone and, although wounded four times, maintained a steady volume of fire at point-blank range until he silenced the enemy weapon."

Honsowetz pulled the surviving members of "B" Company back in reserve and placed it in an open field just to the right of his CP. Suddenly a Japanese six-inch gun—with "an extremely high velocity and a large bursting radius"—opened fire on the exposed Marines. "The shell whistled in with the sound of ripping silk and exploded with a blast that could be felt for one hundred yards." Several men took cover behind a steel donkey-engine dug into a revetment in the center of the field. A report of the incident stated that

> the Japs were using this as a reference point, sending in a barrage of 12 shells, then waiting for several minutes, then another load of shells. One shell burst on the revetment and a man screamed. Second Lieutenant A. A. Hoover . . . jumped to his feet to go to the wounded man just as another shell screamed in and burst thirty yards away. A large fragment cut through Lieutenant Hoover's utility knife, his canteen and belt and tore an enormous hole in his abdomen. Lieutenant Hoover died while being carried back to the Battalion Aid Station. This was the loss of one who had won the respect of every man and officer in the battalion for his courage and judgment in action.

"B" Company's effective strength at this time was two officers and thirty-five men, of which the mortar section consisted of ten men and one officer; the three rifle platoons totaled twenty-five men and the company commander.

SPITFIRE THREE (SABOL)

Third Battalion jumped off in the attack on schedule at 0700, after plastering the area in front of their lines with artillery, naval gunfire and LCI rockets. They quickly gained four hundred yards with light casualties but had to hold up in order to maintain contact with 2/7.

MUSTANG TWO (BERGER)

Lieutenant Colonel Berger's 2/7 started off the day by bombarding the ridges with artillery, mortar and naval gunfire. He also ordered up a platoon of five tanks and an LVT flamethrower. Berger had them standby at his CP, prepared to support the attack scheduled to commence at 0700. All companies were in line—"E" Company on the left, "G" Company in the middle and "F" Company on the right flank.

The attack kicked off on time and immediately ran into a buzz saw. Heavy Japanese artillery, mortars and small-arms fire blanketed the assault. Private First Class Russell J. Massaro "voluntarily and without hesitation took an automatic rifle and courageously made his way toward a concealed Japanese machine gun nest. Upon locating the emplacement, he skillfully delivered intense, accurate fire into it, effectively silencing the enemy weapon," according to his posthumous Navy Cross citation.

Berger sent the armored vehicles forward in support—one tank and the LVT to "E" Company, and two tanks to work the draws west of the ridge. The battalion reported that "the terrain was rugged, visibility exceedingly poor, there were only poor fields of fire and it was very difficult for the companies to use their mortars and automatic weapons to full advantage." The Japanese did not have this problem and continued to pour in a searing fire. Private First Class George Lilja "ranged the entire front area, carrying his unwieldy [bazooka] and heavy ammunition load up and down the ridge . . . blasting the heavily defended Japanese caves, neutralizing many strong points. When his company was held up by deadly volleys from a powerful enemy pillbox, he valiantly proceeded under the withering hail to an exposed position

■ A tank platoon and a rifle company advance into the Horseshoe. The ridge on the left was named the Five Brothers, while Walt Ridge is on the right. Note the white smoke from an exploding white phosphorus shell. *Marine Corps History Division*

■ The Sherman tanks and the infantry continue to advance at the base of Five Brothers. At any moment the Japanese might open up with mortars and artillery—deadly to the men but seldom fatal for the armored machines. *Marine Corps History Division*

. . . and silenced the heavy Japanese installation," as his posthumous Navy Cross citation stated.

"E" Company's tank drew such accurate mortar fire that it was pulled back—tanks were both a blessing and a curse for the infantry. On one hand they were great for knocking out enemy strong points, but on the other hand they attracted "the eye," becoming a magnet for artillery. Armor protected the crew, while the infantry could only dig in.

By mid-morning, the companies reported small gains—"E" Company 75 yards, "F" Company 150 yards and "G" Company made it to the top of a small ridge. All companies were maintaining contact but at a very

■ This photo shows the deadly blast cloud of an exploding artillery shell. The men immediately around the lead tank are seeking cover, while several men can be seen putting distance between themselves and the tanks. *Marine Corps History Division*

high price—"F" Company reported only one hundred effectives left. Artillery forward observers were busy picking out targets for counter-battery fire. Suddenly a message was received that friendly artillery was "falling short and hitting into our front lines." A cease fire was ordered. The friendly fire was a tragic mistake that was unavoidable for, as the battalion reported, "It became increasingly obvious that the maps covering this sector of the island were quite inaccurate."

The tanks became even more valuable because of their direct fire capability. "E" Company reported its tank "proved effective against three enemy caves and the base of Hill 200" but that one tank had been "knocked out by enemy mortar fire." Late in the afternoon a battleship turned its secondary battery on the Japanese. It worked over the ridges in an attempt to knock out "suspected enemy mortar positions." The ship's guns "worked forward slowly a distance of 500 yards." One officer described naval gunfire support as "simply magnificent."

At 1700, Berger halted the advance. His men had seized the forward slopes of Hills 200 and 260, a gain of 300 yards against fierce resistance. He said that the gains did not look like much on a map, "but to those of us who were on the ground and knew the terrain, it was a miracle!" O. P. Smith reported that, "In the center the 2nd Battalion drove forward 300 yards against stiff resistance and seized the high ground fronting the China Wall. Between their position and the Wall was a deep ravine with sheer cliffs 150 feet high on either side. The battalion was effectively stopped. No other unit ever succeeded in pushing the advance further. The final advance came from the east."

The battalion dug in and established security for the night. "E" Company settled in on its hard-won ground. Captain Warrick G. Hoopes established his CP about seventy-five yards behind the front lines on a small piece of high ground. Company linemen laid wire to each of his platoons for communications. At 2030, a platoon commander, Lt. Frank J. Miller, reported over the telephone, "Unable to establish contact with 'F' Company . . . just detected a Jap patrol of approximately thirty strong in rear of lines." Hoopes acknowledged the report and said, "Frank, draw back your right flank a little. Cover down with automatic-weapons fire and keep me informed." Unbeknownst to the two officers, the Japanese knew the password and were in the process of closing in on the company commander's position.

Suddenly a Marine heard movement and yelled, "What's the password?" The battalion report noted, "Japanese walked into the 'E' Company CP shouting the pass word for the night and commenced throwing hand grenades." The sudden onslaught overwhelmed the CP security and wounded Captain Hoopes in both legs. The executive officer and three other officers were fatally wounded, as were several enlisted radio operators and headquarters personnel as the Japanese infiltrators overran the CP. It was reported that one of the Japanese got as far as the battalion aid station. He was shot and killed by a pistol-wielding doctor. Another infiltrator came upon an abandoned telephone shouting, "This Easy Company, This Easy Company." An irate Marine told him to get "the hell off the line," which he did, inexplicably leaving the instrument intact. Three heroic Marines dragged a machine gun forward and sprayed the enemy-held CP area. In the light of a parachute flare, they noted the Japanese, "stacked like cordwood." Thirty dead Japanese were later counted in and around the CP site. Battalion casualties for the day amounted to seventy-one wounded and sixteen killed in action. Enemy dead were estimated at three hundred.

SPITFIRE TWO (HONSOWETZ)

Honsowetz's men were next up in a futile attack. "Except for small counterattacks, we could not see the enemy. The cliffs and swamps kept us from enveloping them. Their mortars were cutting our lines to pieces. It was a matter of moving forward and accepting the losses." Russell Davis watched "one man bend, straighten, and club and kick at something that attacked his legs like a mad dog. He reached and heaved, and a Japanese soldier came end-over-end down the hill. The machine gunners yelled encouragement."

Shortly after 1200, "C" Company, commanded by Capt. Everett P. Pope, was attached to 2/1 and ordered to seize Hill 100, northeast of Bloody Nose Ridge. Hill 100 was called *Higashiyama*, East Mountain, by the Japanese. "We had taken a lot of hills and I thought this was just another one," Pope said. Regiment assumed Hill 100 was just an isolated knob, which in Marine hands would dominate the East Road and the low ground to the battalion's right front. This would allow them to oversee the whole battlefield, according to Pope. It was adjacent to Hills 205 and 210, which had cost so many American lives.

Technical Sergeant Joseph L. Alli, a combat correspondent, wrote that "To Pope and his troops, it was Bloody Nose Ridge or one of the Five

■ Waiting for the word to move out. The dense undergrowth could conceal anything from snipers to bunkers containing automatic weapons. Note that most of the men are facing outboard in case of enemy action. *Marine Corps History Division*

Sisters or Five Brothers, depending on the man you talked to. Regardless of what you called it, it meant another grinding, hot, brutal day of hard fighting, heavy losses, and trouble from the word 'go.'" Pope's bone-tired, under-strength company had at that point just 90 men of the 235 that he had taken in—"obviously we had suffered a lot of casualties." It had been shot to pieces in four unbelievably bloody days of brutal combat. The men were looking forward to a few hours of sleep and a hot meal. Pope's command to "saddle up" was a shock, almost too much for some.

The company worked its way forward, well dispersed, knowing full well what would happen to it if it bunched up. The men took advantage of the sparse cover, ducking behind shattered trees and rocks, slipping into shell and bomb craters, as they cautiously advanced through a debris-filled, foul-smelling swamp. When they reached the road at the base of the hill, two Japanese machine guns opened fire, forcing the company to go to ground. As an assault squad gathered to take out the two pillboxes another machine gun suddenly poured a deadly fire into

■ Two men skirt the swamp behind the protection of a causeway. Japanese fire kept Everett Pope's company from advancing. Hill 100 looms to their left . . . and just ahead can be seen the hull of the Sherman that slipped off the causeway. *The Old Breed: A History of the 1st Marine Division in World War II*

them, causing several casualties and pinning them down. The offending Japanese gun was located across a small pond only fifty yards away, in a position that was unassailable—"We could not reach it and we could not lay fire on it," Pope explained. "C" Company's advance was stopped cold and it was now burdened with casualties, many of whom were severely wounded and had to be evacuated quickly. Pope sent an urgent request for "stretchers and bearers, as well as more corpsmen." Volunteers rushed forward from 1/1, "ten men and one officer from the intelligence section" and succeeded in evacuating them. Three of the volunteers were cited for "outstanding work."

With the approach to Hill 100 blocked by enemy fire, Pope requested permission to withdraw the way he had come, pass to the left of the main lagoon and attack up the road to the base of the hill. "The road at this point angled sharply to the east, on a causeway across the mouth of a wide draw . . . Beyond that, it skirted the base of the objective where the company had previously been pinned down, then angled to the north-eastward." Because this route forced the company to cross open ground and the narrow causeway, Pope asked for tank support. Honsowetz quickly approved but emphasized that " 'C' Company will take the ridge before dark."

By the time the company was able to withdraw and the tanks came up in support it was late afternoon. "It was one of those days when everything went wrong," correspondent Alli reported. "The first tank slipped over the side of the causeway and was immobilized. The second tried to pull it out, but slid over the other side. Neither could move, blocking the passage to the other Shermans." After waiting two hours and suffering heavy casualties Pope said rather laconically, "So much for the tanks." The armor was under heavy fire the entire time, except when they slid off the road. "The Japanese apparently believed that they had knocked them out and stopped firing at them."

Pope gambled that the company could cross the causeway in squad rushes without excessive casualties and decided to continue the attack. "We can either sit here and keep taking casualties while we wait to see if those tanks can be cleared out of the way, or we can take our chances and run across on foot a few men at a time." His attached mortar observer team blanketed the hill with 81mm smoke rounds to conceal the movement. At Pope's signal, small groups of men scrambled across the causeway in a mad dash to throw off the aim of the Japanese gunners. "We'll go one squad at a time. Just run as fast as you can, and don't slow down till you get to the foot of the hill." Sergeant John W. Bartlett was the first to go. His Navy Cross citation stated that "he quickly rose up under the hail of small arms fire and started across the fifty-yard stretch of exposed causeway . . . followed by his squad and the rest of the company."

The improvised maneuver worked and not one man was lost in the frantic dash. Pope quickly reorganized his remaining men and signaled them to storm the hill—"The roar of the battle was too loud for oral orders and arm signals were the only means of control." Pope remembered that, "It wasn't actually occupied but when we went up the hill we were exposed to every available Jap gun . . . artillery and machine guns . . . and we lost a lot of men." Their rush carried them to the top.

"Second Lieutenant Francis T. 'Frank' Burke gallantly led his platoon in a furious attack and reached the summit," reported his Navy Cross citation. "Immediately coming under a heavy caliber field piece which caused numerous casualties, he quickly consolidated the nine remaining men of his platoon into a defense of the forward portion of the hill." First Battalion reported that "L" Company, 3rd Battalion, 5th Marines, cheered them as they charged up the steep ridge." Pope's elation at taking the hill turned to dismay. "The maps were wrong. It was not actually the high point; it was merely the nose of a long ridge." The position was dominated by a higher knoll some fifty yards to the front. Pope realized that he and his men "were in pretty bad trouble."

The Japanese counterattacked, supported by fire from the higher ground and crossfire from a parallel ridge. The Marines were cut off; the only thing they could do was find cover in the jumbled rocks—"Rude shelters were thrown up of the loose rocks that covered the ground"— and try to stave off the enemy attack. Pope sent an urgent message. "The line is flimsy as hell, and it is getting dark. We need reinforcements and grenades badly." Honsowetz replied, "Grenades coming up but we have no men to reinforce you with." Barnett "Barney" Bell went for help. "Our sergeant asked for a man to find the battalion CP and ask Colonel Honsowetz direct if they could get some help up to 'C' Company." Bell volunteered. "I found the colonel in a kind of plank lean-to. I said, 'Colonel, Captain Pope needs help bad on the ridge,' and he said, 'No way son.' I hated that 'son' stuff, so I answered, 'Bullshit,' and left before anything else was said."

Just before dark it was reported that

> Six Japs cut off by the attack tried to regain their own lines and were challenged by the crew of a machine gun protecting the rear of "C" Company and the road. The number 2 man of the gun walked over with a belt of ammunition in his hands, to investigate. When he saw they were Japs, he slapped the lead Jap in the face with the end of the belt and knocked him out. The next Jap fired, but missed and shot Lt. Walter Shaffner through the jaw, killing him. Before he could fire again, the gun crew bayoneted him and the others.

Casualties mounted on the hill—"The dead and wounded were now in our front and then in our rear"—but the survivors beat off attack after attack. Ammunition ran short. "Essentially we were out of ammunition," Pope reported. "Squads of the enemy broke through our line in several places, and the fight was literally hand-to-hand. They were good troops, well led, well trained and determined to die." Two Japanese jumped Lieutenant Burke and Sgt. James P. McAlarnis, bayoneting the officer in the leg. Burke grappled with his assailant and beat him senseless. McAlarnis, according to his Navy Cross citation, "engaged the enemy in fierce hand-to-hand combat and, when his leader was wounded and pinned to the ground by a bayonet in the hand of a Japanese, boldly rushed to his comrade's aid. Throwing himself upon the enemy, he beat him into submission and hurled him over a cliff."

"The edge of the fight rolled backward and forward like a wave," Pope recalled. "It was pitch black except for light from exploding shells. We didn't want illumination support because it would expose our position." The 81mm mortar platoon pumped out shell after shell. Mortar man Bell "figured we fired more than 3,000 rounds that day and night. We knew Captain Pope needed all the help he could get, and we did our best to provide it." Howitzers were firing from positions near the airfield, but "it wasn't a broad enough target and they missed," Pope explained. "The target was just too small, and we got hit by short rounds."

The Japanese kept attacking. "These guys weren't just sneaking around," Pope explained; "They were coming down the ridge firing. We did not have any ammunition, [but] they did! So we did what we had to do, we threw rocks! Not so much to try and hit them . . . but you throw a rock and they wouldn't know if it was a grenade or not and they'd wait a minute to see if it was going to explode. Throw three rocks and then one of your remaining grenades and slow them down a bit." The Japanese also used hand grenades. One Marine kept throwing them back, "Until one exploded in his hand," Pope recounted. "Then he picked up a rifle and used that until he was too weak to load his weapon. I had one round left in my .45. I wasn't going to let the Nips take me." Russell Davis was close enough to hear the wounded "crying and pleading for help, but nobody could help them . . . [A]ll through the night we could hear them screaming for corpsmen, as the Japs came at them from caves all around them on the hillsides."

At dawn the Japanese infantry broke off, but their artillery immediately began pounding the tennis-court-size position. Pope was down to eight men, several of them wounded, including him—sometime during the night he had taken a spray of shrapnel. That was when he decided enough was enough and ordered the survivors off the hill—"I saw no good reason for us all to die there . . . We just pulled off the hill, ass over tea kettle. I don't believe we left any wounded, but we left the dead."

267

■ Captain Everett P. Pope received the Medal of Honor while commanding "C" Company, 1st Marines, on 19–20 September 1945. *Marine Corps History Division*

MEDAL OF HONOR CITATION, CAPT. EVERETT POPE

For conspicuous gallantry and intrepidity at the risk of his life above and beyond the call of duty while serving as Commanding Officer of Company C, First Battalion, First Marines, First Marine Division, during action against enemy Japanese forces on Peleliu Island, Palau Group, on 19–20 September 1944. Subjected to point-blank cannon fire which caused heavy casualties and badly disorganized his company while assaulting a steep coral hill, Captain Pope rallied his men and gallantly led them to the summit in the face of machine-gun, mortar and sniper fire. Forced by widespread hostile attack to deploy the remnants of his company thinly in order to hold the ground won, and with his machine guns out of order and insufficient water and ammunition, he remained on the exposed hill with 12 men and 1 wounded officer, determined to hold through the night. Attacked continuously with grenades, machineguns and rifles from three sides, he and his valiant men fiercely beat back or destroyed the enemy, resorting to hand-to-hand combat as the supply of ammunition dwindled, and still maintaining his line with his eight remaining riflemen when daylight brought more deadly fire and he was ordered to withdraw. His valiant leadership against devastating odds, while protecting the units below from heavy Japanese attack, reflects the highest credit upon Captain Pope and the United States Naval Service.

Pope was the last man to leave the position. As the survivors scrambled down the hillside, the Japanese immediately moved into their old position. "Only seconds after we had abandoned the summit," Pope recalled, "the enemy . . . put a light machine gun into position." It singled him out but he was able to take cover with his men behind a stone wall near the causeway below. Pope said, "My most vivid memory, after being driven off the hill, is that of expecting Puller to have me court-martialed for having failed to hold . . . for not having died up there." After limping into an aid station, Pope appropriated a pair of pliers and pulled shrapnel out of his leg.

Late on the afternoon of the next day, Puller ordered Pope to take the hill again. "It was a suicide mission," he said angrily. "The trouble is, it was our suicide, not Puller's, you see." Reluctantly Pope gathered his men together—twelve men and two officers—and reported to battalion. "As we made ready to go, the lieutenant was needlessly killed. I then received orders to abort the attack. Why Puller wanted us all dead on the top of that hill has never been clear to me." (In a *St. Petersburg Times* interview with Pope dated August 28, 2005, Christopher Goffard reported that "Pope wants it understood, up front, that he has small regard for Puller, whom he thinks recklessly fed so many good men into Peleliu's death traps. 'Puller had a poor grasp of the island's terrain,' Pope said. 'Send enough men to their slaughter up the hill, Puller's strategy went, and a few are bound to make it. The adulation paid to him these days sickens me.'")

The regiment's gains for the day were negligible—four hundred yards on the left and five hundred yards on the right, but the middle had been stopped cold.

CHAPTER 17

D + 5

REGIMENT OF SURVIVORS

"We're not a regiment, we're the survivors of
a regiment!"
                    —Anonymous infantryman, 1st Marines

Despite the horrendous casualties, Puller's orders stood: "Resume the attack with maximum effort." One of his battalion commanders privately told writer Bill Ross that Puller's "failure to recognize soon enough that we were a shot-to-pieces outfit—while still ordering us to do impossible things with the worn-out, pitifully few men we still had—was a sign that he was no longer in touch with the realities of the situation." Bruce Watkins remarked sadly, "we were a remnant rather than a regiment."

O. P. Smith outlined the day's objective. "[T]he attack jumped off in an all-out effort to regain Walt's Ridge [Hill 100]. The 1st and 2nd Battalion [the two had been combined] reinforced by the Division Reconnaissance Company were used. Men from Headquarters were fed into the battalions. A provisional machine gun group . . . was formed from cooks, communication personnel and quartermaster personnel." Every available man in the regiment went into the lines. Additional tanks, LVT(A)s, half-tracks, 37mm guns and mortars were brought up to support the attack.

271

Honsowetz prowled the lines trying to encourage his men. Russell Davis watched him speak to a grizzled veteran of five days on the line. "The colonel was talking to him as he got ready to lead his squad up the hill. The rifleman said, 'Colonel, we can go up there. We been up there before. And we'll go on up again until there's no one left. But we can't hold that ridge, Colonel. We can't hold it unless there's more of us, sir. We can't hold it at all, sir.' The Colonel turned away without answering. He was on the verge of exhaustion himself."

The combined 1st and 2nd Battalions jumped off on schedule at 0700. They were immediately taken under intense mortar fire. "F" Company reported that it was pinned down, taking heavy casualties and had to withdraw. It only had 10 men left in the line and only 150 effectives left in both battalions. Honsowetz ordered, "Maintain your position at all costs," and headed out to them. "Colonel Honsowetz showed up waving his .45 in the air and shouting for us to move up the ridge,"

■ Thirty-seven-millimeter anti-tank gun supporting an attack on the ridge in the background. This direct-fire weapon was too light to penetrate hardened structures but could be effective against hastily erected field works. *Marine Corps History Division*

Watkins recalled. "We rose up then . . . by individuals and little groups and started up the hill . . . There was no real organization, there was only the discipline and purpose, not even pride anymore, just what the Corps had drilled into us."

Watkins "wet, filthy, lips burnt and cracked," advanced with the survivors of his platoon—maybe twenty men. "As the first tremendous rain of bullets hit us, you could feel more than see as people dropped around you—and yet we went on. Soon we were crawling up on our bellies until at last it seemed there were very few moving at all . . . [O]ur

■ Moving out. A Marine looks back for a signal from his unit leader, while a flamethrower operator on the left remains behind cover. The rifleman on his right crouches forward as he advances. *Marine Corps History Division*

drive wore down and stopped perhaps one hundred feet up the slope." One of the "B" Company survivors, Pfc. Boone T. Harris, became a one-man army after several of his buddies were hit. "[He] boldly returned to the area through intense fire from automatic weapons emplaced in caves on the crest of a ridge and single-handedly turning on the first cave, emptied his pistol into the enemy gun crew," his Navy Cross citation recorded. "After silencing the weapon with hand grenades, he picked up an automatic rifle and, delivering intense fire into a second Japanese position, enabled two men . . . to crawl to safety. Then, under cover of smoke grenades, he seized a third casualty and carried him across his shoulders out of the fire-swept zone."

The indescribably brutal combat had taken its toll. "As the riflemen climbed higher they grew fewer, until only a handful of men still climbed in the lead squads," Russell Davis wrote, appalled by the losses. "These were the pick of the bunch—the few men who would go forward, no matter what was ahead. There were only a few. Of the thousands who land with a division and the hundreds who go up with a company of the line, there are only a few who manage to live and have enough courage to go through anything. They are the core structure of a fighting unit. All the rest is so much weight and sometimes merely flab. There aren't more than a few dozen in every thousand men, even in the Marines. They clawed and clubbed and stabbed their way up."

Russell Davis had lost all sense of humanity.

> I picked up the rifle of a dead Marine and I went up the hill. I remember more than a few yards of scarred hillside, blasted white with shellfire and hot to touch. I didn't worry about death anymore. I had resigned from the human race. I only wanted to be as far forward as any man when my turn came. My fingers were smashed and burned, but I felt no pain. I crawled and scrambled forward and lay still, without any feeling toward any

human thing. In the next hole was a rifleman. He peered at me through red and painful eyes. Then we both looked away. I didn't care about him. He didn't care about me. I thought he was a fool and he probably thought I was the same. We had both resigned from the human club. As a fighting unit, the 1st Marine Regiment was finished. We were no longer even human beings. I fired at anything that moved in front of me. Friend or foe. I had no friends. I just wanted to kill.

O. P. Smith noted sadly that "Although some gains were made, the ground was untenable. The attack lost its drive and bogged down." Casualties increased. The exhausted survivors fell back. Russell Davis didn't recall coming off the hill. "I remember sitting by a roadside, in tears. I don't know why." Bruce Watkins pulled his people back. "Slowly . . . in bits and pieces we began our way down dragging the wounded over the rough ground . . . [F]or the first time we left our dead behind . . . until finally what was left reached partial shelter in the ditches and shell holes we had left. First Platoon was now down to nine, and there was only one other platoon leader left of the twelve who had set out with our battalion. We didn't comprehend it then, but the First Regiment was done. There was no effective organization left."

MUSTANG TWO (BERGER)

In the center, 2/7's attack did somewhat better. "E" Company, because of its losses the previous night, was combined with "G" Company under one of the few surviving captains in the battalion. The combined company shifted the direction of attack to "seize the high ground comprising Hill 200." "E" Company's surviving mortar crews were sent into the lines as riflemen—in the Corps, then as now, every man is considered a rifleman. Artillery and naval gunfire laid down a curtain of fire as the attack started. The company reported "moving ahead slowly about fifty yards against heavy opposition, consisting of artillery, mortars and small

■ Stretcher bearers near a destroyed Japanese searchlight wait for the word to move forward. Note the collapsible stretcher and the cloth belt of machine-gun ammunition lying on the ground. *Marine Corps History Division*

■ Dirty, stinking—hollow-eyed after days of little food or water, nights filled with terror—this infantryman's face reflects the stress of combat. *Marine Corps History Division*

arms fire." An urgent request for more corpsmen, morphine, and stretcher bearers was sent to the medical battalion. To make matters worse, "F" Company reported that 2/1 was firing into them. The fire was so heavy that runners could not get through. A messenger dog was sent forward because "it could get through much better than runners." The attack continued to move forward, albeit very slowly and came to a stop as dawn approached.

CHAPTER 18

D + 6

ENOUGH IS ENOUGH

DAY OF DECISION

Shortly before noon on D + 6, Geiger appeared at Puller's advanced command post. As usual, it was so close to the front lines that the sound of the action could plainly be heard. Small-arms and machine-gun fire cracked just ahead—and the crump of mortars and grenades sounded loud in the sweltering heat. The regimental commander was on a field telephone barking orders to Honsowetz. He looked drained, "very tired," according to one of Geiger's small escort. Puller was shirtless, bareheaded, boots unlaced and barely able to walk. He finished the conversation and noticed Geiger for the first time. "What can I do for you general?" he asked. "Just thought I'd drop in and see how things were going," Geiger replied. In typical Puller fashion, he shot back, "We're still going in but some of the companies are damn small."

Geiger pulled him aside for a private conversation. A witness recounted that the discussion was brief and heated. "It became rapidly apparent that the regimental commander was very tired; he was unable

■ Khaki-clad Maj. Gen. Roy Geiger making the rounds during the fighting. Geiger was known for suddenly appearing at command posts . . . often within small-arms fire. *Marine Corps History Division*

to give a very clear picture of what his situation was and when asked by the Corps Commander what he needed in the way of help, he stated that he was doing all right with what he had." Geiger believed that he had lost all touch with reality. Within minutes of arriving, he was on his way to the division command post and a showdown with Rupertus.

■ An exhausted Chesty Puller confers with his army counterpart, while Maj. Gen. Paul J. Mueller looks on. By this time, Puller could hardly walk due to the Guadalcanal wound. *Marine Corps History Division*

Lieutenant Colonel Harold O. Deakin was present at the confrontation. "It wasn't what you'd call a really stormy session, although it had some very tense moments. Johnny Selden, Jeff Fields, and the general were going over the situation map when Geiger showed up and asked to see the latest casualty reports from Lewie Puller's outfit." They were appalling: 1,672 men had been lost—more casualties than any regiment in Marine Corps history. Geiger told Rupertus, "The 1st Marines are finished"; he wanted to relieve it with an army regiment. Jeff Fields watched the confrontation. "General Rupertus didn't want the army regiment, so of course he said no." Fields, however, disagreed:

281

The 1st Marines were pretty well shot up. They weren't fire eaters anymore. They needed to be replaced. I felt that we could get more impetus if we had fresh troops moving to the area, and we want to go and push up north. So I told General Geiger and General Rupertus, we had to take them, and let them pass through the 1st Marines and move to the north. Without further discussion General Geiger turned to Rupertus and ordered him to act immediately.

Late in the afternoon, Puller informed Honsowetz and Berger that their battered men would be relieved sometime in the afternoon. Honsowetz immediately called his company commanders and shared the news with them—but he cautioned them to "hold fast, do not withdraw." Bruce Watkins and two others were the only ones left out of twelve who landed. "Lieutenant Schleip of 'F' Company and Robbie Robbins were still there and we looked at each in numbed silence." Robert Fisher

"heard rumors that we were to be relieved by another outfit before darkness." Ray Davis verified Fisher's rumor. "We began wearily to gather up what gear we had left and waited for the arrival of the fresh troops." At 1600, 1/7 started taking over the lines, under a heavy

■ Major General Roy Geiger on the left and Maj. Gen. William Rupertus on the right. Geiger was forced to order Rupertus to bring in the army's 81st "Wildcat" Division to replace the badly shot-up 1st Marine Division. *U.S. Marine Corps*

barrage of smoke, to conceal the relief. Berger's battalion was relieved by 3/7. His stint with 1st Marines was at an end. His men headed for a much needed rest and hot food.

Sabol's 3rd Battalion remained in the line for two more days patrolling the western flank of the ridge system, as far as the village of Garekoru, about halfway to the island's northern tip.

Smith related that "the first regiment of the 81st Division under Colonel Dark relieved Lewie Puller. By this time, Puller had 1,749 casualties in the regiment. I had hoped personally that with Dark relieving Lewie, maybe with his help we could finish the job, but our troops were too badly beaten down to do it. The first thing that Colonel Dark did was to move his CP one thousand yards back. He wasn't going up there and relieve Puller where he'd been. I think Puller was the most aggressive of the regimental commanders."

RELIEF

Bruce Watkins led his nine men, all that were left, toward the rear. "First Platoon hung together as we moved slowly along, passing our relief column going the other way. I remember the shocked look on their faces as they passed us, now and then inquiring about someone they knew." E. B. Sledge passed them as they came out:

> As we walked along one side of the road, the 1st Marines filed along the other side to take over our area. I saw some familiar faces as the three decimated battalions trudged past us, but I was shocked at the absence of so many others whom I knew in that regiment. During the frequent halts typical to the movement of one unit into the position of another, we exchanged greetings with buddies and asked about the fate of our mutual friends. We in the 5th Marines had many a dead or wounded friend to report about from our ranks, but the men in the 1st Marines had so many it was appalling. "How many

■ Exhausted survivors "take ten." *Marine Corps History Division*

men left in your company?" I asked an old Camp Elliott buddy in the 1st Marines. He looked at me wearily with bloodshot eyes and choked as he said, "Twenty is all that's left in the whole company, Sledgehammer. They nearly wiped us out. I'm the only one left out of the old bunch."

Ray Davis led the pitiful remnants of his battalion back behind the lines. The thin ranks attested to the week of hard fighting. The battalion was no longer recognizable as the same highly trained outfit that landed on White Beach 1. The men were grimy, bearded and visibly emaciated. Many had not had a meal, other than a combat ration, since landing. Their faces were sunburned, eyes bloodshot and lips cracked and bleeding. Salt from sweat crusted their uniforms, leaving white circles under the arms, "like the rings on a tree," according to one veteran. The heavy herringbone twill of their uniforms was torn and frayed at the knees and elbows from the rough-edged coral. Blouses hung open from missing buttons. Their sturdy cord-soled field shoes were falling apart at the seams, and their combat gear bore mute testimony to hard service— helmets dented, cartridge belts torn, the non-essential thrown away or lost. An observer seeing the condition of the men would characterize them more as skid row bums than elite combat troops.

There were so few men left that Davis had to form the battalion into two rifle companies and a small headquarters detachment. He disbanded "D" Company and assigned the pitifully few men to "A" and "C" Companies. Even with this drastic step, "A" Company mustered only 122 enlisted and 4 officers, while "C" Company numbered 117 enlisted and 4 officers. Everett Pope was the only original company commander left. The line companies consisted of clerks, cooks, mess sergeants, jeep drivers, mail orderlies and communicators. Stevenson compared the final muster roll with the 930 enlisted men and 37 officers who made the initial landing. One of the last casualties happened to be the indestructible Platoon Sergeant McAlarnis, who was wounded by a Japanese grenade. He was evacuated under protest. Two others were listed as missing in action when they climbed a ridge in search of Japanese snipers.

Honsowetz received orders to assemble his shot-up battalion at Purple Beach. As the ragged files slowly made their way back along a dirt road, the lead elements were heartened to find several beat-up trucks along the roadway. The men quickly hustled aboard the idling vehicles, gave a shout and the small convoy roared away. Upon arrival at Purple Beach, Honsowetz established a defensive perimeter and sent out local patrols. Although the beach was considered a rear area, the debris-strewn terrain and shattered emplacements harbored Japanese holdouts. Within hours, one of the few remaining lieutenants was "wounded by a Jap sniper who was hiding in a cave in the middle of the battalion area. Several grenades were thrown into the cave and the sniper was killed." The next day a sniper killed a man from "F" Company. A patrol discovered a "well-fed enemy soldier armed with a rifle, carrying grenades and a pack." The interloper was killed.

■ A cautious rifleman approaches a badly damaged concrete emplacement. Even behind the lines, one had to be careful because of bypassed enemy or infiltrators. The charred remains of a Japanese soldier lie underneath the barrel in the foreground. *Marine Corps History Division*

Days later the regiment boarded amphibian DUKWs for the trip to the transports. Richard Watkins was the only officer left in his company.

> We pulled up to the overhanging bow of the *Tryon*. Extending above us was twenty-five feet of cargo net. As the seas were running fairly well, the DUKW would rise and drop about six feet with every wave. Everyone was pretty well exhausted and climbing that net after timing the wave was no joke. I was the last to go up . . . I remember being very tired, but determined . . . [W]hen I finally reached a spot where my head was even with the ship's rail, I knew I could go no further . . . [T]wo sailors were staring me in the face as I said to them, "I don't think I'm going to make it." They reacted instantly, each grabbing a piece of my jacket and literally heaving me over the rail.

■ Memorial service at the division cemetery. Rupertus is in the center of the photo, Puller just to his right. O. P. Smith stands to the left of the chaplain. *Marine Corps History Division*

Another bedraggled, worn-out Marine dragged himself up the cargo net. Upon reaching the top, "he was approached by an eager, clean, close-shaven, immaculately dressed young navy officer. 'Got any souvenirs to trade?' The soaked, exhausted, combat-battered Marine stood silent for a moment, then reached down and patted his own rear end. 'I brought my ass outta there, Swabbie. That's my souvenir of Peleliu.'"

The survivors were transported back to Pavuvu to begin the process of rebuilding. Many were traumatized by the brutal combat. Veterans like Russell Davis dreaded the first few days.

> I knew the first night back in the rest area was always bad. The brothers and buddies and the cousins from other outfits came by to ask about the wounded and the dead. I didn't want to go through it. I didn't want to talk about the wounded and the dead or even think of them. But I knew I would have to because it was a duty that those who had lived had to fulfill. We would have to talk, and say nice things about the dead, just as old people did at a wake, back home. Then, afterwards, we'd go out to other regiments and ask about our own friends. I dreaded that too. The whole First Division had been badly hit.

He told a friend, "If I can get through tonight, I'll be all right, when the wake is over."

The official casualty figure for the 1st Marine Division was 6,526, of whom 1,252 were killed in action—1st Marines, 1,749; 5th Marines, 1,378; 7th Marines, 1,497. It was reported that "the 1st Marines killed an estimated 3,942 Japanese and reduced the following major enemy positions and installations: 10 defended coral ridges, 3 large blockhouses, 22 pillboxes, 13 anti-tank guns, and 144 defended caves.

POSTSCRIPT

A week after the 1st Marines were pulled out, Harold Deakin recounted how "Rupertus and I were sitting on his bunk, alone, and he had his head in his hands and he said, 'This thing has just about got me beat.' I hadn't been, at that point, what you'd call a friend of Rupertus', but I found myself with an arm around his shoulder comforting him, and telling him, 'Now, General, everything is going to work out.' . . . I was kind of half staff officer, half chaplain, and I guess deacon."

After the campaign ended, Rupertus returned to Washington where he met with Vandegrift. His old friend and mentor recalled, "I had no choice but to relieve Rupertus of his command . . . I knew the Peleliu campaign must nearly have exhausted him. He, of course, did not see things my way, but he quieted down a little when I gave him command of the Marine Corps Schools heretofore run under my direct aegis." As an additional reward, Vandegrift gave him the Distinguished Service Medal: "Major General Rupertus gallantly maneuvered his command over swamps, rocky and precipitous slopes and through dense jungle

The President of the United States takes pleasure in presenting the
Presidential Unit Citation to the
First Marine Division (Reinforced)
For service as set forth in the following
Citation:

For extraordinary heroism in action against enemy Japanese forces
at Peleliu and Ngesebus from September 15 to 29, 1944. Landing
over a treacherous coral reef against hostile mortar and artillery fire,
the First Marine Division, Reinforced, seized a narrow, heavily mined
beachhead and advanced foot by foot in the face of relentless
enfilade fire through rain-forests and mangrove swamps toward
the air strip, the key to the enemy defenses of the southern Palaus.
Opposed all the way by thoroughly disciplined, veteran Japanese
troops heavily entrenched in caves and in reinforced concrete pillboxes which honeycombed the high ground throughout the island,
the officers and men of the Division fought with undiminished spirit
and courage despite heavy losses, exhausting heat and difficult terrain, seizing and holding a highly strategic air and land base for future
operations in the Western Pacific. By their individual acts of heroism,
their aggressiveness and their fortitude, the men of the First Marine
Division, Reinforced, upheld the highest traditions of the United States
Naval Service.

growth in a relentless advance, resolutely withstanding repeated counterattacks to annihilate a fanatically determined enemy or drive him
back into a defensive pocket in the centrally located hills in the center
of the island."

Seventy-two days after the American landing, Colonel Nakagawa
committed ritual suicide after burning his colors. In one of his last
messages to General Inoue he announced, "All is over on Peleliu."

O. P. Smith talked with an Associated Press correspondent years
after the battle:

There were actually two Pelelius after the first two
weeks of the battle. One Peleliu was the flat ground we

had captured on the southern third of the island. There we went about the job, all but unmolested, we'd been sent to do—seize the airstrip, and bring in our men and planes so that the Japanese couldn't use the island to interfere with MacArthur's operations in the Philippines. The other Peleliu began at Bloody Nose Ridge and extended northward through the Umurbrogols to Ngesebus Island. This was a brutally different extra-inning ball game, one where the score was kept in the number of ridges taken and how many Marines were killed or wounded in the seemingly endless process.

A friend later said that Smith "often wondered why we didn't simply leave the highlands to the Japanese, keep shelling and bombing them from offshore and the part of Peleliu we held until there were too few left to continue the fight."

BIBLIOGRAPHY

Alexander, Joseph H. *Storm Landings: Epic Amphibious Battles in the Central Pacific.* (Annapolis, MD: Naval Institute Press, 1997).

Bronemann, Leroy B. *Once Upon a Tide: Tales From a Foxhole in the South Pacific.* (Bryn Mawr, PA: Dorrance & Company, Inc., 2000).

Cameron, Craig M. *American Samurai: Myth, Imagination, and the Conduct of Battle in the First Marine Division 1941–1945.* (New York: Cambridge University Press, 1994).

Cook, Haruko Taya and Theodore F. *Japan at War: An Oral History.* (New York: The New Press, 1992).

Daugherty, Leo J., III. *Fighting Techniques of a Japanese Infantryman 1941–1945.* (St. Paul, MN: MBI Publishing Company, 2002).

293

Davis, Burke. *Marine! The Life of Lt. Gen Lewis B. (Chesty) Puller USMC (Ret.)* (Boston: Little, Brown and Company, 1962).

Davis, Russell G. *Marine at War.* (Boston: Little, Brown and Company, 1961).

Davis, William J. *The Story of Ray Davis, MOH.* (San Diego: Privately Published, 1990).

Drea, Edward J. *MacArthur's Ultra: Codebreaking and the War Against Japan, 1942–1945.* (Lawrence, KS: University Press of Kansas, 1992).

Edgerton, Robert B. *Warriors of the Rising Sun: A History of the Japanese Military.* (New York: W.W. Norton & Company, 1997).

Fuchida, Mistuo and Masatake Okumiya. *Midway: The Battle that Doomed Japan.* (Annapolis, MD: United States Naval Institute, 1955).

Gailey, Harry A. *Peleliu 1944.* (Annapolis, MD: The Nautical & Aviation Publishing Company of America, 1983).

Giblin, Tucker. *The Class of '42: Marines in World War II.* (Edina, MN: Beaver's Pond Press, Inc., 2002).

Hallas, James H. *The Devil's Anvil: The Assault on Peleliu.* (London: Praeger, 1994).

Harries, Meirion and Susie. *Soldiers of the Sun: The Rise and Fall of the Imperial Japanese Army.* (New York: Random House, 1991).

Hayashi, Saburo. *Kogun: The Japanese Army in the Pacific War.* (Quantico, VA: Marine Corps Association, 1959).

Heinl, Robert Debs. *Soldiers of the Sea: The U.S. Marine Corps, 1775–1962*. (Annapolis, MD: United States Naval Institute, 1962).

Hoffman, Jon T. *Chesty: The Story of Lieutenant General Lewis B. Puller, USMC*. (New York: Random House, 2001).

———. *Once a Legend: Red Mike Edson of the Marine Raiders*. (Novato, CA: Presidio, 1994).

Holmes, W. J. *Double Edged Secrets: U.S. Naval Intelligence Operations in the Pacific During World War II*. (Annapolis, MD: Naval Institute Press, 1979).

Hough, Frank O. *The Assault on Peleliu*. (Washington, D.C.: GPO, 1950).

———. *The Island War*. (Philadelphia, PA: J. B. Lippincott Company, 1947).

Hunt, George P. *Coral Comes High*. (New York: Harper and Brothers, 1946).

Isley, Jeter A., and Philip A. Crowl. *The U.S. Marines and Amphibious War: Its Theory and its Practice in the Pacific*. (Princeton. NJ: Princeton University Press, 1951).

Johnston, James W. *The Long Road of War: A Marine's Story of Pacific Combat*. (Lincoln, NE: University of Nebraska Press, 1998).

La Bree, Clifton. *The Gentle Warrior: General Oliver Prince Smith, USMC*. (Kent, OH: Kent State University Press, 2001).

Lea, Tom. *Battle Stations: A Grizzly from the Coral Sea, Peleliu Landing*. (Dallas, TX: Still Point Press, 1988).

Leckie, Robert. *Strong Men Armed: The United States Marines Against Japan.* (New York: Random House, 1962).

McMillan, George, C. Peter Zurlinden, Jr., Alvin M. Josephy, Jr., David Dempsey, Keyes Beech, and Herman Kogan. *Uncommon Valor: Marine Divisions in Action.* (Washington, D.C.: Infantry Journal Press, 1946).

McMillan, George. *The Old Breed: A History of the First Marine Division in World War II.* (Washington, D.C.: Infantry Journal Press, 1949).

Myers, Bruce F. *Swift, Silent, and Deadly: Marine Amphibious Reconnaissance in the Pacific, 1942–1945.* (Annapolis, MD: Naval Institute Press, 2004).

O'Sheel, Patrick, and Gene Cook. *Semper Fidelis: The U.S. Marines in the Pacific—1942–1945.* (New York: William Sloan Associates, Inc., 1947).

Prados, John. *Combined Fleet Decoded: The Secret History of American Intelligence and the Japanese Navy in World War II.* (New York: Random House, 1995).

Prange, Gordon W. *Miracle at Midway.* (New York: McGraw-Hill Book Company, 1982).

Pratt, Fletcher. *The Marines War: An Account of the Struggle for the Pacific from Both American and Japanese Sources.* (New York: William Sloan Associates, Inc., 1948).

Ross, Bill D. *Peleliu Tragic Triumph: The Untold Story of the Pacific War's Forgotten Battle.* (New York: Random House, 1991).

Rottman, Gordon L. *Japanese Pacific Island Defenses 1941–1945.* (New York: Osprey Publishing, 2003).

Rottman, Gordon L. *World War II Pacific Island Guide: A Geo-Military Study.* (Westport, CT: Greenwood Press, 2002).

Sherrod, Robert. *Tarawa: The Story of a Battle.* (New York: Duell, Sloan & Pearce 1944).

Sledge, E. B. *With the Old Breed at Peleliu and Okinawa.* (Novato, CA: Presidio Press, 1981).

Sloan, Bill. *Brotherhood of Heroes: The Marines at Peleliu, 1944—The Bloodiest Battle of the Pacific War.* (New York: Simon & Schuster, 2005).

Smith, H. M. *Coral and Brass.* (New York: Charles Scribner's Sons, 1949).

Smith, S. E. *The United States Marine Corps in World War II.* (New York: Random House, 1969).

Strauss, Ulrich. *The Anguish of Surrender: Japanese POWs of World War II.* (Seattle: University of Washington Press, 2003).

Watkins, Richard Bruce. *Brothers in Battle: One Marine's Account of War in the Pacific.* (Self-published, 1992).

Willock, Roger. *Unaccustomed to Fear: A Biography of the Late General Roy S. Geiger.* (Princeton, NJ: Privately Published, 1968).

Woodard, Larry L. *Before the First Wave: The 3rd Armored Amphibian Tractor Battalion—Peleliu & Okinawa.* (Manhattan, KS: Sunflower University Press, 1994).

ARCHIVAL SOURCES

Located at Quantico, Virginia, the Marine Corps University archives, which are maintained by the Alfred M. Gray Marine Corps Research Center, provide a rich source of material for researchers of Marine Corps history including nearly four thousand collections of papers donated by active-duty and former officers and enlistees, documenting every conflict involving Marines. Of particular importance to this book were the oral histories that have been conducted by the Marine Corps History Division over the years.

Buse, Lt. Gen. Henry W., Jr. Marine Corps Historical Division. Oral History Interview, 1986.

Davis, Gen. Raymond G. Marine Corps Historical Division. Oral History Interview, 1978.

Deakin, Brig. Gen. Harold O. Marine Corps Historical Division. Oral History Interview, 1973.

Fields, Lt. Gen. Lewis J. Marine Corps Historical Division. Oral History Interview, 1976.

Honsowetz, Col. Russell E. Marine Corps Historical Division. Oral History Interview, 1990.

Silverthorn, Lt. Gen. Merwin. Marine Corps Historical Division. Oral History Interview, 1973.

Smith, Gen. Julien. Marine Corps Historical Division. Oral History Interview, 1973.

Smith, Gen. Oliver P. personal papers, Gray Research Center archives.

PUBLICATIONS

Alexander, Joseph H. "Peleliu 1944: 'King' Company's Battle for 'The Point.'" *Leatherneck* (November 1996): pg 18.

The Old Breed News, August 2000 through September–October 2006

UNPUBLISHED MATERIALS

Davis, Gen. Raymond G. personal interview with author.

Honsowetz, Col. Russell E. personal interview with author.

U.S. GOVERNMENT PUBLICATIONS

Dictionary of United States Military Terms for Joint Usage. Joint Chiefs of Staff, Washington, June 1948.

"Handbook on Japanese Infantry Weapons, Special Series, No. 19." Dated 31 December 1943. Prepared by Military Intelligence Division, War Department.

"Handbook on Japanese Military Forces, TM 30-480." War Department, May 14, 1941.

Historical Branch, G-3 Division. *A Brief History of the First Marines.* (Washington, D.C.: GPO, 1968).

History and Museums Division. *The 1st Marine Division and its Regiments.* (Washington, D.C.: GPO, 1999).

Hough, Frank O., and J. A. Crown. *The Campaign on New Britain.* (Washington, D.C.: GPO, 1952).

"Notes for Task Force Commander in Pacific Theaters." War Department, 1943.

INDEX